To David

With best wishes

Rodney Ashwood
2011

For Queen and Country

"A new and fascinating angle on the history of the Anglo Zulu War."

Ian Knight
Zulu War Author and Broadcaster

"A moving tribute to bravery."

Brian Best
Chairman Victoria Cross Society

"Heaton's Zulu War diary adds an important social dimension to one of the most dramatic colonial wars in British military history."

Dr Adrian Greaves
Anglo Zulu War Historical Society

For Queen and Country

the Zulu War diary of Lieutenant Wilfred Heaton 24th Regiment of Foot 1879

Rodney Ashwood

Foreword by Nicky Rattray

DELFRYN PUBLICATIONS

First published in 2005
by Serendipity

This edition published in 2011
by Delfryn Publications
14 Camden Road
Brecon
Powys LD3 7RS
United Kingdom

Copyright © Rodney Ashwood 2005, 2011

Rodney Ashwood has asserted his right under the Copyright, Designs
and Patents Act 1988 to be identified as the author of this work

A CIP catalogue record for this book
is available from the British Library

ISBN 978-0-9568177-0-9

This book is sold subject to the condition that it shall not,
by way of trade or otherwise, be lent, resold, hired out,
or otherwise circulated without the publisher's prior
consent in any form of binding or cover other than that
in which it is published and without a similar condition,
including this condition, being imposed on the
subsequent publisher.

Printed and bound in the United Kingdom
by CPI Antony Rowe, Chippenham and Eastbourne

In proud memory of
David Grey Rattray
1958 – 2007
Zulu War historian and Regimental friend

Not theirs to save the day but where they stood,
falling, to dye the earth with brave men's blood
for England's sake and duty.
Be their name sacred among us
neither praise nor blame add to their epitaph
but let it be simple as that which marked Thermopylae.
Tell it in England, those that pass us by,
here, faithful to their charge, her soldiers lie.

from an inscription
on the Regimental memorial
at the battlefield of Isandlwana

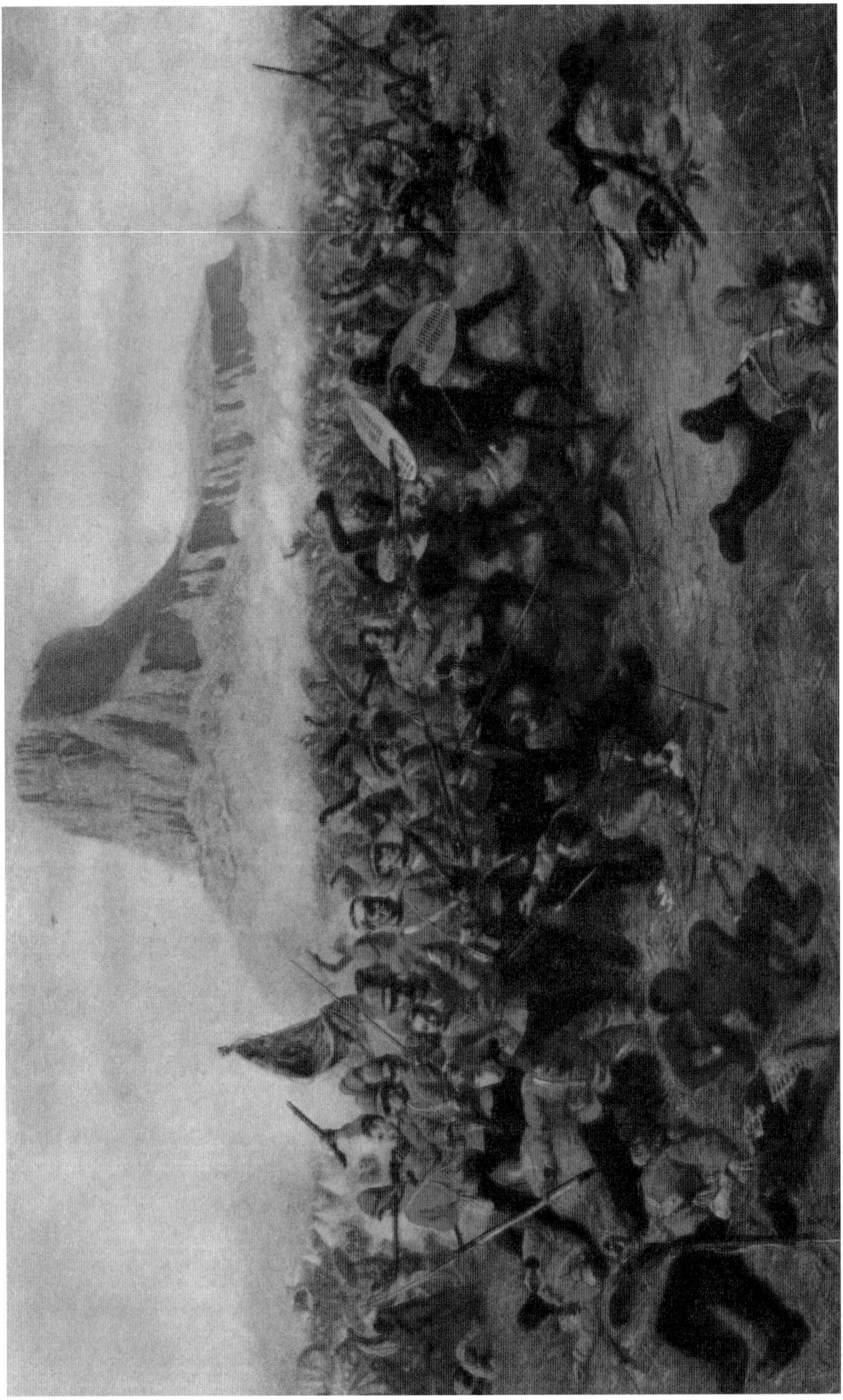

FOREWORD
by Nicky Rattray

The Anglo-Zulu war of 1879 has gripped the imagination of countless numbers of people over many years and none more so, perhaps, than my late husband David. With our home at Fugitive's Drift Lodge on the battlefield itself, David had the greatest respect and admiration for both the mighty Zulu nation, who suffered so much as a consequence of the conflict, and for the Welsh soldiers of the 24th Regiment of Foot, whose heroic exploits in such battles as Isandlwana and Rorke's Drift ensured their immortality in the annals of British military history. No wonder then, that David made the study of this campaign a lifetime commitment in a spirit of peace and reconciliation.

Shortly before his tragic death in January 2007, David published a book about the war which featured the magnificent water colours, sketched and painted during the campaign, of Lieutenant William Lloyd who was serving in the 24th Regiment at the time. By good chance, Rodney Ashwood had also just published this book, *For Queen and Country*, which was the Zulu war diary of Lieutenant Wilfred Heaton, a fellow officer and friend of Lieutenant Lloyd. By following the dates and places in this diary, David was able to identify with considerable accuracy the locations from which Lloyd made his paintings, which was invaluable to his research and for which he was most grateful to the author for giving him unlimited access to his work in its early stages.

It therefore gives me great pleasure, and in many ways in memory of David, to recommend the second edition of this book to you. Described originally by Ian Knight, the well known author and broadcaster as *"a new and fascinating angle on the history of the Zulu War,"* this diary is a warm and personal insight of the life of a young officer on active service in South Africa. Well researched, it chronicles the highs and lows of everyday life while taking part in colonial warfare and it complements the more formal

---

Opposite. *The Last Stand at Isandhula* by Charles Edwin Fripp (1854 – 1906). Fripp covered the Zulu War for *The Graphic* newspaper and exhibited this painting at the Royal Academy in 1885. It is now owned by the National Army Museum who received it as a gift from the 21st Special Air Services Regiment. (The unusual spelling of Isandlwana was thought to be correct at the time.)
(Courtesy Director of the National Army Museum)

detailed accounts of the war by professional historians. David found this book to be most useful to him and I know that he enjoyed reading it. I hope you will too.

Fugitives' Drift Lodge
Kwa-Zulu Natal
South Africa
2011

An Appreciation
by Richard Heaton

The title of this book is taken from an inscription on a stone cross over the grave of Lieutenants Melvill and Coghill at Fugitives' Drift in South Africa, where these two officers gave their lives in an attempt to save the Queen's Colour of the 24th Regiment after the battle of Isandlwana in January 1879. The Colour was eventually recovered from the Buffalo River near where they died and returned to the Regiment at Helpmekaar where it was received by their friend and brother officer called Lieutenant Wilfred Heaton. That young man was my grandfather.

That he should be the subject of this book is a matter of great pleasure to my family as he too served his country with honour and distinction under three monarchs for almost 45 years. Commissioned in 1874 he saw active service in South Africa and Burma under Queen Victoria until 1896. He then returned on the Reserve of Officers to command the Royal Garrison Regiment from 1901 to 1905 in Malta and South Africa during the short sovereignty of King Edward VII and finally served under King George V during the First World War, not in uniform but as a postal vetting security officer.

Grandfather Wilfred was a man of great honesty and integrity, whose watchwords were duty and service. While in uniform he followed the flag to India and it was there that he met and married my grandmother Florence. They returned to North Wales in 1891 when he inherited *Plas Heaton* on the death of his father and although he still had military responsibilities he threw himself into the management of the estate with customary vigour and dedication. He was also very active in the local community where he was highly respected.

During most of his adult life my grandfather kept a series of annual diaries and some years ago my mother and I gave the one for 1879 to the South Wales Borderers Museum in Brecon. I am very grateful to Rodney Ashwood for transcribing this diary and for his meticulous research into my grandfather's military career. I am delighted to commend this book and am quite sure that it will be thoroughly enjoyed by all those who have an interest in the Anglo Zulu wars or in military history generally.

Plas Heaton
Denbighshire

List of Contents

Preface	xiii
David Rattray – A Personal Tribute	xvii
Chronology of Main Events	xxv
List of Illustrations	xxix
Prologue	xxxi
Chapter 1 – Stepping Out	1
Chapter 2 – The Noble 24th	4
Chapter 3 – Prelude to War	11
Chapter 4 – Unexpected Disaster	17
Chapter 5 – Setbacks and Recovery	61
Chapter 6 – The Second Invasion	78
Chapter 7 – Returning Home	104
Chapter 8 – On Extended Leave	116
Chapter 9 – The Later Years	133
Epilogue	142
Notes	146
Bibliography	151
Index	153

Preface to the Second Edition

When the first edition of this book was published I had no idea how it would be received, being my initial foray into the literary world. Happily, sales went well and it was not long before I had sold the complete first print run. Delighted by this success I contacted my publisher for more copies, but just as I needed their services they went into administration and ceased trading. However, encouraged by repeated requests for further copies of the book, this second edition is now up and running. Also since the original publication, the international Zulu War fraternity has endured the tragic loss of David Rattray, who was the world's leading authority on the campaign of 1879, and I have taken the opportunity to include my own personal tribute to the person who was the inspiration behind my book in the first place. At this point I would like to express my sincere gratitude to Nicky Rattray, David's widow, for her enthusiastic support and for kindly agreeing to write the foreword. I must also record my indebtedness to His Royal Highness The Prince of Wales for kindly giving me permission to quote from a letter he sent to David's funeral.

As I have said before, this project could not have happened without the help of a considerable number of people. I must record my sincere thanks to the Trustees of my Regimental Museum for giving me unlimited access to the original manuscript and for their permission to publish the diary in full. I am also very grateful to Major Martin Everett, the Museum Curator and to his Customer Services Manager, Mrs Celia Green, for their full and willing co-operation as my research expanded the diary into a biography of the life of Wilfred Heaton, in whose successor Regiment I had the privilege to serve. I must also express my gratitude to Mr Richard Heaton who with kind hospitality, generosity and patience helped make this task so pleasurable. I am also deeply indebted to Dr Adrian Greaves of the Anglo Zulu War Historical Society, to Mike Snook, a regimental colleague and friend, Jane Brunning, archivist at the Denbighshire County Records Office, Terry Rogers from Marlborough College and Simon Fenwick, historian to the Postal and Courier Service. I also consulted a number of Regimental Headquarters about Wilfred Heaton's later years of service. To all these very helpful people I offer my sincere thanks. In addition I have received much practical advice and assistance from Peter Jenkins, Robert Curtis, John Whitchurch, Haydn Adams, Eleanor Potter, Rita Pace, Lesley

Cadmore and Jessica Lyons for which I am most grateful. As always I have enjoyed the continued support of my wife Jackie and finally, thanks are due in no small measure to Christopher Jones, Ken Fricker, Mark Radley and Geoff Fisher of Antony Rowe Printers for getting me back on the road again.

Wilfred Heaton was an Army officer who served with the 24th Regiment of Foot, later to become the South Wales Borderers and now amalgamated into The Royal Welsh, between 1874 and 1896. For most of his adult life he kept a series of annual diaries and on his death in 1921, these were deposited in the library of the family home in North Wales. There the diaries remained undisturbed until 1966 when his grandson, Mr Richard Heaton, donated the diary covering the year of 1879 to what was then the South Wales Borderers Museum in Brecon. Once again, the diary was to remain virtually unopened for a further 37 years until I undertook its full transcription as part of my degree course studies in 2003.

In transcribing the diary, every effort has been made to keep the document in its original form. It has not been possible to decipher every word and a series of dashes have been inserted where this is the case. The diary has been published verbatim and is most absorbing to read on its own, but I have attempted to provide a commentary from my own military experience where I consider a particular entry needs explanation or amplification. Any errors or inaccuracies of interpretation are mine alone. Like most diarists, the entries were written for his personal use only and he would never have imagined for one moment that some day they would be published in full for anyone else to read, nor was it ever meant to be a military record for historical analysis. Consequently he tended to write in short, often unconnected sentences; nevertheless, as one reads his diary an image emerges of a dedicated professional officer who genuinely cared for his soldiers and who worked hard for the benefit of others. The son of a vicar, he comes across as a sincere man of high principle but with a warm sense of humour. To set the scene to his diary, an introduction to his early years and the Regiment in which he served has been included; likewise a brief explanation of the causes of the Zulu War and the conduct of the campaign is necessary to put his comments into context. The book then concludes with the main events of his career after 1879 to provide a more complete biography. This unique document gives an account of a young man's experiences and activities during the Anglo-Zulu Wars in South Africa and it is hoped that it will add a social dimension to the wealth of material published already on one of the most dramatic colonial wars to have taken place in British military history.

In recent years there has been a plethora of books, documents, commentary, debate and analysis on the whole of the Anglo-Zulu War and one recurring criticism is that not enough weight is given to the Zulu perspective of this fascinating campaign. This is a fair comment which others more qualified than myself are better placed to address, but if this book is guilty of the same omission it is only because Wilfred Heaton, like so many of his fellow officers, saw the war from his viewpoint only and his diary was written not for academic study with the benefit of hindsight, but for his own pleasure. Likewise, this book is intended to be enjoyed by those readers who have a general interest in the Anglo-Zulu war of 1879 or in the military history of the Victorian era. It does not aspire to any lofty academic status, nor do I claim to have re-written the history of this conflict, but some notes and a select bibliography have been included at the end for those who wish to research this absorbing subject in more detail. Every effort has been made to obtain the necessary permissions with reference to copyright material, both illustrative and quoted. I apologise for any omissions in this respect and will be pleased to make the appropriate acknowledgements in any future editions.

Rodney Ashwood
Brecon
2011

DAVID RATTRAY

(Photo courtesy of Jack Crutchley)

XVI FOR QUEEN AND COUNTRY

David Rattray
– A Personal Tribute

For all of us left behind in a world grown darker by his enforced absence, we have to find a way of coming to terms with this most dreadful of tragedies.

His Royal Highness The Prince of Wales
from a message delivered at David's
funeral in February 2007

Just four days after the 128th anniversary of the Immortal Defence of Rorke's Drift, on Friday 26th January 2007, terrible news flashed across the Internet telling us that David Rattray, the world's leading authority on the history of the Zulu War had been killed at his Lodge at Fugitives Drift, Kwa Zulu Natal, South Africa. At a stroke, his wife Nicky and her three sons Andrew, Douglas and Peter were robbed of a treasured husband and father, the world wide Zulu war fraternity was denied forever that unique knowledge and understanding that only David possessed and my former Army Regiment lost a close friend and ally who never ceased to promote the illustrious deeds of the 24th Regiment of Foot during the Anglo Zulu War of 1879. All of the main British daily newspapers immediately carried his obituary, a measure of his international reputation and standing and Royal Princes made arrangements to attend or be represented at his funeral the following week.

So, who was David Rattray and how did he rise to such world wide stature, lecturing to thousands of people on the history of the Anglo Zulu war of 1879, whose gifted oratory could reduce even hard nosed military generals to tears; who also rubbed shoulders with such dignitaries as His Royal Highness The Prince of Wales who invited him on a number of occasions to Birkhall in Scotland and as a guest at Her Majesty The Queen Mother's funeral in 2002; and with Prince Mangosuthu Buthelezei, traditional chief of the Zulu nation? What was it that made the Royal Geographical Society in 1999 present him with the unique Ness Award in recognition of his work in widening popular understanding of Zulu culture in southern Africa, a beautiful country still bearing the scars of apartheid?

David Grey Rattray was born on the 6th September 1958 at Johannesburg where his father Peter was a lawyer and his mother Gillian a noted writer and artist. He was educated at St Albans College in Pretoria and then attended the University of Natal at Pietermaritzburg where he read entomology, graduating in 1982 at the age of 24. One would have thought that his degree might have been in history, given what was to follow but interestingly this was not his first choice. I use the word interestingly deliberately because David's passion for the Zulu wars dates back to his childhood when his father bought some land in the 1960s with an old farmhouse, adjoining the Mzinyathi river, or the Buffalo river, which used to be the natural border between Zululand and the colony of Natal and close to the crossing where the survivors of the Battle of Isandlwana fled to safety, now known as Fugitives' Drift. David always had difficulty with this name as he said it implied that they were trying to escape the arm of the law, which could not have been further from the truth. He would visit there regularly during the school holidays, learning the Zulu language, in which he became fluent and listening to the stories of a local man, Mnandi Ngobese, whose grandfather was a powerful chief and friend of James Rorke and whose father had fought in the Ngobamakosi Regiment at Isandlwana. What he heard completely changed his view of what had happened some 130 years beforehand.

For all this however, David first set out to become a game ranger and subsequently General Manager at Mala Mala Game Reserve, having married Nicky whom he had met at University. They also set up a tourist lodge business in Namibia, not in battlefield tours but on the wild game trail. Tragically their second son James was killed in an accident there as a very young boy and they returned to South Africa in 1989 moving into the farmhouse on David's father's land. At this point, David was at a crossroads and it was as if his whole life so far had led him to what was to become his destiny. Such was his obsession with what he considered to be the untold story of the Battle of Isandlwana, when over 600 men of the 1st Battalion the 24th Regiment of Foot were wiped out by 20,000 Zulu warriors from the mighty army of King Cetshwayo, and the Immortal Defence of Rorke's Drift when just 100 men of B Company, 2nd Battalion the 24th Regiment of Foot held out against a force of some 4,000 warriors, that David determined to make it his life's study.

As Mao Tse Tung is quoted as saying, *each journey begins with the first step* and it was from here that David and Nicky started their guest lodge and battlefield tours and it was not long before David's natural gift of story telling gathered momentum. I first met David and Nicky in July 1994, not long after I had taken over as the Curator of the South Wales Borderers Museum in Brecon. David was making the first of many trips to the home of the Regiment and being rather inexperienced at this stage I felt somewhat daunted at the thought of hosting such an illustrious visitor, but he immediately put me at my ease. I had the advantage of having served in the successor Regiment to the 24th of Foot he told me, something he had never done and he wanted to learn all he could from the coal face as it were. Flattery indeed, but we then enjoyed an unforgettable day looking at primary source documents, the Regimental collection of the original Victoria Crosses of the Zulu War and the Queen's Colour in the Regimental Chapel at Brecon Cathedral, which Lieutenants Melvill and Coghill had given their lives to try and save and who are now buried close to his Lodge. It was moving for both of us and this was a day I will always treasure.

To me, David was the ultimate orator and his gift of story-telling was unique. He never used slides, maps or other high tech teaching aides; he just created a picture in the mind's eye. I listened to David lecture on numerous occasions before my wife Jackie and I visited his lodge in 2001, yet every time he spoke I felt I knew the ground intimately and could feel the warmth of the sun and smell that distinctive aroma which to me, having lived in Kenya as a young boy, was uniquely Africa. I often felt that he had some form of hypnotic power over his audience but when I asked him about this on one occasion he just smiled and changed the subject. He had a rich, melodious voice with a lilt to his attractive South African accent, which would have been equally at home in Wales. With success came the opportunity to expand the Lodge into a very high grade and comfortable establishment, but one that never lost its colonial appeal and African atmosphere. For those of you who have not been there, Fugitives' Drift Lodge is way off the beaten track and it is a 20 minute ride from the nearest village along a bumpy road to get there. The Lodge itself is not far from the river and the spot where Lieutenants Melvill and Coghill, the officers who gave their lives attempting to save the Queen's Colour of their Regiment, are buried. The main building is a large room that serves as the dining room and sitting room, full of Zulu war artefacts and very tastefully decorated. French windows let out onto a large stone patio where a log fire is burnt in the centre each evening to keep the insects away and there is a low stone wall surrounding the patio on which one can sit watching the sun go down over the hill of Isandlwana in the distance. Within the grounds there are a number of buildings, which are the double bedrooms, all within a short walk of the main lodge while David and Nicky had their own house tucked away behind some bushes. When I visited, there was no mains electricity and the generator would be turned off at 11pm sharp and we reverted to oil lamps; it was also a means of ensuring everyone went to bed at a reasonable hour!

People of all walks of life have been enthralled by the manner in which David brought this fascinating campaign to life such was his gift as a story teller – an occupation by which he described himself on his tax return apparently. But it was more than that. As he told me once, it was a passionate love affair, a love of South Africa, a love of the Zulu nation and a love of the Welsh soldier who came from the South Wales valleys and who went out to that war in 1879 from the Barracks in Brecon where I used to work each day. David loved South Africa, the country of his birth. He often described it as the most beautiful place on earth and it was his avowed intention to do all that he could to ensure it did not go the way of other unfortunate African states. He saw so many opportunities for the development of tourism and his contribution was to promote the battlefield tours of the Zulu war era – a campaign that contained so many amazing stories of individual bravery, so many amazing stories of hope and despair and so many opportunities for peace and reconciliation. He also loved the Zulu nation. Their history is an oral one, passed down faithfully from generation to generation with incredible accuracy and David was weaned on this from a very young age. He became conscious of the fact that the majority of the Zulu war historical archives had a very white colonial bias, which did not pay sufficient tribute to the incredible acts of bravery on the other side as it were. Take for example Ntingshwayo kaMahole Khoza, the 65 year old commander of the Zulu army in the field who walked and ran every inch of the 50 miles from Ulundi to Isandlwana along with the 20,000 men he was about to lead into battle and who masterminded the greatest ignominy ever inflicted upon an Imperial army on the 22nd January 1879. Yet the history books make scant reference of the role he played on that fateful day and it was David who redressed the balance by describing this battle not as a British defeat but rather as a great Zulu victory. David had nothing against the British – far from it – but he wanted to restore pride to a once mighty nation which shaped the military hierarchy of South Africa and who were humiliated and broken up because of a totally unjustified war which was never of their making.

 He spent a lot of time and effort in trying to improve the welfare of the local Zulu people at Rorke's Drift and he was instrumental in finding the money to replace the stolen computers which the Rotary Club of Brecon helped to install at the local school there some years ago. And then he loved the Welsh soldier who fought so bravely in a war he probably never understood, in the most unforgiving of conditions in a land so very far away from home, a large number of whom were never to return. While of limited military experience himself, David instinctively understood the mutual respect which often exists between soldiers of opposing armies and he knew that the British soldier respected the Zulu warrior and he emphasised this in every talk he gave on this war, once again in a spirit of reconciliation which became his watchword. It is also a fact that he always promoted my Regiment and my town, whether talking to a small group of people on a dusty battle field tour on the South African veldt or to a packed house at the Royal Geographical Society in London, exhorting them all to come and visit Brecon, the Museum and the Cathedral and I have no doubt at all that many, many people have done so.

The huge attendance at David's funeral is testament to the high regard in which he was held and how his loss was painfully felt across South Africa and indeed the world. Prince Mangosuthu Buthelezei said these moving words in his funeral address – *David will never be replaced, nor will he be forgotten. I will remember him always, with affection and sometimes as one of his stories is retold, with a sense of wonder. David's rousing oratory will never be forgotten by those who heard it. He invoked the fierce warrior pride of the Zulus and the quiet bravery of the British regiments in truly spectacular fashion.*

And then in April of 2007 there was a memorial service at Southwark Cathedral in London, attended by Nicky and members of her family, which was packed to standing room only. By tradition, British Royalty are usually represented at such services but on this occasion The Prince of Wales was there in person. Given David's affection for Brecon, the local Aberhonddu Choir had been invited to sing and Brigadier Robert Aitken, a former Colonel of the Regiment concluded his Address with these remarks – *It is probably true to say that the history of my Regiment was an important part in David's life. It is certainly true to say that David is now part of my Regiment's history. He will live there forever.*

While there had been a number of Services to commemorate David, it was felt, regimentally at least, that there should be some tangible memorial to honour his name in perpetuity. I was asked to head up the project and on the 26th January 2009, the second anniversary of his death, a memorial plaque was dedicated in the garden of the Regimental Museum in Brecon. Having travelled from South Africa for the occasion Nicky, accompanied by her sons Andrew and Douglas and David's mother Gillian, unveiled the plaque in the presence of numerous military dignitaries and members of the public. The Dean of Brecon, The Very Reverend Geoffrey Marshall then dedicated the plaque and a Regimental bugler sounded the traditional and moving military laments of *Last Post*, to honour the fallen, followed by a period of silence to revere their memory and then *Reveille* to look forward to a new day. Made of Welsh slate and carved by a local stonemason, the plaque is fixed to the garden wall and the inscription reads:

In Proud Memory Of
Dr David Grey Rattray
1958 – 2007
Fugitives' Drift Lodge, South Africa
Zulu War Historian and Regimental Friend

The Memorial Unveiling Ceremony at Brecon on 26 January 2009. (From Left to Right) Rodney Ashwood, Jackie Ashwood, Andrew Rattray, Sergeant David Joseph with the Regimental Mascot, Douglas Rattray, Gillian Rattray (David's mother), Nicky Rattray. (Photo courtesy of Martin Everett)

XXII For Queen and Country

On her return home, David's mother Gillian wrote to say – *what a wonderful occasion the unveiling of the memorial to David was. It was so beautifully done and of course very moving and I would have travelled twice the distance to be there. Thank you for arranging it. David's father Peter joins me in sending greetings. We are both so proud that there is a small part of grey slate in Wales that honours our own son.*

And what of the future without David? For some time he had been grooming a number of tour guides to take over the bulk of the lecturing and battlefield tours eventually. As part of his attempt to promote the Zulu side of the battle he had trained up a local Zulu member of his staff, named Joseph Ndima, who came to visit Brecon for the first time in 2008 and if you were to close your eyes when you listened to him speak it was just as if David was there in the room, such was his command of the subject and the mannerisms of speech. Another figure crucial to the success of the Lodge is Rob Caskie, who has been part of the team for some 10 years and as the senior lecturer has been very much the anchor man since David died. He has steered the ship with unflagging commitment recently and his support has been quite outstanding. The Lodge remains as busy as ever and Nicky is determined that David's life work should advance unabated. She has launched the David Rattray Foundation, the funds from which will be used to carry on his community work and which is a project worth supporting and Nicky is confident that the mighty oaks, which grew from the little acorns David sowed over 20 years ago, will continue to flourish.

For those of you fortunate enough to have heard David talk at any time, you will recall that as an act of homage to the memory of all those who had perished in the Anglo Zulu war, he always drew his presentations to a close with these immortal lines of the poet Laurence Binyon:

> *They shall grow not old as we that are left grow old,*
> *Age shall not weary them nor the years condemn.*
> *At the going down of the sun and in the morning,*
> *We will remember them.*

David's race is over but, for those of us whom he touched, his legacy will never diminish. We will always remember him with great pride and may he rest in peace.

Rodney Ashwood
Brecon
2011

Chronology of Main Events

1854
7 June — Wilfred Heaton (WH) born at Llangedwyn, Montgomeryshire

1868
August — Started school at Marlborough College, Wiltshire

1873
12 November — Commissioned into the Royal Carnarvon Rifle Corps

1874
12 January — Resigned from the Royal Carnarvon Rifle Corps
28 February — Commissioned into the 24th Regiment of Foot
2 June — Reported for duty with the 1st Battalion 24th Foot in Gibraltar
30 November — Departed Gibraltar for South Africa

1875
1 January — Arrived at Cape Town

1877
August — Ninth Frontier War began

1878
June — Ninth Frontier War ended
25 September — WH departed King Williams Town for East London en route for Durban
25 November — Arrived at Durban, Natal
11 December — British ultimatum delivered to the Zulus

1879
7 January — WH began move from Durban to Helpmekaar
11 January — Ultimatum expired. Central column crossed into Zululand at Rorke's Drift
21 January — WH arrives at Helpmekaar
22 January — Battle of Isandlwana (Central column)
22 January — Battle of Inyezane (Coastal column)
22/23 January — Defence of Rorke's Drift

12 March	Battle of Ntombe Drift
28 March	Battle of Hlobane
29 March	Battle of Khambula
2 April	Battle of Gingindlhovu
13 April	Lord Chelmsford reorganized his Columns into Divisions in preparation for the second invasion
28 May	WH moved from Helpmekaar after 3 months to Kopje Alleine
31 May	Second invasion began
1 June	Prince Imperial killed
20 June	First attempt to bury bodies of the 24th Foot at Isandlwana
4 July	Battle of Ulundi
8 July	Lord Chelmsford resigned and is replaced by General Wolseley
10 July	WH began withdrawal from Zululand back to Natal
17 August	WH camped on the outskirts of Durban
27 August	Began homeward journey with 1st/24th Foot to England by sea
28 August	King Cetshwayo captured and taken into exile at Capetown
2 October	WH arrived at Portsmouth, England
15 October	Went on leave at home for 8 weeks, via Brecon
15 December	Reported for duty at Brecon

1880

4 September	Promoted to Captain

1881

1 July	24th Foot became the South Wales Borderers (SWB)

1882

25 April	WH posted to 2nd Battalion SWB in Gibraltar
6 August	2nd Battalion presented with new Colours to replace those lost at Isandlwana
1 September	WH arrived in Bombay for service in the East Indies

1884

February	Battalion moved to Madras. WH detached to the Andaman Islands

1885

25 November	Promoted to Major

1886
May   2nd Battalion in Rangoon for the Burma campaign

1888
June–December   WH in temporary command of the Battalion

1889
8 July   Married Florence Church at Bareilly, India

1890
5 June   First son, Wilfred John, born at Rhaniket, India

1891
1 July   Daughter Florence Catherine born. Died 3 weeks later and buried at Allahabad
19 December   Inherited *Plas Heaton* on the death of his father

1892
April   WH and family returned to England
7 July   Second son, Hugh Edward, born at *Plas Heaton*

1896
30 September   Retired on half pay as a Lieutenant Colonel

1901
13 September   Assumed command of the 4th Bn The Royal Garrison Regiment

1902
May   Moved to Malta with the Battalion
18 October   Promoted to the rank of Colonel on the Reserve of Officers

1904
August   Moved to South Africa with the Battalion and took responsibility for the Harrismith District

1905
10 February   Relinquished command of the Battalion and returned to England

1914 – 1918   Returned to the Reserve of Officers during World War I to work for the Postal Censorship Unit in London

1921
29 September   WH died of a heart attack at the Beechwood Hotel, Harrogate
3 October   Funeral service at Henllan, Denbighshire

List of Illustrations

Frontispiece
The Last Stand at Isandhula by Charles Edwin Fripp (1854 – 1906). Fripp covered the Zulu War for *The Graphic* newspaper and exhibited this painting at the Royal Academy in 1885. It is now owned by the National Army Museum who received it as a gift from the 21st Special Air Services Regiment. (The unusual spelling of Isandlwana was thought to be correct at the time). (National Army Museum)

1. Plas Heaton, the family seat at Henllan Denbighshire, which Wilfred Heaton inherited in 1891. (Author's collection)
2. Llangedwyn, Montgomeryshire, birthplace of Wilfred Heaton, 7th June 1854. (Author's collection)
3. The parish church at Llangedwyn where Wilfred Heaton's father was vicar and where Wilfred was baptized. (Author's collection)
4. Principal towns, roads and routes together with main actions during the Anglo-Zulu War of 1879. (Anglo-Zulu War Historical Society)
5. The Battle of Isandlwana showing the Zulu army 'horns of the buffalo' battle formations. (Anglo-Zulu War Historical Society)
6. A sketch map of the Battle of Isandlwana 1879, drawn shortly afterwards by Captain William Penn Symons 2/24th Regiment. He rose to the rank of Lieutenant General and died of wounds sustained at the battle of Talana Hill in October 1899 during the Boer War. (Royal Welsh Museum)
7. *The Defence of Rorke's Drift*. Painted in 1880 by the French artist Alphonse Marie de Neuville (1835–1885) this famous picture encapsulates the variety of action during the defence of Rorke's Drift at some point just after 6pm when the hospital was set on fire. There are two 'original' paintings – this one is an original (owned by The Royal Welsh) and is believed to be his rough work prior to painting the full sized picture which is now in the Art Gallery of New South Wales in Australia. (Royal Welsh Museum)
8. A plan of the defensive position at Rorke's Drift, 22nd January 1879 by Lt John Chard VC, Royal Engineers and the officer in

charge during the battle. It shows the direction of the Zulu advance from Isandlwana and the line of the defences which were hastily erected. (Royal Welsh Museum)
9. A young Victorian officer, drawn by Lieutenant William Whitelocke Lloyd, who served in D Company 1st/24th Foot with Wilfred Heaton. There was no such officer as 'Tomkins of B Company,' so it is quite possible that this is a caricature of Wilfred as the two officers were very close friends. (Royal Welsh Museum)
10. Life on active service, captured by William Lloyd. (Royal Welsh Museum)
11. The trials and tribulations of living in the field, giving an indication of Lloyd's sense of humour. (Royal Welsh Museum)
12. In contact with the enemy – caught off guard or William Lloyd giving rise to that well known expression . . .?! (Royal Welsh Museum)
13. School of Musketry, Hythe Kent 1880. Wilfred (with drooping moustache) is seated on the left of the third row looking directly at the camera and just below the left elbow of the officer standing with his arms folded. (Royal Welsh Museum)
14. Line Laying Course, School of Military Engineering, Chatham Kent 1880. Wilfred is seated second from the right, looking away from the camera. (Line laying was for communication purposes, with the advent of the electronic field telephone). (Royal Welsh Museum)
15. The Heaton brothers in 1897. Rear L – R: Ernest, Wilfred (then age 43) and Bernard. Front L – R: Gilbert and Kenneth. Bernard was the last survivor who died in 1959. (Richard Heaton's collection)
16. Colonel Wilfred Heaton, as a reserve officer in 1911 at the age of 57, from a family oil painting. (Author's collection)
17. Mrs Florence Heaton, from a family portrait, painted in 1911 at the age of 41. (Author's collection)
18. The parish church at Henllan, where Wilfred was a warden for some years and where many of the Heaton family are buried. (Author's collection)
19. (Foreground centre). The final resting place of Wilfred and Florence Heaton, Henllan parish church cemetery. (Author's collection)

Prologue

It was going to be another hot day, but at least it had stopped raining. As dawn broke over the South African colony of Natal on Wednesday 22 January 1879, Lieutenant Wilfred Heaton rose early from his makeshift bed at the administrative base at Helpmekaar, high up on a windy escarpment looking down towards the Buffalo River which was the border between Natal and Zululand. Not yet 25 years old but already an experienced junior officer in the 1st Battalion the 24th Regiment of Foot, Wilfred had arrived there late on the previous evening with his Company, having spent the last 10 days moving up country from the coast at Durban along very poor tracks made even worse by the incessant rain in recent weeks. Although he had the relative comfort of riding a horse while his soldiers marched on foot, he was no doubt ready for a short break, a good meal, the comfort of a hot bath and a change of clothes. None of this was possible for the time being, however, as the long awaited invasion of Zululand had begun and he and his men were under orders to move on a further 10 miles or so with another Company to assist in the security of a stores depot and a makeshift hospital close to a shallow crossing point into Zululand across the Buffalo River, known as Rorke's Drift.

Wilfred was no stranger to South Africa, having been there for the last four years. Most of this time had been spent in the Cape Colony much further to the south where he had been involved in security duties in Griqualand West following the discovery of diamonds there in 1876 and then more recently on active service during the ninth frontier war. This was the culmination of a long period of territorial dispute between white settlers and the tribes of the indigenous Xhosa people around the Great Kei River along eastern boundary of the Cape Colony, stretching back 100 years to the first frontier war in 1779. As this war drew to a successful conclusion in the summer of 1878, Wilfred was then told that his Battalion was to move north to Natal to join a large Imperial force being gathered in preparation for a possible campaign against the Zulu nation of King Cetshwayo. One of the reasons given for this likely confrontation was that their aggressive war-like behaviour and large standing army of native warriors was a threat to the way of life of the white colonial settlers living in neighbouring Natal. This was not perceived to be a problem however as the Regiment had dispensed with their native adversaries in the ninth frontier war with ease and an army of Zulus equipped only with shields and spears would hardly be a match for disciplined British infantrymen armed with the latest Martini-Henry rifle.

When Wilfred arrived at Durban in December 1878, he learnt that an ultimatum had been delivered to the Zulu King. Unless Cetshwayo disbanded his army in the next 30 days, British forces would have no alternative but to invade his country to do this for him. The 1st and 2nd Battalions 24th Foot were now at the coast and had begun to move north west ready for the inevitable conflict, while D Company, of which he was part, and G Company of the 1st Battalion remained behind to assist in garrison administration and were then to follow on behind. Like any young officer at the time Wilfred did not wish to miss out on the action and was keen to move forward himself as soon as he could. The 30 day period of the ultimatum expired with no response from King Cetshwayo and on Saturday 11 January 1879 Lord Chelmsford, commander of all the British forces in South Africa, advanced into Zululand intent on breaking up this defiant army which had chosen to ignore him. His only fear was that he might not actually be able to get the Zulu army to fight.

There were three Columns advancing simultaneously into Zululand along different routes and Lord Chelmsford had decided to attach himself and his headquarters to the central Column which had passed through Helpmekaar in the previous week and had crossed into Zululand at Rorke's Drift. Wilfred Heaton's Company was also part of this Column and by early afternoon on 22 January he was about ready to continue the advance. Equipment had been reduced to the bare minimum so that each man was carrying just his backpack with essential items, plus a blanket to act as his bed at night and 70 rounds of ammunition in his pouches. The remainder of the Company's baggage would be loaded onto the large trek wagons, pulled by 16 oxen and which would make their way slowly behind the marching men under the supervision of a transport conductor and a military escort. All the troops were dressed in their one and only style of uniform, a bright red thick serge jacket and blue trousers with heavy leather boots, and the only concession to the sub-tropical sun was a white topee helmet which might be stained with tea as an attempt at camouflage. Their uniforms were already beginning to show signs of wear and tear as the facility for re-supply was limited, but as they were convinced that this campaign was going to be short and sharp the existing clothing would make do for now.

As he had arrived at Helpmekaar only the night before, Wilfred had little idea where the central Column was, or whether it had seen any action so far. With only native runners or mounted infantrymen to carry despatches, the passage of information was sometimes quite slow, but as his Company paraded in the early afternoon for the march to Rorke's Drift, a number of strange and ominous reports started to come in. Riders came galloping up to say that the main Column was camped about 20 miles away at a hill feature called Isandlwana and had suddenly been attacked that morning by a massive Zulu army and all but a few white men and native levies had been slaughtered in the space of just a few hours. Given the size of the force and the firepower that Lord Chelmsford had under his command no-one could believe that such a catastrophe was possible, particularly against an adversary armed primarily with only shields and spears, but there was no doubt from the horrifying reports of those lucky enough to have escaped with their lives that it was true. A compulsive diarist for most of his life, Wilfred Heaton was about to record a year he was unlikely ever to forget.

CHAPTER 1

STEPPING OUT

In the quiet unspoilt countryside of North Wales there is a small village near Denbigh called Henllan and while most pleasant and well kept, it would be quite unremarkable save for the presence of the large, attractive country estate just on its outskirts, close to the road leading to Treffnant. Here lies *Plas Heaton*, seat of the Heaton family, who have been associated with the county of Denbighshire for the last 800 years. The family can trace its heritage back to the Hetons of Heton in Lancaster and they first came to Wales as soldiers in the 13th century. They were given land at Lleweni Green by King Edward I and by inter-marrying with other notable families in the area, such as the Myddletons of Gwaenynog, the Griffiths of Garn, the Wyns of Voelas and the Lloyds of Foxhall, they acquired further properties and extended their influence in Denbighshire. Such was their standing that in 1572 the Heaton family incurred the displeasure of Robert Dudley, Earl of Leicester who complained to the burgesses of Denbigh that the Heatons had taken it upon themselves to choose a burgess to represent them in Parliament without his consent! In the early 18th century they also became Lords of the Manor of Wareham in Norfolk through marriage, but Denbigh remained the centre of their interests. Members of the family have served as High Sheriff and Deputy Lieutenant of Denbighshire and John Heaton (1787–1855) was Chairman of Quarter Sessions for 18 years and also Chairman of the Committee of Visitors of the North Wales Lunatic Asylum. In 1805 the family purchased the impressive manor house at Henllan, then known as *Plas Newydd*, which they renamed *Plas Heaton.*

Although the Heaton family tree can be traced back in outline to about 1475, the most verifiable records are to be found in the front pages of a magnificent leather bound family bible published in 1727 during the reign of King George II, which is kept in the library at *Plas Heaton*. Here, generations of the family have lovingly hand-written their lineage in great detail since 1736 when John Heaton married Martha Adamson in that year. They were living in London at the time when the infant mortality rate was high, as the first entry in the family bible records:

> *'John the son of John Heaton and Martha his wife was borne on Saturday the third day of January 1736 at half an hour after four of the clock in the morning and was baptized by Mr Withers the curate of St Mary Woolnoth*

London on Wednesday the fourteenth day of Janry aforesaid. Jack dyed and was buried at Wearham in Norfolk October 1737 sadly was brought to God when 2 years and ½ old of a boy who dyed in the night.'

John and Martha Heaton were to have four children, but as their first born son John, referred to above, died in infancy, inheritance went to their second son, Richard. He married Sarah Venables in 1783 and they had five children of which John, their third child but the first born son, continued the family lineage. Later, this son John was to marry Elizabeth Jones of *Cefn Coch* on 2 August 1814 and they had six children. Sadly Elizabeth died in 1822 at only 28 years old and two years later John married again, this time to Anne Eliza Henniker, daughter of the Right Honourable Lord Henniker of Major House, Suffolk. They were to have a further 10 children, but the succession was to be through the descendants of John Heaton's first marriage. While the custom and practice of primogeniture would normally apply, John's sixth child and youngest son of the first marriage, Hugh Edward, born on 13 May 1821, was to outlive his brothers who had either died in infancy or who had left no descendants themselves and in 1855 he inherited *Plas Heaton* on the death of his father. A few years earlier in 1852 Hugh had married Catherine Maria Craven and they were to have a total of 12 children. There were nine boys, two of whom died at a very early age and two who died as young 20 year olds and three girls, but it is their first born child who as son and heir is of particular interest to us. [1]

Hugh had been ordained into the priesthood and was the vicar of the parish church at Llangedwyn, Montgomeryshire when his first son Wilfred Heaton was born on Wednesday 7 June 1854 at *Plas Uchaf*, the vicarage in the village. Wilfred was baptized by his father a month later in his parish church on 2 July 1854. According to the family bible, the godparents – or sponsors as they are referred to – were John Richard Heaton (his uncle), the Revd George Powell and Margaret Craven (his aunt). The family then lived at *Plas Uchaf* until Wilfred was five, when his father returned to Denbighshire in 1859 to take up the appointment of vicar at Bettws yn Rhos, not far from *Plas Heaton*, where he remained until he retired in 1885. It was here that Wilfred was to grow up in the close companionship of his own large family and with other relatives and friends who lived on the local country estates such as *Garn, Galltfaenon, Garthewin* and *Cefn Coch*. Fond of the outdoor life, he took part in the traditional country pursuits of hunting and shooting and was to develop an abiding love of horses, which he was to continue into his adult life. During the winter months he would enjoy nothing better than skating on the frozen ponds of *Cefn Coch*.

At the age of 14, Wilfred went away to boarding school and in August 1868 he started at Marlborough College in Wiltshire, one of England's premier public schools. Set up originally for the sons of the clergy, facilities at Marlborough were fairly spartan in an attempt to keep the fees to a minimum. His boarding house for the next four years was called C2, so named as it was in a complex of three such purpose built houses, (the initial letter representing the original Church House) and his house master was Mr A H Beesley, who taught classics. Having just arrived at the College he was then away for most of the Michaelmas term between September and December 1868 with various ailments, but for the rest of his time there he maintained a respectable average of middle of the class for academic studies. Tall, slim and naturally fit, Wilfred made the College 1st rugby team in his final term, where the College magazine described him as ' – *a good forward of some strength who plays well on the ball, but should try to use his head more.*' By this stage, he was also showing an inclination towards soldiering and he joined the College Rifle Volunteer Corps, becoming a member of the Corps Shooting XI. Annual reports were written on individual progress within the Corps and there is an entry about a certain Private W Heaton who ' . . . *often shines at the long ranges, but stands in need of further improvement at standing ones.*' [2] He obviously took this advice to heart and made the further improvement necessary, for within three months of leaving school in the summer of 1873 the army had become his chosen profession and he was about to embark upon a long and distinguished period of service.

When Wilfred decided upon a military career, he chose well. His first experience in uniform was with the Royal Carnarvon Rifle Corps, a Militia Regiment in North Wales, which he joined on 12 November 1873 when not yet 20 years old. This was a temporary expedient only, while he waited to take the Civil Service Commissions examination, which was held at Burlington Gardens in London on 2 January 1874. Out of 80 candidates he came a modest 62nd having passed English, Maths, Latin, French and Geometrical Drawing. [3] This enabled him to resign from the Militia on 12 January 1874 and one month later he was commissioned into the 24th Regiment of Foot on 28 February 1874. The purchase of commissions had been abolished some three years previously and although he did not attend the Military College at Sandhurst he was obviously considered ready to join a regular battalion. As a descendant of well established landed gentry in Denbighshire he could have chosen one of many Regiments, infantry or cavalry, but by now the 24th Regiment of Foot was well ensconced in Wales, with a Depot in Brecon since the previous year and it was recruiting throughout most Welsh counties. The next 20 years of his life were to be inextricably linked with one of the most famous and distinguished Welsh regiments, as fate was soon to determine.

1. *Plas Heaton*, the family seat at Henllan Denbighshire, which Wilfred Heaton inherited in 1891. (Author's collection)

2. Llangedwyn, Montgomeryshire, birthplace of Wilfred Heaton, 7th June 1854. (Author's collection)

3. The parish church at Llangedwyn where Wilfred Heaton's father was vicar and where Wilfred was baptized. (Author's collection)

CHAPTER 2

THE NOBLE 24TH

While the heritage of the 24th Foot and its successor Regiments is now an inextricable part of Wales, this was not the case at the time that Wilfred joined, when its origins were very much elsewhere. Some 200 years previously in 1689, King William had signed a Proclamation for the raising of 10 Regiments of Foot to serve in Ireland and in March 1689 Sir Edward Dering, a Kentish Baronet who owned the manor of Surrenden near Ashford, raised one of these Regiments. A commemorative stone at Pluckley Church records the event and by 28 March 1689 Dering's Regiment, as it was then known, took its place in the Infantry of the Line. At the time, an infantry regiment was very much the preserve of its Colonel who was at liberty to determine its uniforms and Colours and the expenditure of Government funds for the clothing, quartering and pay of his unit was left entirely in his hands. It is worth noting at this point that the Colonelcy of a Regiment then bore little resemblance to the honorary appointment that it is now. Today the Colonel of the Regiment is more often than not a retired senior officer acting as the regimental figurehead, while the battalions are commanded by lieutenant colonels, usually aged about 40. Until the mid 18th century the colonel of the regiment was the *de facto* commanding officer, with all the training and administrative responsibilities of that appointment, including active command in the field. It would be customary for him to appoint a lieutenant colonel as his second in command. [1]

Less than 5 months after the first muster parade, Colonel Dering's Regiment found itself on active service. In August 1689 King William despatched a large expeditionary force to Northern Ireland to counter the Catholic uprising there and on 13 August the Regiment landed at Bangor. Sir Edward Dering's tenure was short-lived as he died of fever at Dundalk in September 1689 and his brother Daniel succeeded him, thus perpetuating the family name embodied in the Regiment. This was to be the custom for the next 50 years as the Regiment's title changed with each new Colonel. Returning from Northern Ireland in 1691, the Regiment was stationed briefly in Somerset but soon moved to the south coast of England following threats of French invasion. For the next 5 years it saw service on the continent until returning to Ireland once again, this time to Dublin having been transferred to what was called the Irish Establishment as a result of recently imposed cuts in strength.

In 1702 the Colonel of the Regiment changed over once more, this time to the illustrious John Churchill, 1st Duke of Marlborough, who was Colonel of the Regiment from 1702 to 1704. Then followed the War of the Spanish Succession when such famous battles as Blenheim, Ramilies, Oudenarde and Malplaquet were enshrined in the annals of the Regiment's history. Another notable figure was Colonel Thomas Howard who was Colonel from 1717 to 1737 and whose name gave rise to the regimental nickname of 'Howard's Greens' from the green colour of the uniform facings and a colour which remains associated with the Regiment to this day. The practice of name changes ceased in 1751 when a Royal Warrant directed that henceforth all regiments were to be designated by a number according to their seniority in the Line; that is the date on which the regiment was first raised. [2] Thus Colonel Ancram's Regiment, as it was then known, became the 24th Regiment of Foot. Old habits die hard of course but before long this became the accepted practice and the new title became synonymous with the Regiment and continues to do so, even after a number of reforms and amalgamations. During this period other events of significance in the Regiment's history took place. With the Seven Year's War with France looming, in 1756 the Government ordered the raising of a further 15 battalions, one of which was the 2nd Battalion the 24th Regiment of Foot. Recruited mainly from the Midlands, this battalion assumed its own identity in 1758 when it became the 69th Foot. Much later it was to be subsumed into the Welch Regiment which in turn amalgamated with the South Wales Borderers (24th Foot) in 1969, thus returning to the fold once more; but that is another story.

Also towards the latter part of the 18th century a regimental colonel was rarely the actual commanding officer as he had been in Marlborough's day and before. Nearly always a general officer by now, he was usually found some staff appointment which supplemented his pay as colonel; without such appointment he received no pay of general's rank. From this stage onwards therefore, the active command of the regiment devolved to the lieutenant colonel, as it has been ever since. Then at about the same time infantry regiments were allotted specific recruiting areas and the counties of Devon, Cornwall and Somerset were assigned to the 24th Foot. [3] However, the Regiment spent little or no time in this area and was in fact otherwise serving in such places as Cartagena, Minorca, Gibraltar, the war on the continent against the French and eventually in the American War of Independence from 1775 to 1781. Here the Regiment fought with great distinction but sustained heavy casualties during its 6 years in North America, either in action or through disease and sickness.

The 24th Foot returned home to a major change in the Army's recruiting policy, which was to have a significant bearing on its title for the next century. A Royal Warrant of 31 August 1782 conferred county titles on all regiments which did not have a Royal designation already and the 24th Foot was arbitrarily assigned to Warwickshire. It was apparently intended that regiments should cultivate a recruiting connection with counties whose name they took and the 24th Foot, which became the 2nd Battalion the Warwickshire Regiment (the 6th Foot being the 1st Warwickshires) were ordered to send a recruiting party to Tamworth. However, no special link with the county militia was established, nor were any Depots or permanent recruiting centres set up. [4] This county link was to remain in the regimental title for virtually 100 years, but as most infantry regiments continued to use their numerical title in preference anyway, it is fair to say that Warwickshire itself did not play a significant part in its Regimental history. As we will see later, the Regiment established a more lasting affiliation with the Marches of South Wales where its depot was to be established in 1873.

The beginning of the 19th century saw an increase in the Regiment when the Additional Forces Act of 1803 raised the 2nd Battalion 24th Foot. As was customary practice extra battalions would be raised in time of need only to be disbanded when the crisis was over and the Government could no longer afford to maintain them. This was the fate of the 2nd Battalion, which was disbanded in 1814 after the Peninsular Wars only to be raised again in 1858 when commitments in India and elsewhere demanded a larger army once more. While these two battalions had links in title, their fortunes took them in different directions around the globe. Of particular interest is the 1st Battalion's service in India during the Second Sikh War and the Battle of Chillianwalla in January 1849. While the outcome of the battle was eventually a success, the 24th Foot took very severe casualties including the loss of its Colours. Flags, banners and standards have long been rallying points on the field of battle and over the centuries they have come to embody the honour, pride and spirit of a regiment. Each infantry battalion would have two such flags, or Colours as they are correctly called; one being the Queen's (or King's) Colour bearing the Union Flag, the other being the Regimental Colour which is unique to that battalion. Battle Honours awarded by the Sovereign would be emblazoned on the Colours and until the time of the Boer War they were carried into battle, closely guarded by two officers and three senior non commissioned officers (known as the Colour Party, so giving rise to the rank of Colour Sergeant) as it was a disgrace for the

Colours to fall into the hands of the enemy. During the battle, the Queen's Colour disappeared completely, allegedly wrapped under the tunic and around the chest of an officer whose body was lost under the mud of the battlefield; at least it was not captured. When Ensign Collis fell bearing the Regimental Colour of the 24th Foot this was bravely rescued by Private Perry who was awarded a gallantry medal for his courageous action. [5] This Colour (known as the Chillianwalla Colour) continued in service until 1868 when it and the missing Queen's Colour were replaced by new ones which were to become immortalized 11 years later in 1879. The Chillianwalla Colour was laid up in the Beauchamp Chapel of St Mary's Church in Warwick where it remained for the next 60 years until the Regiment (by now the South Wales Borderers) requested its transfer in 1925 to its newly appointed Chapel in Brecon Cathedral. There followed an 11 year struggle with the Church authorities in Warwick for its release until the Chillianwalla Colour eventually returned to the spiritual home of the Regiment in 1936. This was not the first time the Regiment had lost its Colours, however – nor was it to be the last. During hostilities against the French in 1810, the 1st 24th Foot were en route to India by sea when their ships were engaged in the Mozambique Channel. With *HMS Ceylon* about to be taken captive, the commanding officer had the Colours with regimental books and records thrown overboard rather than surrender them to the enemy. [6]

Later the 2nd Battalion moved to Mauritius and then to Burma from 1865 to 1873 where the Regiment gained the first five of its 23 Victoria Crosses, the nation's highest possible accolade for valour and the highest number won by any single infantry regiment. Investigating a report that the crew of a British ship had been massacred by natives on one of the Andaman islands, a company of the Battalion became trapped on the beach, unable to get back to their own ship anchored off-shore because of bad weather. In high running seas, the battalion doctor, Assistant Surgeon Douglas and four men ran a gig, or small boat, back and forth through the heavy surf from ship to shore, saving almost 100 soldiers of the Battalion from being massacred, putting their own lives at risk in the process. All five men were awarded the VC for their undoubted courage and while this incident may not have met the prime requirement of conspicuous bravery in the face of the enemy in combat, it must be remembered that the carefully selective procedures which now determine the award of this medal had not then been introduced. [7] In 1873, the 2nd 24th Foot returned home to Aldershot at the same time as the Brigade Depot at Brecon was set up in the town barracks as part of the Cardwell reforms. Recruiting in the counties of Brecon, Radnor, Cardigan and Monmouth, from this period the Regiment began the development of its Welsh identity. However, the two battalions were not to serve together until early 1878, when the frontier wars of the Cape Colony (or the Kaffir wars as they were also referred to) called for more infantry battalions to be posted to South Africa.

In the meantime, Wilfred had undergone a period of training at the Regimental Depot and on 2 June 1874, one week before his 20th birthday, he reported for duty with the 1st Battalion in Gibraltar along with Lieutenants Edgar Anstey, James Daley, Nevill Coghill, William Spring, George Hodson and Charles Atkinson. Little did they realize that less than 5 years later, only two of them, Wilfred and Lieutenant Spring, would still be alive. (Even Spring was to die seven years after the war in 1886 at the age of 31, presumably of some illness, at his home in Harrogate.)

One of these officers, Nevill Josiah Aylmer Coghill to give him his full name, was to rise to great fame as we shall learn later on. Born in 1852 in Dublin and the son of a Baronet, he went to Sandhurst in 1871, having served for 2 years in the County of Dublin Militia. He was then commissioned in the 24th Foot in 1873. [8] There was not a lot of time to enjoy the delights of a Mediterranean posting, however, as the next few months were spent preparing the Battalion for its forthcoming move to South Africa. By the autumn, more drafts had arrived under Captain William Degacher and at the end of November 1874 they set sail for South Africa in the troopships *Simoon* and *Himalaya*, arriving in Cape Town on New Year's Day 1875. It was while serving at the Cape that Wilfred was to witness the sad death of one of his fellow officers of the 1st/24th Foot in a swimming accident. On one particularly hot day on 31 January 1877, he and Sub Lieutenant Richard Grenvill Deane went for a swim in the Liesbeck River. Richard dived in but did not surface, having probably struck his head on the river bottom, and Wilfred immediately went to his aid. He managed to drag Richard to the riverbank and tried to resuscitate him, but unfortunately he had drowned. [9] At the age of only 21, Lieutenant Richard Deane was buried at the Claremount Cemetery in Capetown, where his grave can still be found.

After helping defuse the confrontation between the Cape authorities and the dissident prospectors in the diamond fields of Kimberley, over the next three years Wilfred was to experience his first taste of active service in what was known as the ninth frontier war. This was the culmination of a long period of territorial dispute between white settlers and the tribes of the indigenous Xhosa people around the Great Kei River along eastern boundary of the Cape Colony, stretching back 100 years to the first frontier war in 1779. Most of these engagements were inconclusive but the pattern of cattle raid, destruction, reprisal and atrocity was to repeat itself regularly. On this occasion the war varied between such actions as native attacks on British and Mfengu entrenched positions in the Amathole Mountains and skirmishing tactics against the Ngicka army in the Perie Bush. As this particular war was drawing to its successful conclusion, events to the north in the colony of Natal were leading to an inevitable confrontation, this time with a much more aggressive and disciplined army – the Zulus of King Cetshwayo. The 24th Foot were highly praised for their professionalism during this frontier war, but their success was to create a false illusion. The ninth frontier war was won by a relatively small number of troops and at a low cost in white lives. The battle at Quintana (or Centane), for instance, was hailed as a model action against numerically superior but poorly armed forces. It resulted in a euphoric overestimation of the potency of disciplined infantry armed with the Martini-Henry rifle, an error which played a part in the terrible mismanagement a year later at Isandlwana. [10]

While Wilfred was serving in the Cape Colony, another officer who was to become a close friend was in the process of joining the Regiment. Two years younger than Wilfred, William Whitelocke Lloyd was born on 5 May 1856 in Ireland. His father, George Whitelocke Lloyd, had his main property at Strancally Castle near Villierstown in County Waterford and he also had an estate near Calton in Yorkshire. A Deputy Lieutenant and High Sheriff of the West Riding of Yorkshire, George married Selina Jane Henry, daughter of Arthur Henry Esq. of Lodge Park, County Kildare on 14 September 1854. In addition to William, there were three daughters – Eveline, Augusta and Selina. Their mother died in 1860 when William was only three and in 1861 their father remarried, his second bride being Lady Anne Margaret Butler Somerset, daughter of Richard Somerset, Earl of Carrick. [11] William's first military experience was with the Carlow Rifles Militia and on 12 June 1878 he was commissioned into the 24th Foot. A month later he set sail in the SS *Balmoral Castle*, to join the Regiment in South Africa as it came to the end of the ninth frontier war in the eastern Cape. He caught up with them at East London as they waited to embark on HMS *Tyne* to make their way north to Durban in anticipation of coming conflict with the Zulu army of King Cetshwayo. William was assigned to D Company where he first met Wilfred.

Meanwhile, Nevill Coghill who had served on the staff of the field force commander, General Sir Arthur Cunnynghame, as his Aide-de-Camp during the frontier war, returned to England briefly in 1878, only to return again as preparations for the Zulu war began, this time as ADC to the High Commissioner in South Africa, Sir Bartle Frere. So keen was he to be involved in any likely action he was granted permission to return to his Battalion, this time as an ADC to his commanding officer, Colonel Glyn. At the same time, a brother officer whose name was to be linked with Coghill was also in the Cape Colony. Lieutenant Teignmouth Melvill was 10 years older than Coghill, having been born in 1842 in London. After a university education at Cambridge he was commissioned into the 24th Foot in 1865 while the Regiment was in Ireland during which time the Battalion received its new Colours with which his name was to be forevermore associated, as we shall see. By 1873 he was the Adjutant in the rank of Lieutenant, serving with the Battalion as they embarked on the ninth frontier war. While in South Africa he married Sarah Elizabeth Reed in 1876 and also passed the examination for the Staff College in England, to which he returned in January 1878. Clearly not to his liking he immediately volunteered to return to the Cape Colony on learning of fresh hostilities there, arriving back with his Battalion a month later. [12] Having made this decision, little did he realize that fate was to determine an eternal place in Regimental history for himself and Lieutenant Coghill soon after the beginning of the Anglo-Zulu war.

CHAPTER 3
Prelude to War

There are a number of interpretations as to the causes of the Anglo–Zulu War, but most seem to agree that the seeds were sown when Shaka kaSenzangakhona ascended to the Zulu throne in 1816. In the space of 12 years, he took a hitherto obscure tribe and created a mighty Zulu nation, whose army was to strike fear and awe throughout the whole of Southern Africa. Described both as a great military leader and as a despotic tyrant, Shaka never fought against the British. It was his half brother and assassin, Dingane, who plotted Shaka's death in 1828 who was to breed the lasting distrust between black and white when he opposed the Boer trekkers as they attempted to settle along the borders of Zululand. One of the Boer leaders, Piet Retief, was murdered by Dingane in an act of treachery in February 1838 but the Boers took their revenge in the humiliating defeat of the Zulu army at the Battle of Blood River later that year in December 1838. This led to a shift in the balance of power in favour of the Boers who sided with Dingane's younger brother Mpande, who succeeded to the Zulu throne in 1840 when Dingane was eventually usurped and later murdered. [1]

There was an uneasy peace during the reign of Mpande, but the neighbouring colony of Natal never felt secure with such a large standing army of fearsome reputation along its border. This unease was not helped with the power struggle between Mpande's two sons Cetshwayo and Mbuyazi for succession to the throne, when at the battle of nDondakasuka in December 1856, some 20,000 natives were killed in some of the worst inter-nicene blood-letting witnessed in Zululand in living memory. King Cetshwayo finally inherited the Zulu throne in 1873 at the age of 41 on the death of his father. Although he had no intentions of invading the colony of Natal, British imperial aspirations and Boer territorial intransigence along the Transvaal border with Zululand meant that the stage was set for inevitable conflict before too long.

From a British perspective the catalyst for this conflict was the discovery of diamonds at Kimberley in the virtually uninhabited Griqualand West in 1867. This area was not under British jurisdiction, but this was relatively easy to resolve and in typical colonial fashion British administrators simply reassessed the border and adjusted their maps to bring the diamond fields under direct British control. [2] This was in keeping with progressive British foreign policy towards confederation as a means of successfully administering its many and diverse colonies. Confederation was the unification of a collection of neighbouring territories and then grouping them under one central administration. This policy had been successful in such places as India, Australia and Canada and the powers-that-be in the Cape Colony saw no reason why such a policy should not work in Southern Africa as well. However, as well as a perceived danger of Zulu aggression, a stumbling block to this policy was the potential threat of the Boers and their recently established independent state of the Transvaal on the borders of Natal and Zululand, and the British solution to this problem was the arbitrary annexation of the Transvaal. While it was in Britain's wider interests to control the mineral wealth beginning to emerge from Southern Africa through a policy of confederation, the long standing border dispute between the Boers of the Transvaal and Zululand was now Britain's problem. The annexation of what was admittedly a bankrupt administration effectively destroyed the existing system of checks and balances. Previously, Natal had been safeguarded from potential Zulu attack by the existence of an independent Transvaal, but the change of flag in that area now made it impossible for Natal to pursue its hitherto successful but risky policy of employing the long standing enmity between Boer and Zulu to secure for herself immunity from Zulu aggression. [3]

The newly arrived High Commissioner for South Africa, Sir Henry Bartle Edward Frere, sent to accelerate the pace of confederation after his recent successes in India, was caught between a rock and a hard place. Now that Britain had assumed responsibility for the perpetual Boer-Zululand strife, Frere faced the choice of conflict with either the Boers or the Zulus. He allied himself with the Boers and soon became convinced that the independence of the Zulu kingdom posed a threat to his policies. By breaking up the Zulu kingdom Frere hoped not only to intimidate opposition but also to demonstrate British strength. The 'Zulu problem' would have to be resolved as a pre-requisite to confederation so in this respect Frere considered the chain of events he was now about to set in motion as being quite justified and in Britain's wider interests. Frere was quick to decide that a powerful independent Kingdom had no place in the proposed Southern African union. He therefore attempted to persuade the British Government that peace in southern Africa was seriously threatened by Cetshwayo and his army. [4] While Lord Carnarvon was in office at home as Colonial Secretary there was active support for the policy of confederation, but in 1878 he was replaced by Sir Michael Hicks Beach, who was more cautious in his approach to colonial affairs. It was therefore incumbent upon Frere to paint as dark a picture as possible of the situation on the ground with the intention of winning Government support and justification for his actions.

Towards the end of 1877, King Cetshwayo was convinced that the diplomatic understanding he had tried hard to reach with Natal was in ruins and in his desire for moderation and peace he turned to Sir Henry Bulwer, Natal's Lieutenant Governor. Bulwer had become increasingly disturbed by the attitude of Frere towards the Zulu and was already considering some form of mediation. He therefore appointed a Boundary Commission to inquire into the disputed territories between the Boers and the Zulu. The Commission met at Rorke's Drift in March 1878 and for the next few months took statements and reports from both sides. [5] In June the Commission presented its report and to Frere's horror and dismay found in favour of the Zulus. This impartial judgement was a considerable setback to Frere, as it could well inflame the Boers to take retaliatory action against Natal, but he had no intention of changing his position. He suppressed the findings of the report and meanwhile made political capital out of such border incidents as the stoning to death of two of Chief Sihayo's absconding wives in July 1878. In a well-orchestrated atmosphere of political spin, he appealed for British troops to be sent to the area in the light of the deteriorating situation. During this time, the Honourable Sir Frederic Augustus Thesiger CB assumed command of the Imperial forces in South Africa, in the local rank of Lieutenant General, having replaced Sir Arthur Cunnynghame. Born on 31 May 1827 he was gazetted into the Rifle Brigade in 1844 as a very young Ensign. He went on to see service in the Crimea and in India where he eventually commanded his Regiment. In 1866 he married the daughter of an Indian Army General and in 1877 was himself promoted to the rank of Major General. [6] His career had been varied, light on action and heavy with peacetime staff duties, but he was deemed to be competent and reliable and although reserved by nature he was a popular officer. In October 1878 he succeeded to the title of Lord Chelmsford on the death of his father.

On 9 October 1878, an incident occurred which precipitated action by Frere. A local chief led his warriors through the Pongola valley in the area under dispute, attacking immigrant Boers and natives and stealing herds of their cattle. This played right into Frere's hands and was to form the basis of the first item of the infamous ultimatum, which led to the invasion of Zululand. From its very conception, the ultimatum issued to King Cetshwayo's representatives on 11 December 1878 by the banks of the Tugela River was a very devious act by Frere. Under the pretext of delivering the findings of the Boundary Commission, the Zulus were told that reparation must be made for the excesses of the various border disputes in recent months. This was tolerable and seen as fair game, but what was to follow was quite different. In stunned silence, the Zulus were told that their army was to disband, the Zulu military system was to be abandoned and all Zulu men were to be free to marry. Furthermore, if these conditions were not met within 30 days then an invasion of Zululand by British forces under the command of Lord Chelmsford would immediately follow. [7]

In devising this ultimatum, Frere knew from the outset that King Cetshwayo could not comply with these demands. Unlike its western counterpart, the Zulu army was part and parcel of the fabric of Zulu society and existed not just for military purposes. To disband it would mean the destruction of the Zulu way of life and Cetshwayo would be handing his kingdom to the British on a plate. This of course is exactly what Frere wanted, but it is a sad indictment of his motives that he had to back the Zulu king into a corner to achieve his own ends. If the Zulus were the threat they were made out to be then there would have been no need for an ultimatum. As it was, the Zulus posed no direct threat to the white settlers of Natal and were not planning to launch a pre-emptive strike on their neighbours. The war was prosecuted to further the policy of confederation, to subdue the Zulus in order to repress widespread black resistance to expanding white domination, and to prevent the Zulu blocking British progress and ultimate expansion to the north. There was also personal prestige to be gained for Frere and for Lord Chelmsford, and it would eventually free Zulu manpower resources for labour hungry European commercialism. [8] It is no surprise that the 30 day period passed without resolution and on 11 January 1879, the invasion of Zululand began.

In anticipation of such an outcome, Lord Chelmsford had already drawn up his invasion plans. The lesson he had learned from the ninth Kaffir war was that the first blow in native warfare must be a heavy one and that success depended upon his ability to smash the Zulu army and capture the King. This necessitated an assault upon King Cetshwayo's capital at Ulundi and while a single heavy column might be able to achieve this, it would solve nothing by merely occupying the royal kraal. If it was too massive it might never be attacked by the Zulus, which would negate the prime objective of bringing the enemy to battle. The Zulu army had to be destroyed and victory in the field was necessary to assert ascendancy. Chelmsford therefore decided to invade with three main columns and two smaller columns in reserve. The first column on the right flank would cross into Zululand at the Lower Drift on the Tugela River, close to the coast and move northwards via Eshowe. The second, or central column would advance north east from a central point along the border with Zululand, crossing the Buffalo River at Rorke's Drift, while the third column on the left flank would move south east from the north, in the area of the disputed territories around the headwaters of Blood River. Of the two reserves, one was stationed at the Middle Drift of the Tugela below Kranz Kop and the other to the north on the Transvaal border, both being a guard against any possible counter-invasion. [9]

Chelmsford's strategy was to entice the Zulu army to attack one or more of the columns as he was convinced that the Zulu would discover to their cost that the numerical inferiority of the apparently weak columns was more than compensated for by the superior firepower and tactics. The army was equipped with an excellent .45 calibre, single shot, breech loading 1871 model Martini-Henry rifle, and Chelmsford believed that a disciplined British force, properly positioned and handled so as to give maximum effect to the destructive capabilities of such modern, rapid firing weapons was normally invulnerable against the poorly armed mass attacks of warriors such as the Zulu. [10] The main striking force of Chelmsford's army was the regular Imperial British soldier. However, given the fact that the British Government was neither expecting, nor had sanctioned, a war in South Africa and with more pressing commitments elsewhere such as Afghanistan, Chelmsford had only eight Battalions at his disposal, totalling about 5,400 men. Facing a potential threat of up to 40,000 Zulus, he augmented his force by raising the Natal Native Contingent (NNC) – ironically themselves Zulus who were resident in Natal – numbering about 10,000 men in nine Battalions, but they were poorly armed and trained and consequently of doubtful morale. A far better fighting force, but underestimated by the British regulars, was the locally raised colonial militia cavalry units, about 1,200 strong, which the initial lack of regular cavalry made essential for patrol work. This was critical for reconnaissance purposes and the absence of sufficient horsemen was one of the greatest defects in Chelmsford's army. Just as he was disparaging about Boer tactics, the British officer did not hold his colonial counter-part in high regard. This was a poor error of judgement and valuable local knowledge was wasted as a result.

Both battalions of the 24th Foot were to serve together in the central column and by September of 1878 the 1st Battalion was ready to move north from the Cape Colony to Natal. One of the first companies to move was D Company, in which Wilfred Heaton and William Lloyd were subaltern officers with Major Upcher as their company commander and on 25 September they moved on foot from King William's Town to East London on the coast and then by sea northwards to Durban. By mid December 1878, Colonel Richard Glyn, formerly commanding the

1st/24th Foot, had taken over command of the central column and both battalions were assembling in Natal. Born in India in 1831, Richard Thomas Glyn initially purchased a commission in the 82nd Foot (the South Lancashire Regiment) in 1850 and transferred to the 24th Foot in 1856, by which time he was a Captain. He had seen service in the Crimea and in India and in 1867 he became the commanding officer of the 1st/24th Foot, a position he held for 13 years until 1880, during which time he reached the rank of Colonel. [11] Despite the fact that he was described by some as a 'short grouchy officer, inclined to need urging and forever at odds with his own officers and superiors' Lord Chelmsford wanted Colonel Glyn to command the 3rd column when drawing up plans for the invasion of Zululand. Clearly he could not command his Battalion at the same time, so this task devolved to Henry Burmeister Pulleine in the brevet rank of Lieutenant Colonel (a form of acting rank where an officer was required to fill the next higher rank where a vacancy had occurred, often on active service). On Pulleine's death at Isandlwana, Wilfred's company commander Russell Upcher took over temporary command of the Battalion for most of the remaining period of the Zulu war.

As the new year of 1879 dawned over the colony, the 2nd/24th Foot was ready to join the central column while the 1st/24th Foot was at, or moving towards, Rorke's Drift, with the exception of two of its companies. Of these, G Company was in the process of moving from Pietermaritzburg to Helpmekaar, while Wilfred and William were still on the coast at Durban with D Company. As far as the 24th Foot was concerned, the year about to unfold was to be one of the most dramatic in the Regiment's history, so we will let Wilfred recount his own experiences through the pages of his diary.

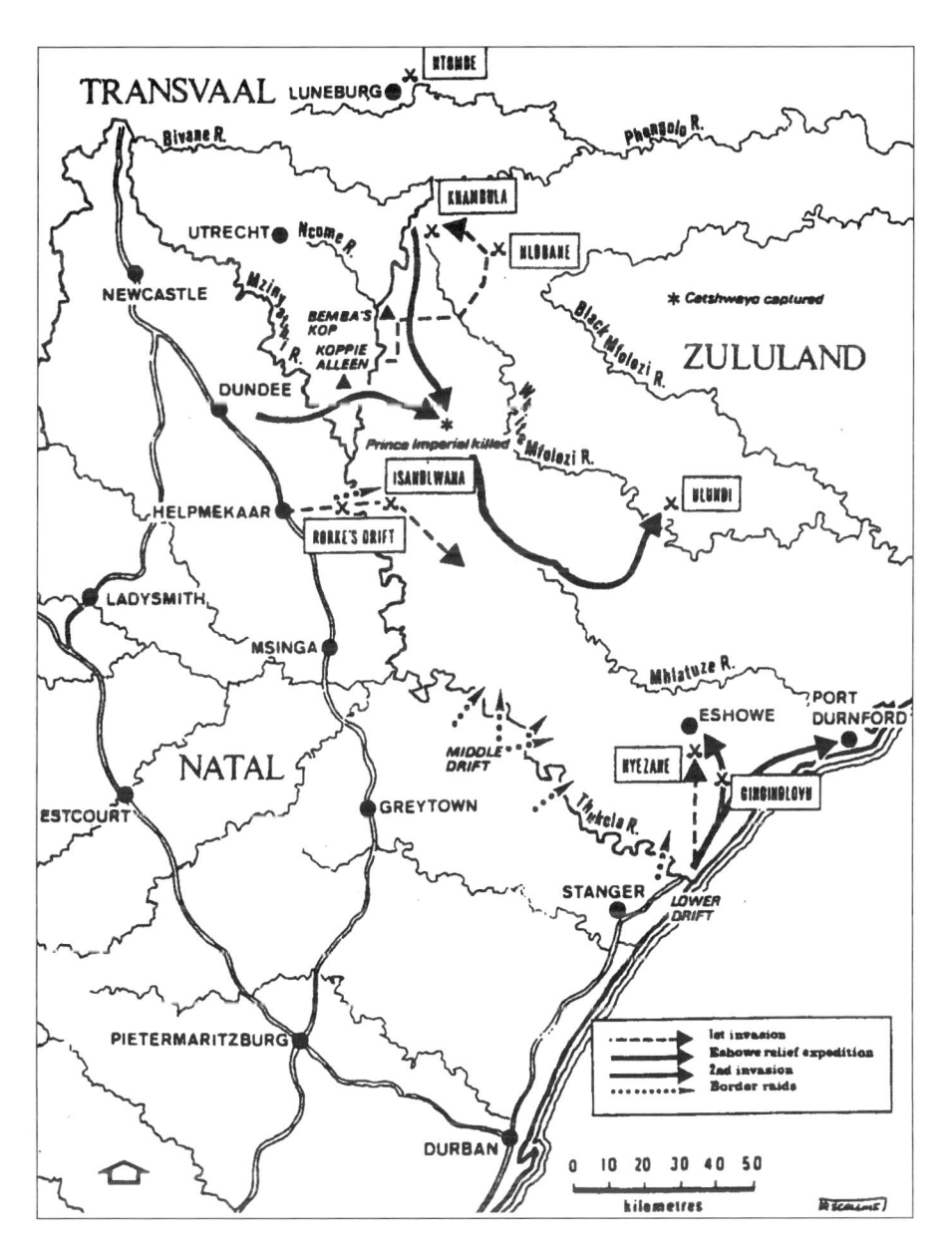

4. Principal towns, roads and routes together with main actions during the Anglo-Zulu War of 1879. (Anglo-Zulu War Historical Society)

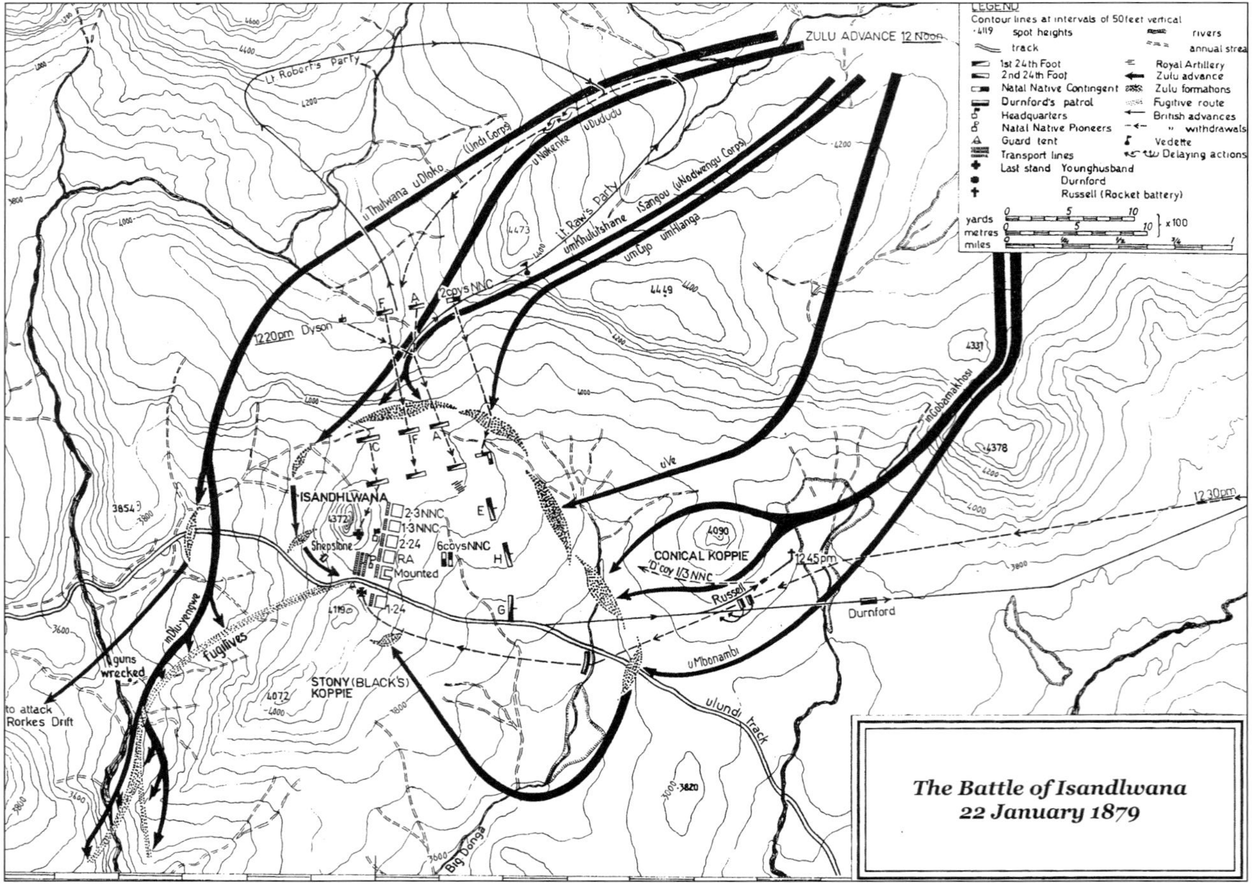

5. The Battle of Isandlwana showing the Zulu army 'horns of the buffalo' battle formations. (Anglo-Zulu War Historical Society)

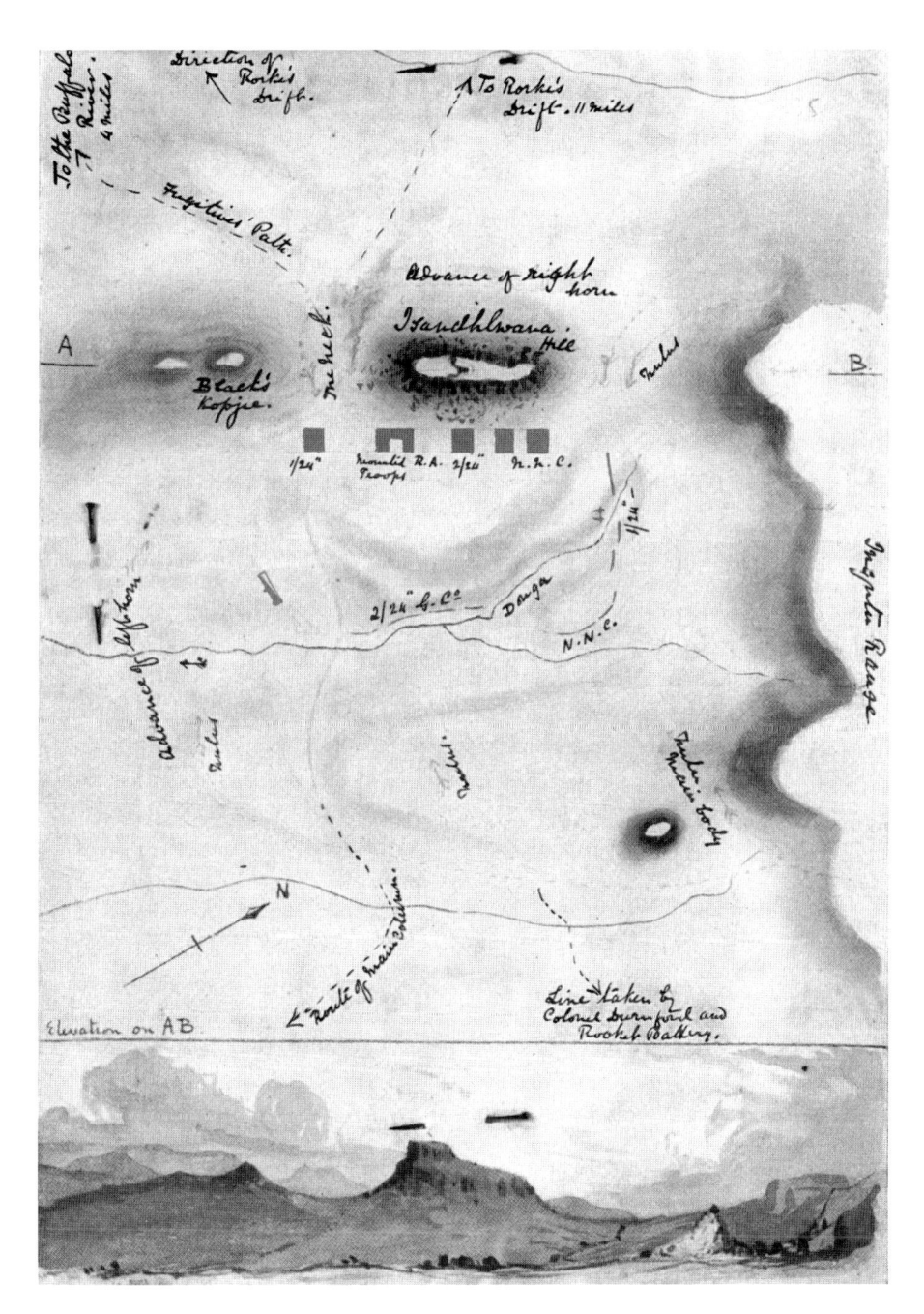

6. A sketch map of the Battle of Isandlwana 1879, drawn shortly afterwards by Captain William Penn Symons 2/24th Regiment. He rose to the rank of Lieutenant General and died of wounds sustained at the battle of Talana Hill in October 1899 during the Boer War. (Royal Welsh Museum)

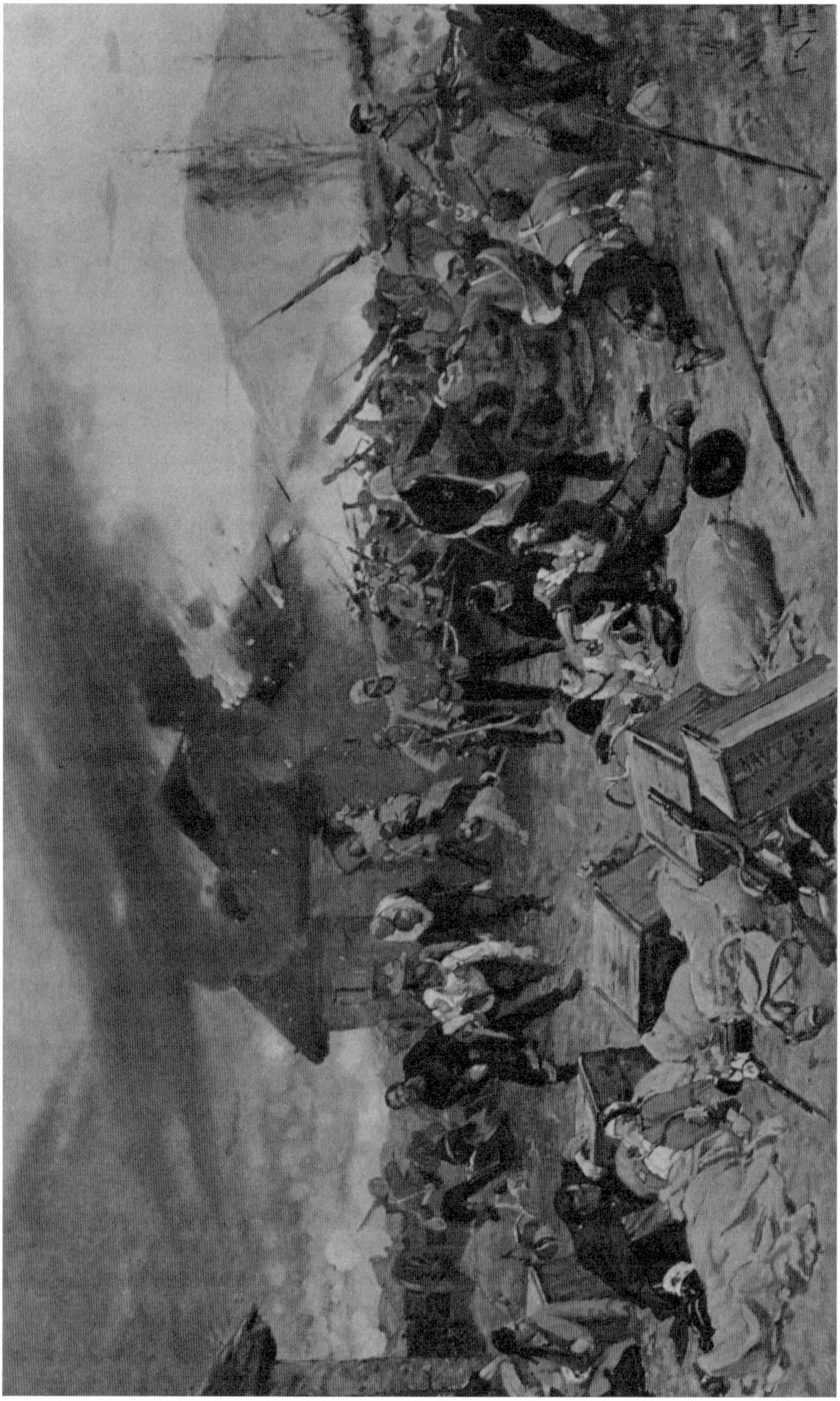

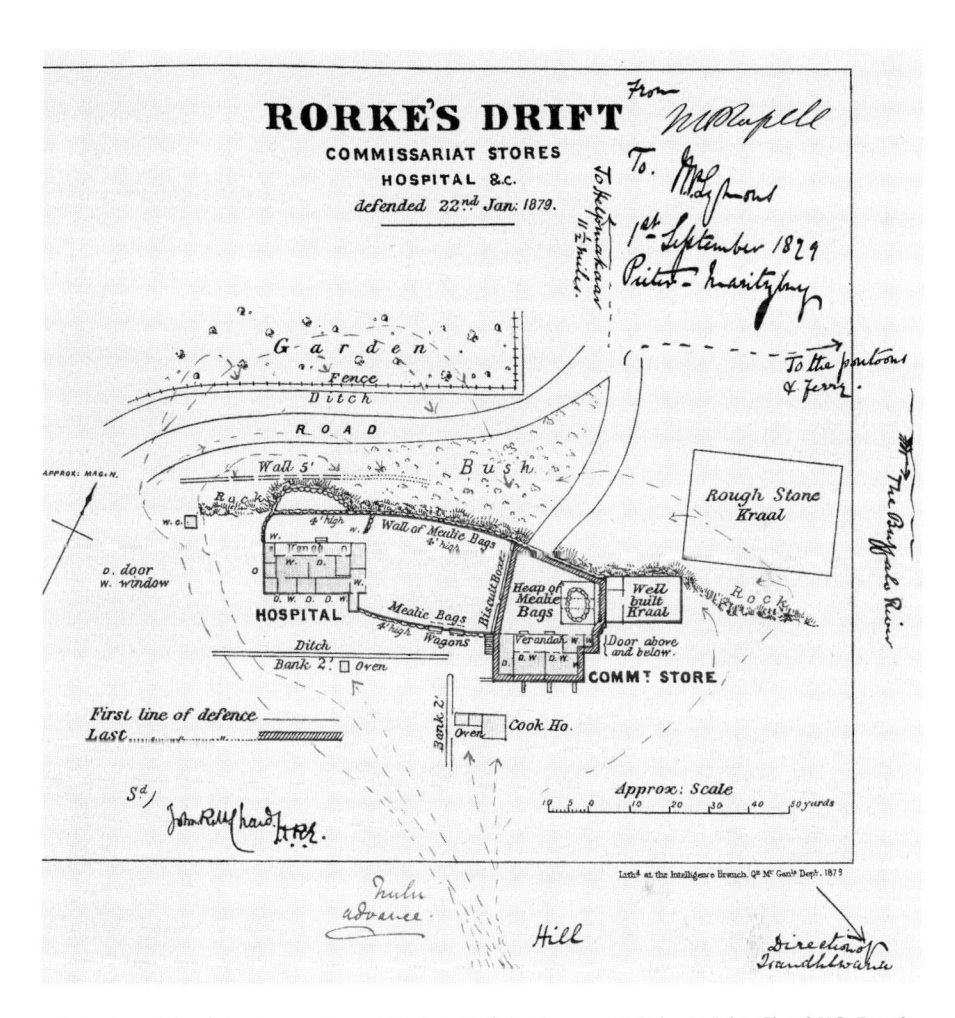

8. A plan of the defensive position at Rorke's Drift, 22 January 1879 by Lt John Chard VC, Royal Engineers and the officer in charge during the battle. It shows the direction of the Zulu advance from Isandlwana and the line of the defences which were hastily erected. (Royal Welsh Museum)

Opposite 7. The Defence of Rorke's Drift. Painted in 1880 by the French artist Alphonse Marie de Neuville (1835 – 1885) this famous picture encapsulates the variety of action during the defence of Rorke's Drift at some point just after 6pm when the hospital was set on fire. There are two 'original' paintings – this one is an original (owned by the Royal Welsh) and is believed to be his rough work prior to painting the full sized picture which is now in the Art Gallery of New South Wales in Australia. (Royal Welsh Museum)

9. A young Victorian officer, drawn by Lieutenant William Whitelocke Lloyd, who served in D Company 1st/24th Foot with Wilfred Heaton. There was no such officer as 'Tomkins of B Company,' so it is quite possible that this is a caricature of Wilfred as the two officers were very close friends. (Royal Welsh Museum)

10. Life on active service, captured by William Lloyd (Royal Welsh Museum)

11. The trials and tribulations of living in the field, giving an indication of William Lloyd's sense of humour. (Royal Welsh Museum)

12. In contact with the enemy – caught off guard or William Lloyd giving rise to that well known expression . . .?! (Royal Welsh Museum)

CHAPTER 4

UNEXPECTED DISASTER

While the arrival of a new year is usually a time for celebration, the Regiment was far too busy for such festivities at the start of 1879. Most of the 1st and 2nd battalions were gathering on the borders of Zululand for the impending invasion and this particular new year saw Wilfred Heaton at Durban, immersed in the daily routine of his company and receiving drafts for the invasion columns. As his diary for the day records:

Wednesday 1 January
Upcher away at Binns for some shooting. Did Orderly Room for him. Kept in the District Office a long time arranging about tents for the troops to land. Went to the Club and saw about the Governor's horse and started a parcel to Major Black. Went to a picnic in the Botanical Gardens and got nicely wet coming home. Dried at Philips. Letter to Melville this morning about Sergt Bradbury's character.

Major Wilsone Black of the 2nd Battalion was one of the senior officers of the Regiment and we shall learn more of him a little later on. Meanwhile, Brevet Major Russell Upcher was Wilfred's company commander during the initial stages of the campaign, having been the commandant at Durban initially. After Isandlwana, he took over as commanding officer of the 1st Battalion 24th Regiment until such times as the battalion could be reformed again with reinforcements from England. Later on he had the distinction of commanding the 2nd Battalion South Wales Borderers (as the Regiment became in 1881) in Burma from 1886 to 1888, with Wilfred as one of his company commanders. He became a Major General in 1898 and died in 1937 at the age of 93. [1]

Although the Regiment was gathering for war, there was still a need to look after various soldier's careers, as was the case with Sergeant John Bradbury. He had been promoted to Sergeant 6 years earlier in 1873 and as one of his company officers Wilfred was required to send a character reference to the Adjutant, one Lieutenant Teignmouth Melvill, in preparation for his promotion to Colour Sergeant. He was to survive the Zulu war and was awarded the Long Service and Good Conduct Medal in October 1881. Instituted in 1830, and to encourage high standards, this medal was originally awarded to soldiers of exemplary conduct for 21 years service in the infantry or 24 years in the cavalry throughout the

British, Dominion and Colonial Armies. Over the long period in which this medal has been in use it has undergone a number of changes. In 1870, for example, the length of time was reduced to 18 years, while today the qualifying period is 15 years from the age of 17½ or from the date of enlistment if later. The prime criterion is a Conduct Sheet free from any disciplinary entries (like a driving licence without any penalty points) and the medal is often affectionately referred to as 15 years of undetected crime! During the Second World War, commissioned officers were permitted to acquire the medal so long as they had completed at least 12 years of the requisite period in the ranks. What is of particular interest is the fact that in 1950, the South African army replaced this medal with one called the John Chard Medal, awarded for the same purpose, but named after that heroic defender of Rorke' s Drift, such is the esteem in which that immortal action is still held.

Thursday 2 January
Memo to Adjt 2/3rd Buffs. Pte Craney discharged Hosp. Sent back a prisoner. Papers sent by Sergt McClearge Walmer Castle expected Baxter down from P.M.Burg to land his people. Pitched Camp and got wood and water early with sentry on them. Picked up own heavy baggage and tried to store it. Upcher back from Binns lunched there. Answered memo about men A.H.C. taken to drift for – – – . Wrote after supper home. Mother and Bernard, and to Spratt for cart tomorrow. Settled one or two Bills got Club Bill in £15 odd.

Private Craney had been in hospital for some time and whatever his illness, whether it was an injury or enteric fever which was quite common throughout the whole of the army in South Africa, he took no further part in the forthcoming battles. This is deduced by the fact that he was awarded the South African campaign medal for being present in Natal, but without a bar or clasp which would have indicated that he was involved on active service. [2]

Friday 3 January
Lloyd told off to do orderly Officer to the Commandant. Finished preparing the Camp for the Walmer Castle people who arrived about 9.30 but could not land for the bar. Paid up the bills due by canteen and Mess, also Club bill. Called on the Lloyds, Bezanton's, Millars before lunch. Billiards after. Sent old saddle to be sold. Two companies 99th landed, tried to get their Officers places at the Clubs and elsewhere had supper at the club. Strickland and Richardson passed through en route for Tugela.

Meanwhile, Lieutenant J C Baxter of the Royal Engineers had travelled down from Pietermaritzburg to meet some of his soldiers arriving on the troopship HMS *Walmer Castle*. As Lord Chelmsford's forces gathered for the invasion, Durban became quite an active garrison town and Wilfred would have seen many different units passing through as he assisted in preparing their transit accommodation. On this occasion, the Walmer Castle was bringing in companies of the 99th Regiment (The Duke of Edinburgh's Regiment) and on this occasion their landing was hampered by the bar. While Durban (known previously as Port Natal) was an excellent harbour its narrow entrance was impeded by a long sand bar on which many a ship had floundered in the past at low tide. Aware of this natural obstacle, the *Walmer Castle* had to wait off shore for the incoming tide before being able to dock safely.

Commissariat General Edward Strickland was the senior officer in charge of the Commissariat Department for the whole campaign and was also entrusted with the organization of the transport service. He established a number of supply bases along the line of advance and now that the Columns were moving forward he had come to check on their progress. Deputy Commissariat Richardson was his secretary.

> *Saturday 4 January*
> *4 more coys 99th and Engineers and the drafts came ashore. Upchers mare sold for £24.3.0 Sold my old saddle could not buy another pony. Went to the point after lunch to help Upcher. Dined at the Club.*

> *Sunday 5 January*
> *A letter from Bainbridge about Mrs Marvel's box. Got leave from Church parade but had to do a fair bit of other work. Got up the box and found van der lum, milk munch and cake. Orders received for trial of Corpl Roddy and Russell. Spent better part of the afternoon getting up the cases. Supped with the Addisons Met a parson Field and the Pimms. The orders to leave on Tuesday and make all preparations tomorrow.*

Corporal Roddy and Private Russell served in the 1st/24th Regiment and while their offence is not clear, Wilfred was busy preparing the paper work which would lead to disciplinary action being taken against them. By the end of the week, orders had come through for D and G Companies to move up the line of communication to Helpmekaar, as described in the entry for 6 January.

> *Monday 6 January*
> *Upcher sent out to – – – – – – to encamp the 99th. £40 canteen takings for Saturday and Sunday banked it. Prosecuted Roddy and Russell 10am. Got water bottles rigged for saddle. Said goodbye to the Dillons, Grundys and Phillips. Paid Field Officer for the New Year picnic. Had a lot of bother*

about the tents and spades lent to the R.E. Supped at home wrote Bainbridge. Mrs Kingsley, Benningfield about sale of canteen bar stock and a character for Sergt Bradbury. Arranged for Cox to ride the pony to Pinetown and packed Mess and own kit.

As the word Mess, or the Officers' Mess, appears regularly in the diary, a brief explanation of its meaning and significance may be of assistance to put much of what Wilfred describes into context. Class distinction had long been part of the fabric of the British way of life at the time and it was particularly noticeable throughout the Army where men from all walks of life lived and worked much closer together than they would normally have done in civilian society. Officers came primarily from the upper classes, especially when commissions could be purchased and quite often background and breeding meant more than military ability. From 1870 however this started to change when the purchase of commissions was abolished. Officers now had to demonstrate a level of professional competence and the Cardwell Reforms of the Army introduced a more progressive career structure. Consequently, standards began to improve, albeit slowly, but officers remained predominantly young men from public schools and the aristocracy for some time yet. There was also a social hierarchy within regiments, with cavalry and infantry of the line of perceived higher standing than, say, artillery, engineers and logistic support units. Those officers from the landed gentry took staff and servants for granted and on active service they would usually mis-employ soldiers as a man-servant, or orderly, to look after their personal equipment and a groom to tend to their horses. Soldiers on the other hand were very much working class men and under normal circumstances the two groups would seldom mix or spend protracted periods of time together. The officers were responsible for the command of their soldiers, especially in battle, but the daily administration was invariably left to the senior ranks.

While soldiers' living conditions in the field were very rudimentary, the officers of each regiment would live far more comfortably in a facility similar to a small country club, known as the Officers' Mess. This would range from a permanent building in a garrison town at home or abroad in such places as India to a makeshift building or series of tents on active service, but the concept was always the same. There would be a central dining room with as much regimental silver, crockery and cutlery as the regiment had been able to take with them. There would be an anteroom, or lounge, which was as well furnished as was possible and each officer would then have his own room or tent as his bedroom. Soldiers would be employed as the cooks and servants and quite formal codes of behaviour and protocol were expected. Meals would usually be taken together by all Mess members and they would, where practical, dress formally for dinner. The Regimental flags or Colours, about which we will hear much more later, would be housed in the Mess and be on display each day. While in direct contact with the enemy such niceties did not apply of course, but there would be an Officers' Mess somewhere on the line of march and on this occasion the central column Mess was at Helpmekaar. This was a combined Mess for all column officers, (and some civilians deemed suitable to join), irrespective of cap badge and Wilfred was the honorary Mess secretary. As such, he was responsible for ensuring that the Mess ran to the required standard and had the facilities it needed. Officers contributed to the upkeep of the Mess from their own pockets and received a Mess bill at the end of each month for additional items purchased, such as drinks. Getting officers to pay such bills was easier said than done and Wilfred would spend much time and effort chasing various individuals for the sums of money they owed. [3]

Tuesday 7 January
Tents struck at 6am. All baggage at the station by 10. Our Det the drafts and 89th under command of Church. 2/24th off by 11.45 to Pinetown except our truck full that I brought on at 12.15 Pony ridden up by Cox all right. Lunched at Hotel. Waggons not leaving turned up Camped at Station Dined with Martin. Rain hard all night.

Major Hugh Backhouse Church was commanding F Company 2nd/24th but was also in charge of the convoy containing the two companies from the 1st Battalion and elements of the 89th Foot (The Connaught Rangers) for the first stage of the move out of Durban. Private Cox was Wilfred's groom and was given charge of his horse for the move as he had other responsibilities bringing up a wagon load of Officers Mess equipment.

Wednesday 8 January
Rained all day Made Gillets for midday meal. Camped for night at Padleys. Bennett left us today to do Adjt Gen Depot. Lloyd to do duty with Buffs he and I orderly day about. Church and the doctor left their nags at Pinetown 88th kicked up a devil of a row at Padleys had to turn out with the Picquet to bring them in.

If officers enjoyed relatively high standards of living while on campaign, consider for a moment the life of the average British soldier. Described by the Duke of Wellington as 'the scum of the earth' Tommy Atkins as he has been affectionately known (although an expression never used by Wilfred in his diary) came from the working class. Often illiterate and uneducated he originally joined the Army because he was incapable of little other meaningful employment. His interests centred around women and drink, and military history is littered with examples of their excesses as they plundered the spoils of war after a successful campaign. Consequently discipline had to be harsh and swift to keep them focussed on the task in hand. However, the Duke also went on to say that they were the finest fighting soldiers he had come across and when he was advising British ministers intent on reducing the army after 1815 he stated:

> 'My opinion is that the best troops we have, probably the best in the world, are the British infantry . . . this is what we ought to keep up and what I wish above all other to retain.' [4]

Towards the end of the 19th century, soldiers' standards of living, conditions of service and general education began to improve, witnessed by the number and quality of letters written home during the campaign. Their fighting spirit and steadfastness under fire was never in doubt but left to their own devices the devil would find work for idle hands. On this occasion the 89th of Foot were clearly causing problems, fuelled no doubt by alcohol, and the duty guard had to turn out to restore order!

The weather was particularly unpleasant this week which made the move of the wagons over dirt tracks quickly turning to mud very difficult. Eight years older than Wilfred, Lieutenant Levett Holt Bennett was promoted to Captain this month and worked on the Adjutant General's staff during the war, involved in manning and administration. He was to transfer to the Army Pay Department in 1881, reaching the rank of Lieutenant Colonel in 1901. [5]

Thursday 9 January
Horrid wet day sent back from Padleys to Gillets to try for wood could not get any. Outspanned at the old stables opposite Inchanga hotel for night.

Friday 10 January
Left early weather much better. At Campertown got eggs at 3/a dozen On again to Thornville by 4.30 had a tub there and a good dinner

Saturday 11 January
Rouse which should have gone at 2.30 went at 1.30am. Consequently got in to PMB by 6am - - soup before leaving. Breakfasted at the Club. Upcher in orders to take over command of the column. Rushed about the town against time trying to complete own and coy's kit. Church in orders to find his own way up and his draft handed over to me. Drinks with Bennett at the Mess. Upcher back with ague. Doctor sent for.

Rouse, otherwise called reveille, is a military term for the first bugle call of the day, ordering all soldiers in the camp to get up. Most key events during the day, such as meal times, parades and lights out at night were indicated by a bugle call, which would be preceded by a short unique regimental signature to identify the unit concerned if there was more than one regiment or company in the vicinity. The bugle was also essential on the battlefield to give the order to advance, retire or whatever formation was required and soldiers were trained to recognize and respond to such calls. On this occasion, the duty bugler, more often than not a young boy, had sounded off an hour earlier than expected, although it was not unusual for the day to start well before dawn, given the heat of a South African summer. The expression 'outspanned' means the release of oxen from their trek waggons, primarily for grazing, and infers a rest for all concerned.

Sunday 12 January
The detachment inspected by Col Hopton at 7am. Breakfasted in camp and worked till 3 when we fell into march out got no lunch. Heavy thunderstorm road flooded and men got a good ducking. Got part of the way up the Town hill Served out a ration of grog. 2/24th waggon stuck fast Moffat took out a fatigue party to fetch up their blankets at about 10pm Upcher left behind to get all right. Found a Wrexham Guardian in my tent.

Colonel Hopton of the 89th Regiment of Foot was the transport officer on the line of communication between Durban and Helpmekaar and as such would have been responsible for ensuring that independent detachments were properly prepared before moving off. It was a particularly difficult day, hampered by the very wet conditions, and the soldiers would have been soaking wet as a consequence, with little or no spare clothing to change into. The issue of rum, or grog as it was called, was not restricted to the Royal Navy and it would be given out for medicinal purposes by the medical officer or to restore flagging morale when necessary. Captain Herbert Moffatt 1st/24th Foot was employed on duties in Natal. The *Wrexham Guardian* was a local newspaper from his home in North Wales.

Monday 13 January
Got up the Town hill and out spanned at 12 when Upcher joined us. Went on to the Mangeni bridge and dined at the Hotel.

Tuesday 14 January
Breakfasted at Hotel went on to first – – – Spruit for dinners, had a bathing

parade and inspection of feet on to 2nd Spruit crossed and went 3 parts of the way up a long hill. Lloyd left behind to bring up a cow for rations.

While there is an old adage that an army marches on its stomach, alluding to the importance of good food, reality dictates that sound feet are also an essential prerequisite for marching infantrymen. It was essential therefore that their feet were inspected on a regular basis to ensure they were fit to march and they were also made to bathe frequently to keep as hygienic as possible. The daily entitlement of food per person was usually about a pound of fresh meat, a pound and a half of fresh bread or hard dried biscuits, plus fresh vegetables, fruit or lime juice and possibly sugar. [6] This was supplied by the Commissariat Branch and the quality and quantity would vary depending upon availability. Officers were more fortunate in that they could afford to supplement their rations by purchasing additional items locally, one of the tasks allocated to Wilfred. On this occasion however, the Company's rations were being enhanced by a cow, procured by his friend William Lloyd.

Wednesday 15 January
Ordered start for 4.30. Sergt of Guard neglected to call the Bugle. Last waggon not off till 7. lost 3 of its oxen. Breakfasted near the farm of 3 colony Englishmen. Killed Lloyds cow. Got on to a – – at – – – where we camped as the waggons could not get on. Gastern's relief passed on his way to Grey Town where he is to join us. Fed at tent.

Not everything would go to plan and on this occasion the early morning bugle call was very late; no doubt much appreciated by the soldiers who benefited from a few more hours in their tents! While officer accommodation was quite reasonable, for soldiers it was less so. They would sleep in what was known as a bell tent (named after its designer rather than its shape) which would house up to 15 men with all their equipment in cramped conditions. There was no ground sheet and the men had only a blanket or greatcoat to keep warm. Often when on the march there would be no time to erect a tented camp, or lines as they were called, so the soldiers would sleep in the open in all weathers. After a long dry period in the previous year the rain was falling with a vengeance and many a soldier suffered from flu, enteric fever or rheumatism as a result. Surgeon Major WC Gasteen had been appointed as Secretary and Statistical Officer to the Surgeon General of the Forces in the Field, so he was being replaced as one of the Column's medical officers.

Thursday 16 January
Got off at 4 punctually outspanned near a stream for Breakfast. Got into Greytown by 10.30. Had Mr Dodds shoes changed and feet pared. Met

Michel 57th on Transport here asked me to lunch. Warneford Commst Officer Bought a lot of stores at the various stores for the Mess.

Mr Dodds was the name of Wilfred's horse, which he had purchased locally. Some officers brought their own horses with them from England, but they were not accustomed to the harsh African conditions and many were to die as a result. Unscrupulous local breeders and dealers took advantage of this situation and would charge anything up to £50 for an indifferent horse; at least they were tough and reasonably manageable if not well trained. Farriers also did well as they were kept very busy re-shoeing horses and mules throughout the campaign. Deputy Commissariat WJT Warnedford (this is the correct spelling of his name) was the senior commissariat officer at Greytown who would have assisted Wilfred with supplies for the Officers Mess.

Friday 17 January
Left Grey Town 4.30 got to Burrups at about 8 Breakfasted there found a dead horse on the campground made the niggers cart it away with them. Left a waggon behind for rations which came in a couple of hours after us. Camped for the day and night. Michel turned up. Fed 3 meals very good at Burrups.

Saturday 18 January
Left 4.45 for Moir River 12 miles where we had to camp as the coy waggon got off the pont and upset which made us too late to start off again. Thunderstorm passed over grog ration bathing parade. Lucky Lloyd to dive for lost articles in the river did not recover any. One sheep drowned in crossing and one lost. Found a letter at the Hotel for Smith Dorrien took charge of it.

As the column moved off, so the weather changed for the worse and it became a hot, wet and muddy journey. By 18 January, they had passed through Pietermaritzburg and Greytown and were at the Mooi river. As Wilfred recalls, one wagon came off the pont carrying them across the river and his friend William Lloyd had the pleasure of cooling off in the water attempting to retrieve some of the equipment.

Horrace Lockwood Smith-Dorrien was an officer of the 95th Regiment of Foot (later the Worcestershire and Sherwood Foresters Regiment) who came out to South Africa as a volunteer. He was employed as a transport officer, supervising the provision of much needed oxen and wagons for the various columns. He was attached to Lord Chelmsford's column and was fortunate to escape with his life from Isandlwana. He eventually rose to the rank of General, commanding the 2nd Corps of the B.E.F in the First World War. During the retreat from Mons he became cut off from flanking corps by a headquarters error, disobeyed orders and turned to fight. Though his courageous action enabled the B.E.F to extricate itself, he was never forgiven by his superior officer, Sir John French and was hounded out of France the following year. He died in 1930, aged 72. [7]

Sunday 19 January
Left early for Tugela Several Oxen lost Coy waggon started last and trekked right through Outspanned for breakfast at the top of cutting. Got the waggons down to the cutting by 12 and all over but 3 by dark camped anyhow in the Bush. Caught up Sergt Merrissey in charge of an escort with 26 waggons stores boat and ammunition for the front. Lunched in the first house, too tired for dinner so took some biscuits to bed.

To provision his invasion force of some 16,000 fighting men, Lord Chelmsford needed in the order of a 1,000 wagons and mules carts, over 10,000 oxen, some 900 horses and about 450 mules. A full span of oxen to pull a loaded wagon ranged from 14 to 18 beasts and they needed eight hours a day to graze and a further eight hours to rest. With only eight hours left in the day for actual work, progress could be very slow, particularly in bad weather on poor or non-existent tracks. The pressure on these animals was great and their losses were frequent as a result, which slowed up the progress of the columns and the re-supply process. The wagons were heavy and cumbersome so each day was often a long hard slog for all concerned.

Monday 20 January
Tried to get off by 4.45am Very bad start got the remainder of the waggons across and all but 1/13th started up the hill by 8.15. halted on top for breakfasts. Went on after dinners and bivouaced about 3 miles short of Sand Spruit. Had a huge fire and supper long side of it.

The invasion of Zululand had begun a week earlier on 11 January, but such was the passage of information that the event went un-remarked further down the line of communication. By the time that Wilfred arrived at Helpmekaar on 21 January the central column was camped at the small sphinx shaped mountain of Isandlwana – bearing an uncanny resemblance to the cap badge of the 24th – having successfully attacked and destroyed Chief Sihayo's kraal on the way. Helpmekaar was an administrative staging post on a high and windy escarpment looking down towards the Mzinyathi or Buffalo River which was the border between Natal and Zululand. Upcher had shot some pigeons at Sand Spruit on the way, but Company administration was slow and the evening meal took some time to prepare. Wilfred however did not go hungry.

> *Tuesday 21 January*
> *Left about 5 to Sand Spruit where we breakfasted. Got some mess stores from the shop at tremendous prices. Went on 3pm to Helpmakaar got in at 6. Upcher shot 4 pidgeons at Sand Spruit in three shots. Found Rainforth, Palmes and Clements at Helpmakaar men ordered to leave all behind except Blankets waterproofs and field kit. Found the conductor asleep on the waggon coming up the hill and had to shout him out. Dined with Rainforth ie eat his Dinner as mine was not ready.*

Major Thomas Rainforth, aged 37, was the officer commanding G Company who had also moved independently from Pietermaritzburg to Helpmakaar just ahead of Wilfred's Company. The two subaltern officers who were to become close friends of Wilfred's were Lieutenant George Palmes, three years his junior and Lieutenant Arthur Clements, who he often refers to as Clem in his diary and who was the same age. Once these two Companies had met up, they were to prepare to move forward to join the rest of the column, so their kit was stripped down to the bare minimum to make marching easier.

As dawn broke on Wednesday 22 January 1879, Wilfred rose early from his makeshift bed at Helpmekaar. Wilfred had arrived there late on the previous evening with his Company, having spent the last 10 days moving up country from the coast at Durban along very poor tracks made even worse by the incessant rain in recent weeks. Although he had the relative comfort of riding a horse while his soldiers marched on foot, he was no doubt ready for a short break, a good meal, the comfort of a hot bath and a change of clothes. None of this was possible for the time being however as he and his men were under orders to move on another 10 miles or so with D Company to assist in the security of the stores depot and the makeshift hospital at Rorke's Drift. However they were blissfully unaware of the dramatic events unfolding 20 miles away to their front.

With the column encamped on the slopes of Isandlwana, the previous day Lord Chelmsford had despatched Major Dartnell with a force of the Natal Mounted Police and mounted volunteers along the track to the Mangeni river some 10 miles to the south east to look for the main Zulu army. At the same time, Lt Browne took a party of mounted infantry to scout the area of the Isipesi Hill, 5 miles due east of Isandlwana. While the latter consisted of mainly British soldiers, the group commanded by Dartnell and Lonsdale were either colonial irregulars or poorly trained native contingents, yet Chelmsford entrusted the main thrust of his reconnaissance to this force. During that day they encountered parties of Zulus, but they lacked the tactical knowledge, experience and resources to fully understand and react to the scenario unfolding in front of them. What they had seen in fact was the screen (a military term for a force of guarding troops on the flank of a main body) of the main Zulu army moving in a northerly direction across their front to a ravine on the north east face of the Nqutu plateau, but with limited scouting facilities to hand, they had no way of knowing this.

That evening, Dartnell sent a message back to Lord Chelmsford asking for reinforcements as the Zulu force he had encountered had increased to some 1,500. While it was not unreasonable to assume that the vanguard of a Zulu force had been discovered – after all, Chelmsford was aware that Cetshwayo had sent an army to oppose him – this information was accepted at face value and with no corroboration. However, Chelmsford was not prepared to delegate such responsibility to a non-regular officer and decided to take control of the situation himself. In his haste to commit the Zulu army to battle, he then made the cardinal error of deciding to split his column in the face of an unknown enemy force based on unconfirmed intelligence. Of all his failings, this fundamental mistake demonstrated Lord Chelmsford's weakness as a tactical commander.

In the early hours of 22 January, Chelmsford led six companies of the 2nd 24th, a rocket battery and some mounted infantry out of the Camp at Isandlwana to reinforce Dartnell. The force left behind was made up of about 1,700 men, consisting of 5 companies 1st 24th, one company 2nd 24th, three battalions of NNC and a number of irregular units. At this point the command and control arrangements are worth consideration. Although a large proportion of the column remained in the camp, in Chelmsford's mind, no doubt, the main effort was with Dartnell and he was in effect continuing his advance towards Ulundi. He therefore took with him the original column commander, who would have been better employed commanding the substantial element in camp as a reserve in case Chelmsford got into difficulties.

At this point, Colonel Anthony Durnford, Royal Engineers, enters our story. Commissioned in 1846 from the Royal Military Academy at Woolwich, Durnford had served in South Africa since 1871 as a Colonial Engineer. In 1873 he was involved in the abortive Battle of the Bushmans River Pass in the Drakensberg Mountains, having been given the task of capturing a local chief, Langalibalele of the Hlubi tribe, who was wanted by the colonial authorities in Natal for allegedly failing to surrender firearms owned by his young men. During this battle Durnford lost the use of his left arm from an assegai stab wound. He was also romantically associated with a daughter of Bishop John Colenso, the Bishop of Natal, which caused some consternation locally as he was already married.

At the start of the Zulu War, Durnford was given command of Number 2 Column which was made up primarily of three Battalions of the Natal Native Contingent, five troops of the Natal Native Horse and a rocket battery. Positioned originally at a place called the Middle Drift with the task of preventing any diversionary border incursions into Natal by King Cetshwayo, he was then redeployed to Rorke's Drift as the central column moved further into Zululand. As a precaution, on the morning of 22 January Durnford's column was called forward from Rorke's Drift to reinforce the camp at Isandlwana, but in Lord Chelmsford's haste to leave camp the orders given to Lieutenant Colonel Pulleine, now commanding officer of the 1st/24th Foot and to Durnford were unclear. There has been considerable debate over Durnford's role at Isandlwana and it is alleged that he was ordered to command the camp on arrival. Equally, it is contended that Durnford saw his role as that of providing some form of flank protection for Lord Chelmsford who was now separated from the main force, which would explain why he did not remain in the camp to bolster its defence, but moved out along the route towards Lord Chelmsford without delay. The truth may never be known, but this action (which in hindsight was a tactical error) played a significant part in the ensuing battle as we shall see.

At the same time, the commanding officer of the 1st/24th, Lt Col Pulleine, who had joined the column only five days previously, was given vague orders by Chelmsford's staff to defend the camp and yet prepare for its subsequent move. Pulleine, who joined the 2nd/24th Foot in 1858, is often criticized for being a commanding officer with little or no tactical experience, but this is not the case. True, most of his former staff appointments had been in various administrative capacities but during the ninth frontier war he had been called upon to raise two Frontier Corps, one of infantry known as Pulleine's Rangers (afterwards the Transkei Rifles) and the other a cavalry force, which became the Frontier Light Horse. He served with this Regiment until September 1878 when he moved north to Natal in view of the impending hostilities. When the invasion began he applied to rejoin the 24th Regiment, which he did on the 17th January; hardly the inclination of a non-tactical officer. [8]

It had never been Chelmsford's intention to make a stronghold of the position at Isandlwana. It was a convenient bivouac site on the march to Ulundi and Chelmsford saw little point in spending time and resources on its defence, despite all the advice he had been given to the contrary.

To laager the wagons (a term used by the Boers to describe a defensive position, usually made by encircling their trek waggons) would take considerable time and effort and they were needed anyway to ferry stores from Rorke's Drift. The ground was too hard to dig any form of worthwhile entrenchments and by the time all this had been done the column would need to move on again. With two experienced infantry battalions to hand, extensive fields of view and picquets out on the hills at night, Chelmsford did not feel under any specific threat, so his own regulations on field defences were quietly ignored. Some regimental officers voiced their concerns in this respect but to no avail and Lt Col Pulleine saw no reason to question the lead set by his superior officer.

Once Lord Chelmsford had departed, Lt Col Pulleine set about the defence of his camp and in so doing compounded the errors already unfolding. Rather than taking advantage of closed ranks of concentrated firepower in a position of all-round defence, based on the natural obstacle of Isandlwana itself, Pulleine's companies were well forward in an extended arc stretching from the north to the south east of the position. There were three companies of the 1st/24th to the north with two of these companies and two companies of the NNC initially further out as a screen. The other three companies faced east with the rocket battery Royal Artillery facing north-east between these two groups. The balance of the NNC was held centrally behind the main company positions. No attempt was made to strike the camp – a routine procedure in enemy territory – and although each soldier had his standard allocation of 70 rounds of ammunition, no orders were given to open up and distribute the large reserve held centrally. As far as Pulleine was concerned, there was no evidence of an immediate threat and he was under remit anyway to prepare the camp ready to move forward to join Lord Chelmsford when called for.

The paucity of surveillance and lack of any formalized plan to gather intelligence about enemy movements cannot be emphasized enough. Although picquets were put out at night, no one seems to have been responsible for the central co-ordination of this essential element of the battle plan. When reports first came in that Zulus were seen moving to the north of the position, no-one had sufficient information to analyse what this might represent. The companies, quite rightly, stood to (that is, prepared for action) and Pulleine sent a message to Chelmsford to this effect. However, this report gave no indication of alarm and Chelmsford saw no reason to change his original plan, given the sizeable force he had left in the camp. In the event, no attack developed at this stage and the camp carried on with its normal routine.

Later that morning, Durnford's column arrived at Isandlwana, but this did little to improve the situation. It is alleged that Durnford had been instructed to take command of the camp, but if this is so, then it is unlikely that he would have abandoned the camp to move out along the track towards Lord Chelmsford. If he was under command of Pulleine, then he should have remained in the camp to assist in its defence. There was no logic in this action and by moving out and expecting to be reinforced if he ran into trouble, he only weakened the already over-stretched defensive line. There is a parallel here with Chelmsford's actions the previous night. Durnford had received no orders to this effect and there was no Zulu activity to his front at the time to justify it. Once again it can only be attributed to complacency and incompetence, and this from an officer who was reputed to be experienced in Zulu military matters. His cavalier attitude had already incurred the wrath of Chelmsford, normally a mild mannered person, on a previous occasion, yet here he was, taking matters into his own hands, with disastrous consequences. What Durnford did do, however, was to send out some scouting patrols of the 1st/3rd NNC onto the Nqutu plateau to follow up the earlier sightings of Zulus and it was Lt Charles Raw who stumbled across the main Zulu army of over 20,000 warriors in the Ngwebeni valley, five miles to the north east. Herein lies one of the great tactical weaknesses faced by Lord Chelmsford – a lack of regular, professional cavalry for reconnaissance purposes.

Zulu tactics were based on the 'horns of the buffalo' formation, allegedly introduced by Shaka. Regiments of young fleet footed warriors would form the horns, which would sweep out in a semi-circular movement to surround and enclose the enemy to prevent any escape. The chest, made up from the more mature battle hardened Regiments would then close in directly upon their foe to engage them at close quarters with their short, wide bladed assegai to deadly effect. The older veteran Regiments would make up the reserve, held to the rear and made to sit on their shields with their backs to the battle in case they should get swept up in the excitement, ready to be deployed where necessary. All these elements would be controlled by the *indunas*, or chiefs, who would position themselves on a high vantage point from which they could control the battle by hand signals or by the use of runners if the distances were too great. On this occasion the Zulu army had been led into battle by the 60 year old veteran Ntingshwayo kaMahole who had marched every mile of the way from Ulundi with his warriors, and so disciplined were these regiments that the precision and timing of their movement would not have been out of place on a British military drill parade.

The ferocious speed and onslaught of the traditional Zulu horns of the buffalo formation was soon to expose the inadequacy of the British defensive line. Having pushed well forward on the right flank, Durnford came face to face with the left horn and realized that he was in danger of being outflanked. He appreciated that this would leave the main defensive line totally vulnerable, so he began a spirited fighting withdrawal back to the nek (a dip between two hills) to the south of Isandlwana. Unfortunately, Lt Col Durnford's ill considered sortie forced Pulleine to adjust his line in his support and so prevented him from pulling his forces into a tighter formation. Pulleine thus forfeited the overwhelming advantage his men's concentrated firepower would have enjoyed if they had been drawn up in a tight all-round formation. Spread out so thinly in open skirmishing order, his men were placed at an unnecessary disadvantage. At the same time, the two companies on the left flank confronted the full weight of the Zulu right horn and while they were able to put down a massed volley of rifle fire to great effect, they were soon obliged to pull back closer to the hill feature in line with the third Company. As they did so, the two NNC companies, who had never been intended for employment as battle line troops, were forced to pull back with them and became part of the main defensive line. This was a task for which they were ill equipped and as such only added to the vulnerability of the position.

At this point, all companies had withdrawn to a more consolidated position but they were still extended over some 2,000 yards and anything up to 800 yards from the centre of the camp. Heavy volley fire had succeeded in checking the Zulu advance in some places, but its continued impact depended upon ready access to ammunition re-supply. There are fashionable views and theories about the lack of ammunition at Isandlwana, but the reality is more likely a matter of being unable to re-supply an over-extended line fast enough. As the Zulus sensed a decrease in the rate of fire, they re-exerted pressure on the centre of the position and Pulleine had no option but to withdraw his line once again as far back as possible. The companies attempted to withdraw in fighting order, but in no time at all the line broke and once the Zulus were through, firepower was no longer the deciding factor and the British position was rapidly overpowered by sheer weight of numbers. Durnford fought his way back to the nek, but was eventually overcome. Once they saw the inevitability of defeat, the Natal Native Horse and the NNC fled the battlefield, leaving the 24th Foot to its fate. Faced by overwhelming odds, they fought and died together, witnessed by the compact piles of bodies found on the battlefield four months later.

During the battle, a number of messages were sent to Lord Chelmsford by Lt Col Pulleine, but none of them conveyed the urgency of the situation and in any event, Chelmsford believed he had left enough men in the camp to defend it. It was not until later in the day, when more telling reports came in, that the reality of the situation became apparent. In any event, it would have taken up to three hours to send reinforcements back from his location and by then it was too late to influence the outcome of the battle. Of the 1,700 men on the battlefield that day, less than 60 white and 400 black soldiers survived, while Zulu casualties are believed to be about 2,500. [9]

That afternoon, the reserve force of the Zulu army swept on to Rorke's Drift, where B Company of the 2nd/24th, under the command of Lieutenant Gonville Bromhead, had been left to guard the makeshift hospital and store set up at the former Swedish Mission Station. Born in 1845, the third son of Major Sir Edmund de Gonville Bromhead, 3rd Baronet, he joined the 2nd/24th Foot in 1867. Aged 34 and allegedly hard of hearing, Bromhead is often cast as an over-age Lieutenant with little career prospects, consigned to a nondescript appointment of guarding a stores depot; how he was soon to disprove his critics. In overall command was Major Henry Spalding of the 104th Foot (later the Royal Munster Fusiliers), a staff officer from Chelmsford's main headquarters, and earlier in the day he had returned to Helpmekaar to supervise the move forward of D and G Companies, who were due to reinforce the station at Rorke's Drift. At this point in time there was no obvious indication of any immediate threat to his position and he was content to delegate command to Lieutenant Chard, being the senior officer present on site. Although born 2 years later than Bromhead in 1847 and commissioned one year after him in 1868, he was senior only by virtue of his promotion to the rank of Lieutenant. John Rouse Merriott Chard was an officer in the 5th Company Royal Engineers who had arrived at Durban only a few weeks earlier on 5 January 1879. He was immediately assigned to the river crossing at Rorke's Drift to ensure that the ponts were kept in good working order for the forward movement of supplies for the central column.

When Lord Chelmsford began the invasion, a similar air of complacency prevailed at Rorke's Drift. With a strong column to its front, no attack on the position was expected, so little provision was made for its defence. Screened from the line of advance by the Shiyane hill feature, a basic tactic would have been to post a vedette or observation post at its summit. However, no such action was taken and it was not until news of the disaster at Isandlwana reached Lieutenants Chard and Bromhead that they realized the enormity of the threat which faced them. Neither Bromhead nor Chard had been given specific instructions in the event of an attack upon the position, so it was for them and the other officers to decide upon what action was to be taken. Withdrawal was not really an option as there were too many sick people to be evacuated from the hospital building and their movement would have been far too slow to escape the advancing Zulus. It would also have left the way open for a potential assault upon Natal, and while this was not part of Zulu strategy, they would not have been aware of this. They quickly began to design a simple but sound system of all-round defence, linking the hospital to the storehouse with walls of mealie bags and biscuit boxes. A bisecting line was built across the courtyard between the two outer walls, enabling the defenders to cover all lines of approach if necessary and the available ammunition was broken out and either issued to individuals or made accessible for immediate re-supply. This was sound tactical thinking, but a weakness of the position was the fact that it was closely overlooked by the Shiyane hill. The defenders did suffer from sniper fire from its slopes and had the Zulus been more proficient in the use of firearms, this would have spelt disaster.

When the Zulu attacks began, the defence of Rorke's Drift rested upon 100 men of B Company 2nd 24th Foot, with 35 patients in the hospital. With a force of some 4,000 Zulus pitted against them, it was surely only a matter of time before the position suffered the same fate as their comrades at Isandlwana earlier in the day. The difference was the fact that the British were able to put down concentrated volleys of rifle fire from a position of all-round defence and this time the line held. There was no complacency displayed during this battle and Lt Chard was ever conscious of the developing Zulu attacks. Chard, fearing that in their determination the Zulu would get over the wall behind the line of biscuit boxes and breach his position, and anxious at the mounting casualties from the snipers on Shiyane, decided to withdraw to the shorter position he had prepared behind the biscuit boxes.

Wave after wave of Zulu assaults were beaten off as Chard and Bromhead re-deployed their forces to meet the direction of attack, and while it may be argued that the Zulu shield and spear was no match for the Martini-Henry rifle, many outstanding acts of bravery took place during the battle. The evacuation of the sick and wounded from the burning hospital building is testimony to the courage of the individual soldier that night, and it was not until the early hours of the morning that the Zulu attacks faded away. Ammunition had run very low by this stage and there is the view that if the Zulus had returned to the attack the next morning then the position may well have been over-run. As it was, the Zulus themselves were exhausted and had taken heavy casualties. Also, having noticed the arrival of the remainder of Chelmsford's column from the direction of Isandlwana at daybreak, the Zulu force decided to pull out. With the award of eleven VCs to the defenders of

Rorke's Drift it is often argued that this action was played up as a distraction from the disaster at Isandlwana. [10] There may be some truth in this, but it should not detract from the incredible acts of individual heroism which took place that night. The citations of such men as Privates Henry Hook, Fred Hitch, Robert Jones, William Jones and John Williams, Corporal William Allen, and the outstanding leadership of Lieutenant Gonville Bromhead bear witness to unflinching courage and an unshakeable determination to stand by their colleagues at all costs, nurtured by the Regimental system which is still cherished today. There can be little doubt that the success of that battle had as much to do with the bravery of the soldiers who were there that night as it did to the firepower of the .45 Martini Henry rifle. The battle also clearly demonstrated the power and value of massed volley fire from a well defended position. This tactic was to be employed again successfully during the campaign and its implementation at Isandlwana may well have changed the whole course of this war if Lord Chelmsford had listened to the advice he had been given to this effect from the outset.

Wilfred records the fateful day as follows:

Wednesday 22 January
Orders came in for Rainforth's Coy to leave as well as ours. Col Hassard and Baxter came in for breakfast. All goods bar light field kit and one blanket gone with stores. A lot of canteen stores for both Batts came in made arrangements to forward them to the drift. Rainforth's Coy left at 2.30 ours just after 3. Met Spalding outside, after him any number of mounted men flying from the camp at Col Glyn's column which the Zulus had cut up. 5 Coys of ours killed Col Pulleine Wardell Anstey Daly Dyson White Pullen. Coghill and Melville escaped with Queens Colour. Hospital at the Drift and detachment 2/24th cut up. Got orders to retire on Helpmakaar got in about 11. and made Laager there put on outpost duty 12.30 to 3am.

This short but historic entry warrants further examination. Having arrived at Helpmekaar only the night before, both D and G Companies were ordered to move forward to Rorke's Drift the next day, with the intention of eventually joining up with the main part of the column. Consequently, Wilfred would have had little or no time to become acquainted with the current situation. Once all the stores had been prepared, the two Companies moved off at 30 minute intervals and Wilfred is quite specific about this. He then states "– *met Spalding outside, after him any number of mounted men flying from the camp at Col Glyn's column.*" Major Spalding, it will be recalled, was in overall charge of the supply depot at Rorke's Drift and had returned to Helpmekaar earlier that day to hasten the move of the two Companies who had been earmarked to assist him in the defence of that depot. Precisely where they met up is not quite clear, as the word "outside"' could mean anywhere from the Officers Mess at Helpmekaar to somewhere on the track to Rorke's Drift. In his own report submitted after the battle, Major Spalding states that he arrived at Helpmekaar at 3.45pm where he met both Companies, but there would seem to be a discrepancy here. The two companies were not under any orders to wait for Major Spalding, so they had no reason to delay. If Wilfred left at the time that he states in his diary, then they would have been about 3 miles from Helpmekaar on the track to Rorke's Drift when they met up with Major Spalding at 3.45pm. Spalding, however, reports that he met the companies at Helpmekaar at that time. Erroneous accusations of ignorance, incompetence and even cowardice have since been levelled at Spalding for not committing the troops he now had with him to the fighting taking place at Rorke's Drift, but on reflection there is a more reasonable and even logical reason for his subsequent actions that day.

Given the timings in both Wilfred's diary and Major Spalding's report, by the time that he had met up with the two companies and had moved some of the way back to Rorke's Drift, the battle there had clearly begun. Whether his surprise intervention from an unexpected direction with two infantry companies might have influenced the battle at that stage is a matter for debate. It should be pointed out at this juncture that Major Spalding was an administrative officer, responsible for the logistical control of the stores depots at both Rorke's Drift and at Helpmekaar, so the two companies of the 1st/24th Foot were not his to command. Also, it was getting close to nightfall by now and, generally speaking, night fighting was not really a viable option for either the British forces or the Zulus, given their lack of any effective means of communication during darkness. Agreed, most of the fighting at Rorke's Drift took place at night, but this was not a pre-planned action by either side. It was more the consequence of the Zulus being spurred on by the sheer scale of their unexpected victory at Isandlwana earlier that day and they did have some light from the burning hospital to provide them with illumination. The Zulu assault on Rorke's Drift did not follow the traditional horns of the buffalo formation, but was rather a series of sporadic, almost uncoordinated attacks as more and more Zulus made their way across the Buffalo River to join in what they thought might be easy pickings. A better disciplined and traditionally structured assault by the Zulus could well have seen another British defeat that day.

By the time that Major Spalding had joined up with the companies, he would have known about the disaster at Isandlwana from those who had been lucky enough to escape on horseback and it would have been a logical assumption that a similar fate was about to befall the mission station at Rorke's Drift. Indeed, some of the reports he received were to the effect that Rorke's Drift had in fact been taken by the Zulus. Also, we must not forget that he had with him the two company commanders from Helpmekaar, Captains Russell Upcher and Thomas Rainforth, and the three of them would, no doubt, have assessed the consequences of the present situation. Having fought in the ninth frontier war in the previous year, the officers of the 24th Foot had every confidence in their abilities against a native foe, but to commit themselves to battle against an unknown force, in darkness, without being able to co-ordinate their activities with the company already at Rorke's Drift, was fraught with great difficulties and was a recipe for further disaster. Equally, if the Zulu army had crossed the border into Natal and had taken the position at Rorke's Drift as had been reported, then it was logical to assume that their next objective would be the base at Helpmekaar which was now very weakly defended. To lose this position as well could have serious consequences, not only for the logistical supply of the central column, but also for the security of the colony of Natal itself, so its defence was vital. For these reasons it is believed that they all decided that it was essential to return to Helpmekaar as soon as they could and arrived there, according to Wilfred, at about 11 pm.

He then records that ' – *Coghill and Melville escaped with Queens Colour,*' which seems to throw fresh light on the events surrounding this emotive and heroic incident. As explained earlier, flags, banners and standards have long been rallying points on the field of battle and over the centuries they have come to embody the honour, pride and spirit of a regiment. On 22 January, both battalions of the 24th had their Colours at Isandlwana, but for some unexplained reason, the 1st/24th had the Queen's Colour only with them, the Regimental Colour having been left under guard at Helpmekaar. When it was apparent that the camp was about to be overwhelmed by the Zulus, it is alleged that Lieutenant Colonel Pulleine directed the Adjutant, Lieutenant Teignmouth Melvill to take the Queen's Colour of the 1st/24th to a place of safety. With the Colour apparently furled in its leather case, Lieutenant Melvill rode off the field of battle and fought his way along the only escape route until he made the banks of the Buffalo River, which was in full spate from recent heavy rain. Still pursued by Zulus, he plunged his horse into the raging torrent only to become unseated, but he managed to make the comparative safety of a large rock protruding from the water. As we know from the report made by Lieutenant Higginson of the NNC who crossed the river at the same time, Lieutenant Neville Coghill had already reached the safety of the far riverbank, but on seeing Lieutenant

Melvill in trouble and though injured himself, he immediately turned back into the water to assist him. As Melvill and Coghill struggled back to dry land on the Natal side of the river, they lost their grip on the Colour, which was carried away downriver in the fast moving water. As they made their way up the riverbank they were confronted by Zulus who were already on that side of the river and killed. Several authors report that Lieutenant Melvill's watch stopped at 2.20p.m., this being the time that he entered the Buffalo River. While this cannot be accurately corroborated, it is safe to assume that watches in 1879 were not properly waterproof and this fits well with the eyewitness accounts of events on that day.

At this stage, the tragic truth of the events surrounding the Queen's Colour had not yet reached Helpmekaar, so Heaton recorded only that the two officers had *escaped*, hopefully to turn up soon. We must assume that this information came from eyewitness accounts on the battlefield itself, because had it come from witnesses on the banks of the Buffalo River then Heaton would have been told that both officers had already been killed and the Colour lost. It is significant that Wilfred tells us that Melvill and Coghill *escaped* with the Colour, rather than the fact that they were *killed* in their attempt, so it is argued that they left the battlefield together, rather than separately as some historical accounts indicate. This does not have to mean that they rode off side by side, as depicted by Alphonse de Neuville in his dramatic painting, but it does imply that it was their joint endeavour to prevent the Colour falling into enemy hands and as Regimental officers they would have considered this to be their bounden duty. Coghill had injured his leg the previous day in an accident, so he was left behind with the 1st Battalion, rather than join Colonel Glyn when Lord Chelmsford split his column earlier that day. There is no clear record of what tasks he was given, but it is reasonable to assume that he was attached to Lieutenant Colonel Pulleine's headquarters. Some authors assert that Coghill may have been despatched, or decided on his own initiative, to ride to Rorke's Drift or Helpmekaar to give warning of the Zulu advance, or perhaps to call for reinforcements but it would have been impossible for them to arrive in time to be of any value, given the speed and ferocity of the Zulu assault.

There is also an inference that Coghill left the battlefield early to save his own skin, but this is entirely without foundation. Had desertion been on his mind, he would have fled before the right horn of the Zulu army moved round behind Isandlwana, thus blocking the track which led back to Rorke's Drift and the fact that he was forced to use the fugitives' trail can only mean that he was still at Isandlwana in the closing stages of the battle, when any attempt on his part to call for reinforcements would have been entirely superfluous. Great significance also seems to be made of the fact that Coghill was on the home bank of the Buffalo River when Melvill was in difficulty in the water, implying therefore that he had left sometime earlier. We can only imagine the confusion, chaos and terror experienced by those attempting to escape along that rocky and treacherous route and the fact that Coghill was ahead of Melvill, who would have been moving more slowly with the Colour in hand, is perfectly reasonable in the circumstances, despite the fact that Coghill's horse had been struck by Zulu assegais on several occasions. If Melvill was visible to Coghill when he was struggling in the river, then it is logical to assume that Coghill was no distance at all from the riverbank, which suggests that he was only minutes ahead of his brother officer. [11] This scenario is supported by Wilfred's diary entry that Melvill and Coghill *escaped* together with the Colour.

There has been considerable debate about whether Lieutenant Colonel Pulleine actually gave Lieutenant Melvill specific orders to save the Queen's Colour, or if this was his own decision in the absence of his commanding officer, who may well have been killed by this stage. It has also been suggested that Melvill was attempting to rally the troops with the presence of the Colour, but this is highly unlikely. In the early stages of the battle this would have been neither necessary nor practical as the Companies were too far forward and once the withdrawal turned into wholesale slaughter, Melvill would never have risked the Colour falling into enemy hands. For this reason alone, his intention would have been one of saving the Colour. There are also aspersions cast in some quarters about his leaving the field of battle in the face of the enemy. In his report after the war, General Wolseley unkindly remarked that he would have preferred these two officers to have died closer to the scene of battle in the company of the men under their command. In fact, neither was in a command appointment at the time, so there is no question of them abandoning soldiers to their fate. Thankfully, history is more generous and understands the significance of the price they paid for their Regimental pride and loyalty, for which they were subsequently awarded posthumous VCs. What is quite clear is that Lieutenant Melvill would have known full well the intrinsic value and significance of the Colours and it is suggested that there would not be any regimental officer, then or since, who would have questioned for a moment the action that he took, whether or not he was ordered to do so by his commanding officer.

The Colours of the 2nd/24th Foot were lost completely, because it would seem there was no one from that battalion in the camp headquarters at the time who was in a position to make any kind of decision in the heat of the Zulu assault. That said, it is inconceivable that the

2nd/24th would have left the camp with Lord Chelmsford on the morning of 22 January without making some contingency plan for the safekeeping of their Colours by their sister battalion. We will probably never know what those arrangements were but it is hard to imagine that the 2nd/24th Colours would have been consciously abandoned, adding weight to the supposition that when Melvill and Coghill escaped with their Colour it was a final, desperate act in the face of the enemy when all about them was lost. We should also remember that these were hardly two impetuous young men, despite their junior rank of Lieutenant. Coghill was 27 years old at the time of the battle and Melvill was 10 years older. Promotion was much slower in the Victorian army of that era and by today's standards Melvill would have equated to a senior major approaching the rank of Lieutenant Colonel. They had both served long enough to understand the significance of saving the Colour and in their minds there was no other alternative course of action.

There is an associated mystery surrounding the Colour and its case during its immersion in the Buffalo river. We are told that the Colour was furled in its leather sleeve (akin to a close fitting umbrella cover, with a brass hood and draw strings at the bottom) when Melvill left Isandlwana, but when the Colour was found in the river about 10 days later it was not in its case. As most regimental officers will agree, it is exceedingly difficult to insert or remove a Colour from its case single-handed, and it usually takes two people to roll the Colour around the pike and slide it in or out of the case. Clearly Melvill would not have been able to enjoy such luxury during the battle, so if the Colour was cased initially then there could have been no question of him removing the case, by accident or design, while in flight along the fugitives' trail to the river. By the same token, if the raging river was strong enough to pull the Colour out of its tight fitting leather case then the Colour itself, made of fragile silk embroidered with gold and silver thread, would have been torn to shreds and probably never found. This leads to the possibility that perhaps the Colour was not cased after all and maybe de Neuville's painting of an uncased Colour (albeit the wrong one – the painting depicts the Regimental Colour when in fact it should have been the Queen's Colour) leaving Isandlwana is more accurate than at first thought. While it is accepted that the case was found in the same location as the Colour, it is quite possible that Melvill took this with him as well, with the intention of replacing it on the Colour when he reached a place of safety.

Wilfred's entry for this day is also interesting for a number of other reasons. He had received a good public school education and had been tutored by a master of classics, yet his entry for the day in no way captures the high drama of the events that had just taken place. His own company might easily have been at Isandlwana, in which case Wilfred would have been slaughtered along with the rest of his comrades of the 1st/24th, yet the loss of his commanding officer and many of his personal friends seems to have had little impact upon him. Likewise, the survivors fleeing from Isandlwana would have painted graphic details of untold horror, but all of this passes without comment. He would have known virtually every one of the many officers who were killed that day, but he mentions only seven of them by name; perhaps these were the closest to him. No doubt the nature of the Victorian army officer demanded a stiff upper lip and no display of emotion, but it is difficult to comprehend that his only remark in the whole of his diary on the defence of Rorke's Drift was to be ' – *Hospital at the Drift and detachment 2/24th cut up.*' One could argue from this that, perhaps, the action was not as dramatic and significant as historians have since recorded it to be, but even the most dispassionate analysis would refute this view, given what is now known about the events which took place that night. A more reasonable explanation is that, with poor lines of communication and slow passage of information, the full impact of what had happened was not immediately apparent, especially to a junior officer some distance from the battle. Equally, his diary was a personal record only, so this one entry was sufficient to remind himself of all that had happened that day.

As we now know, there was the fear that King Cetshwayo would follow up his success with an invasion of Natal, so there was frenetic activity to strengthen the defences of the laager at Helpmekaar as indicated by Wilfred on 22 January. This continued into the next day.

Thursday 23 January
Some more stragglers came in finished up the laager barricading the waggons with sacks of mealies etc. Got in stock of rifles for unarmed men. Worked all day Orderly Officer by night. Bengough bought up his Battalion and they were told off to the waggons and outpost on the flanks.

This laconic diary entry belies the real fear of further attacks by the Zulu army and every effort was made to reinforce the camp at Helpmakaar. By the word stragglers, Wilfred means some of those who survived the wholesale slaughter at Isandlwana and though they may have been traumatized by their experiences, they were soon put to work. Strong barricades were hastily erected and weapons found for those who may have lost their own the previous day. Brevet Lieutenant Colonel HM Bengough, who had only arrived in Natal the previous month, was the commanding officer of the 2nd Battalion Natal Native Contingent (NNC). Initially part of Colonel Durnford's column, he had been left behind to protect the frontier at Kranz Kop and on learning of the defeat at Isandlwana, he moved towards Rorke's Drift with the intention of joining up with Lord Chelmsford. Instead, he was diverted to Helpmakaar to bolster the defences there. Commandant George 'Maori' Hamilton-Browne (so called because of his service in a volunteer unit in New Zealand) was a hard-bitten colonial Irishman who was locally contracted to command the 1st Battalion of the 3rd Regiment NNC. His force had accompanied the General on his abortive advance away from Isandlwana and was allegedly one of the first to actually witness the battle itself as they made their return journey. When the remnants of the column withdrew to Rorke's Drift the next day, Hamilton-Browne was despatched to Helpmekaar. He had absolutely no regard for the natives under his command and so disgusted was he with their performance that he took the drastic action of arbitrarily disbanding his Battalion. [12]

By this stage, Chelmsford was anxious to return to Pietermaritzburg to give his version of the defeat at Isandlwana, to deflect the blame away from himself. As Wilfred recalls, he had stern words to say before he left:

Friday 24 January
The General and some of the staff came up and fell in Bengough's men who were deserting on 3 sides of the Square. Selves on 4th and threatened to have them all shot unless they went on with duty. Brown came in with his mounted troop also the remainder of Harness's Battery and Natal Carbiniers Worked all day reducing the laager and loop holing the end of one of the flanks joined by a tin store. General went on to P.M.Burg by way of Ladysmith. Colonel Russell staid here to help old Hassard. A Coy of Native Contingent arrived. About 1000 passed on their way home

Helpmekaar was clearly a hive of activity with so many units passing through as the column tried to regain some sense of order. Lieutenant Edward Browne, 24th Foot commanded a unit of mounted infantry, raised to compensate for the lack of cavalry troops in the early stages of the campaign while Lieutenant Colonel Harness commanded N Battery, 5th Brigade Royal Artillery and he too had accompanied Lord Chelmsford away from Isandlwana on that fateful day. The comment about old Hassard relates to the Court of Inquiry initiated by Lord Chelmsford into the events of Isandlwana. Clearly there had to be a post mortem on the debacle and the official instruction to hold a Court of Inquiry was issued at Helpmekaar on 24 January. The officer chosen as the President was the 60 year old Colonel Fairfax Hassard RE, who was commanding the base at Helpmekaar at the time. The other members were Lieutenant Colonel Francis Adeane Law RA and Lieutenant Colonel Arthur Harness RA, who had commanded N Battery at

Isandlwana, but who had accompanied Lord Chelmsford on his advance to the Mangeni river. As he had been a witness to many of Chelmsford's actions that day, he was precluded from giving evidence himself. The mandate given to the Court was to enquire into the *'loss of the camp on the 22nd January.'* The Court, which started on 27 January and sat for only 2 days, was not asked to give an opinion; it only took 8 statements and declined to question or interrogate witnesses. Many key people were not called and it can only be concluded that the inquiry was an attempt to exonerate Chelmsford from any blame and to discredit the likes of Colonels Durnford and Pulleine, on the basis that the dead could not defend themselves. [13]

While the remnants of Chelmsford's column recovered at Rorke's Drift they needed re-supplying and this was one of the tasks which fell to young Wilfred.

Saturday 25 January
General fatigue cleaning up the Camp. Got a wash in Hopes waggon store supplies sent down under escort to the drift. Fatigues of all sorts all day. Tried to make a decent room among the sacks in the store. A false alarm in the afternoon. Attack expected at night. Upcher. Moffatt Cockrane to Drift. Cockrane staid all night.

Lieutenant Francis Cochrane 32nd Foot (The Duke of Cornwall's Light Infantry) had been a staff officer to Colonel Durnford and was one of the few lucky survivors from Isandlwana. The fear of invasion by Cetshwayo was to remain for some time, as indicated by the nervous reaction to false alarms and the punishment inflicted on suspected Zulu spies, brought in by patrols of the mounted infantry. While inexcusable and unworthy in the cold light of day, it is perhaps understandable that the survivors of the column would seek to exact some form of revenge after the debacle at Isandlwana. Any Zulu who gave any indication of having contributed to the death of British soldiers was summarily executed, no doubt without fair trial. Hamilton-Brown in particular had no compunction about executing so-called spies. [14]

There was no running water at Helpmekaar and the opportunity for a hot bath was very limited indeed. However, with some ingenuity and the use of a tin tub, Heaton was able to have a good wash down in the privacy of Assistant Commissary Hope's wagon. At the same time, Colonel Hassard was insistent that the fortifications at Helpmekaar were completed as soon as possible.

Sunday 26 January
Col Bray up from Sand Spruit for a short time. Fatigues cleared up the end of the laager and dried a lot of tents. Several loads of Sergt Morrissey's

ammunition came in and stored. Major Dalrymple from P.M.B Cockrane from drift. Sent down some spare clothing to the fellows at the drift. Fort to be commenced tomorrow and finished so Col Hassard says in 3 days!! Jones and his Coy R.E. in. Stores to drift Clem on escort. Spy hung at the drift yesterday and a suspected one brought in here today and shot. Sick men from the drift. Dalton among them with a wound in his shoulder.

Also, disease, particularly enteric fever, was a major problem throughout the whole invasion and sick men were regularly moved back along the line of communication for further treatment and more often than not, for burial as they succumbed to their sickness. On this day, Commissariat James Langley Dalton, who had been so influential in the defence arrangements at Rorke's Drift and who was to receive the Victoria Cross in due course, was also evacuated having been badly injured during that heroic action.

Monday 27 January
The Col came up from the drift and held a sort of mess meeting about Mr Bourke and others things. The fort begun and got a lot turned out. Clements party came up late at night. The Col joined us for the night on the mealie sacks. Dalys dog Ponto came in with Clem.

His mention of the fort refers to the construction of defences around the camp against the threat of another invasion. Meanwhile, Colonel Glyn came up to Helpmekaar from Rorke's Drift for a Mess meeting to discuss what to do with the personal effects ('others things') of those officers killed at Isandlwana and stayed overnight visiting the men of his Battalion who were on sentry duty on the ramparts; a fitting example of leadership and good man management.

There is also a poignant entry here about Daly's dog Ponto. Lieutenant James Patrick Daly was in F Company 1st/24th Regiment and he had joined the Regiment on the same day as Wilfred five years ago, only to be killed at Isandlwana the previous week. A number of stray dogs were collected as pets by officers during the campaign and Ponto had been left behind at Helpmekaar when the column had advanced into Zululand.

Tuesday 28 January
Col left for the drift. The Mess split into two mounted and infantry. Foraging parties out went with Smith Dorrien and made 5 fowls some eggs and vegetables Major Dalrymple lead a fatigue party and made the store more habitable by shifting some sacks. Made a huge Kaffir cooking pot. Cockrane went off towards Utrecht to see his brother but heard that he had trekked. Sorted out Col Pulleine's kit for sale at the drift took silk pocket handkerchief for self.

As there was no formal welfare service at the time and not all war widows received an army pension, it was customary to auction off the belongings of an officer killed in action and the proceeds sent to the family. Lieutenant Colonel Pulleine had been the commanding officer of the 1st/24th Foot at Isandlwana and Wilfred organized the auction of personal effects which was held at Rorke's Drift. While he mentions that he took Pulleine's silk handkerchief, what he means is that he purchased it and he would no doubt have contributed generously to the proceeds. With no specific duty at this stage and no doubt to recover from the trauma of that battle, Lieutenant Cochrane was given leave to go to Utrecht, about 50 miles to the north, to spend some time there with his brother, only to find that he had moved on (*trekked*). Quite what his brother was doing there is not clear.

The Mess split into two for practical reasons. The infantry officers were primarily those of the 24th Foot companies, who saw themselves as a family regiment and who were together on a regular basis. The mounted officers however were from a mixture of units and by their nature of employment were not regular users of the Mess facilities. Reinforcements were a priority, as were horses for the officers.

Wednesday 29 January
Sent poney to Rainsforth to go out and get some Burrells. He and Clem took over charge of a couple of stray half starved ponies found tied up to the waggons. ½ Coy Engineers 4th K.O. 2 Coys and Sergt Morrisseys party came in from Sand spruit. Col Bray complimented our men very much on their behaviour under his command. Moffat took over the draft 2/24th and gave me the 1/13th one. Marched the former to the drift. Hope back from Ladysmith.

Soldiers are always at their best when kept busy, indicated by Colonel Bray's complimentary remarks. There was also the on-going need to ensure that fresh drafts of manpower reached the right destination and Wilfred took the opportunity to get out of Helpmekaar for a while by taking the new draft for the 2nd/24th Foot down to Rorke's Drift personally. While the Court of Inquiry was in progress, it was essential to compile records of all those who had been killed at Isandlwana.

Thursday 30 January
Upcher spent nearly the whole day making up the list of men and officers killed on the 22nd with the help of escaped men etc. On outlying picquet duty all night

As company commander, Upcher was given this unpleasant task, using company nominal rolls and eyewitness accounts from those who had survived. Meanwhile, the fear of Zulu attack was still a concern.

Friday 31 January
Lonsdale and Gordon NNC came up from the drift Prisoners of 1/13th for loosing a rifle and sleeping on post. Tried to turn in and get a sleep in the afternoon, but something was wanted every 10 minutes. About the time for turning into laarger report came in that the Zulus were crossing below. All horses sent out loose. Slept out with the men in the new South parapet.

Life was clearly very busy for all concerned and sleep was at a premium. Setting a good example, Wilfred gave up the comfort of his own tent to sleep out with the men as they guarded the ramparts against possible attacks.

Saturday 1 February
Orderly Room work in the morning wrote Adjt Gen Depot for 94 – – . DCM: Russell and Ruddy and enclosing defaulters sheets. To Runningfield about sets of saddlery and Canteen Bar stock at Durban and started one home. Had a good sleep in the afternoon.

Discipline has always been the bedrock of military training and it would have been strictly enforced on active service in South Africa. For the previous 100 years at least, Parliament had recognized the legality of military courts on the basis that the civil legal process had little in common with the enforcement of military discipline. There were three levels of military courts, or courts-martial as they were called. The lowest was the Regimental court-martial (RCM), often referred to just as a court-martial. Designed to try soldiers below the rank of warrant officer for lesser disciplinary offence they were easy to convene, proceedings were brief and their sentences could be implemented immediately. The RCM would usually consist of a Captain and three or four Lieutenants from the unit concerned and the extent of their jurisdiction was undefined. As a result, commanding officers sometimes made frequent use of deliberately vague charges such as 'neglect of duty' to conceal the fact that their men were being tried for serious military crimes. The more formal District court-martial (DCM), conducted by senior officers from outside the unit of the accused had wider powers for more serious crimes, but could not try a commissioned officer while a General court-martial (GCM) had the widest powers of punishment, extending to the death penalty if necessary and could try an officer or soldier of any rank. [15] On this occasion, Wilfred was preparing the paperwork ready for a DCM.

Sunday 2 February
Party on the works in the morning and Church parade at 12. Parson came

up from the drift. Issue of clothing to the men from Hopes waggons from Dundee. Foraging parties out Clements 4 fowls Upcher and Rainsforth one Hertebeast 13st 8lbs when cleaned. Major Black, Church and Moffatt up from the Drift. Spalding came in for the night on the way to P.M.Burg, also Gardiner one of farmers horses died in the night.

Monday 3 February
Got the last of the laager waggons out of the fort. The Colonel and some of the 2nd Battn fellows came up from the drift took a fatigue party to the old Regtt store house to look for Orderly room papers but found nothing satisfactory among them. Lunched at the 4th Mess. Some of the farmers of the neighbourhood came up to complain of their new houses being broken into by Officers and NCOs of NNC. The Commissariat Corps Brownrigs in a great state of mind about the meally sacks etc used in the parapet. Complaints by 1/13th draft Sergt Sharps and by Church about some of the things he bought at the Canteen yesterday.

With so much to do, Sunday was no day of rest this time. Uniforms had to be replaced and foraging parties went out to see if they could bag some fresh meat for the cooking pots. Church parade still went ahead though and the service was taken by the Rev George Smith who had worked so hard during the battle on the night of 22 January with ammunition resupply. Work on the fortifications at Helpmekaar continued without let-up and the use of mealie bags for protection was no doubt copied from their successful use at Rorke's Drift. The Commissariat did not appreciate this however.

Discipline was not all that it should be amongst the Natal Native Contingent. Although most of the officers and non-commissioned officers were white colonials the standards they set amongst themselves and the control they had over their native levies did not compare with that of the Imperial battalions. Deputy Commissariat General Brownrigg had been based at Helpmekaar since the start of the invasion and was responsible for replacing losses and restoring the organization of supplies after the disaster at Isandlwana. Having seen the damage done to the mealie bags used so successfully in the makeshift defences at Rorke's Drift he was agitated that a similar thing could happen at Helpmekaar should there be another invasion, thus depleting the food chain for the remnants of the Column.

Tuesday 4 February
Clements had a fatigue party of mounted men cleared out the sacks except one row from the stores we occupy and built up a couple of covers for the men inside the fort. Some letters at last from Mother, Kit and Wolfe also

receipt for the rebate of income tax from V. Holt and Co. Reports in that Zulus to assemble at full moon at Kings Kraal and advance to the attack of this and other forts. Upcher heard from Colonel Queens Colour recovered by Major Black and Melville and Coghill buried. Parcel of clothing from drift for men 2/24th in hosp etc.

In his entry for 22 January, Wilfred thought that Melvill and Coghill had escaped with the Queen's Colour, but when Lieutenant Higginson of the Natal Native Contingent who had witnessed the events at the Fugitives Drift made his report, a search party led by Major Black, a senior major in 2nd/24th Foot, was sent out to see if the Colour could be recovered. The bodies of Melvill and Coghill were soon found as was the Colour, which was wedged against a rock and protruding above the water level now that the flooding had receded. The news soon made its way to Helpmekaar.

The Colour was taken first of all to Rorke's Drift, where amongst emotional scenes it was handed over to Colonel Richard Glyn who had first received the Colour at the Curragh in Northern Ireland in 1866. It was then brought up to the base at Helpmekaar where Wilfred had the great distinction of receiving it into safe custody once more. The cover picture to this book, drawn by William Lloyd and which appeared in the *Illustrated London News* on 29 March 1879 depicts Wilfred taking hold of the Colour. It is also interesting to note his comments about the first prisoners for some days. No doubt the recent battles and fears of further invasion had kept everyone pre-occupied, but as the pace of life began to slow down, so some of the soldiers began slipping back into their bad ways once again.

Family and friends at home were very important to Wilfred and he corresponded with them all as often as he could. As was the custom in the Victorian era his relationship with his parents was quite formal, often referring to *the mother*, but he obviously held them in high regard. Catherine, or Kit, was the eldest of his three sisters while Wolfe was a family friend. He was also very meticulous with his personal affairs, V Holt & Co. being the Army Bankers at the time.

Wednesday 5 February
Lots of letters in for sorting etc. First 24th prisoner for some days. Major Black brought back the Queens Colour from the drift. The Col came up with him and the colour escort. I received the Colour. Col and Black made speeches about finding it in the river and Melville and Coghill's bodies and their burial. Reports of Zulus crossing and advancing on Fort Pine and Utrecht also below and a reverse to Col Pearson's Column from Bengough's Camp. Williams Policeman came in for Drinks. All our

rations for day and part for tomorrow run out by Contingent at lunch. Issue of rum.

The search for security against their hostile neighbours in Zululand was a perennial occupation of the white settlers in Natal and from as early as 1843 fortifications were built as places of refuge in the event of an attack. The first recorded fortification was the 'Old Fort' in Durban and another half dozen were built over the next 30 years, but the onset of war saw a rapid increase in the number of defensive strongholds along the Natal border. By the time of the second invasion in June 1879 there were about 130. These were classed as either permanent, temporary or improvised fortifications and varied in the complexity of their construction and were designed as either defensive positions, staging posts or supply depots. [16]

Fort Pine, initially known as the Dundee Laager, was about 20 miles north west of Helpmekaar on the road to Utrecht. Named after a former Governor of Natal, Sir Benjamin Pine, it was an open square within walls 14 feet high, loop-holed for rifles to fire out from. Intended initially as a post for the Natal Mounted Police, the Buffalo Border Guard and the Newcastle Mounted Rifles were hastily sent to garrison the fort as rumours continued to circulate about a likely attack across the border and even another assault below, by which Wilfred means at Rorke's Drift. None of this of course materialized but the rumours were all taken seriously.

The Colours of the 2nd/24th Foot were lost completely during the battle, but the pikestaff and crown of one was eventually recovered. This and the Colours of the 1st/24th Foot now reside in the Regimental Chapel in Brecon Cathedral. Melvill and Coghill were buried where they had fallen and though there was no provision for posthumous awards at that time it was generally accepted that, had they not died in battle, they would have been recommended for the Victoria Cross. After the Boer War at the turn of the century this policy was eventually reversed and on 15 January 1907, after vigorous representation by the Regiment and their families, these two officers were bestowed with the accolade that their bravery richly deserved. Sadly, Coghill's father died shortly before the announcement was made, but Melvill's widow Sarah and her two sons had the honour of receiving Melvill's posthumous medal from King Edward VII. These medals, along with all but one of those awarded to the 24th Foot at Rorke's Drift – the exception being that of Private Robert Jones which is in a private collection – are now the property of the Regimental Museum at Brecon.

The Battle Honour awarded for this campaign and carried on the

Colours today reads *South Africa 1877–8–9* and the question is often asked why is there no mention of either Isandlwana or Rorke's Drift on the Colours, as the Regiment fought with great honour on both occasions, even though the outcome was different in each case. Battle Honours are not given lightly and are usually awarded only when the whole battalion has been involved and where the action played a significant part in the outcome of the campaign. At Rorke's Drift only one infantry company was involved, so the action did not meet the prime criterion for such an award, despite the heroism that took place that night. However, the numerous acts of individual bravery were acknowledged by the award of the highest ever number of VCs for one action – a total of 11, of which 7 went to B Company 2/24th Foot. Isandlwana was a defeat and while the Regiment remembers it with honour and pride, it was considered more appropriate that the whole period of service in South Africa including the ninth frontier war should be a collective honour.

Queen Victoria bestowed a unique privilege upon the Regiment by placing a wreath of immortelles upon the Queen's Colour which recognized not only the immortal defence of Rorke's Drift but which also paid tribute to those who gave their lives at Isandlwana and during the whole campaign. No other regiment has ever received such an accolade. There was a South African campaign medal with a bar upon the ribbon to denote the actual years of service in that country and Wilfred was awarded his for the period of the Zulu Wars between 1877 and 1879. He was also mentioned in despatches for his attempt to save the life of his brother officer, Lieutenant Deane, who had drowned during a swimming accident while in the Cape Colony in 1877.

By this stage, news of the coastal column was beginning to filter back and it transpired that they too had been in action on 22 January. With Colonel Pearson, 3rd Foot, in command, his column had crossed the Tugela river on 11 January at the start of the invasion. His column was making steady progress towards Eshowe and on the morning of 22 January the leading element had reached the banks of the Inyezane river. Colonel Pearson had been meticulous about his forward scouting and was concerned that his present position was in thick bush and overlooked by the Majia hill, a steep ridge to his front. A few Zulu scouts appeared on the top of this hill so Pearson despatched a company of NNC under Lieutenant Hart to disperse them. As with Dartnell at Isandlwana, this force was ill equipped for the task in hand and the moment they crested the hill a mass of Zulus appeared to their front. Hart beat a hasty retreat, but the main position was now alerted to the threat, which had been a deliberate ambush aimed at outflanking the column and cutting into the line of communication. Supported by artillery and for the first time in this war a gatling gun manned by a Naval detachment, Pearson was able to withstand the assault, which was all over in an hour and a half.

Hart's stand had sprung the trap prematurely and the artillery and rifle fire had broken the Zulu left horn before the full attack was able to develop. By disrupting the progress of the two horns, it was possible to negate the impetus of the main assault and though they considerably outnumbered the British column, the Zulus were forced to retreat. Pearson reached Eshowe the following day, where he set about establishing a strong defensive position while he awaited word of the location and intentions of the central column. [17] Given the poor system of communication between columns, it was to be two weeks before Pearson learned the full extent of the disaster at Isandlwana and with little clear direction from Lord Chelmsford, he had to decide whether to stay put or withdraw to the Tugela river. He attempted to communicate with Chelmsford but was reluctant to retire without explicit permission. The days passed and the loose ring of Zulus on the surrounding hills gradually thickened. No more messages arrived and it became obvious that none could be sent. By mid March, Pearson realized that he was cut off and that Eshowe was in a state of siege.

Chelmsford's tactical plan was now in ruins. His central column had been decimated and his coastal column was trapped. He still had the left hand column under Colonel Evelyn Wood VC, but this was obviously insufficient to continue the advance upon Ulundi. The British Government at home, shocked as it was by the ignominious defeat at Isandlwana, had little option but to restore Imperial credibility and began the task of sending out substantial reinforcements as soon as possible to finish the task, while Chelmsford set about regaining the initiative on the ground.

By now, Colonel Hassard had completed his Inquiry, which he delivered personally to Lord Chelmsford at Pietermaritzburg. News continued to come in from the other columns and the threat of invasion was still prevalent.

Thursday 6 February
Tyrell 1/13th told off for DCM. Col Hassard and Baxter left for P.M.Burg Col Pulleine's poney recovered from one of native contingent riding down to drift. Two contingent men to Breakfast. Heard all sorts about other columns and intended inroads on Natal by Zulus.

During the battle of Isandlwana, the Zulus would have slaughtered almost everything in sight, be it human or animal. Lieutenant Colonel

Pulleine's horse survived, or was more than likely used by a fugitive escaping the battlefield. Someone clearly recognized the horse and it was returned to the fold to be used by another officer later on. Rumours continued about a possible invasion of Natal by King Cetshwayo and more reports were filtering in about the fate of the coastal column and Colonel Wood's activities to the north.

Friday 7 February
Hardish day's work took stock of Degacher and Younghusbands kit Arranged for Corpl Keon to be tried by detachment am tomorrow. Wrote to Mother. Lloyd making sketches to send home for the Illustrated Papers. Shelters just up by the traverses for the men in reserve to be under by night.

The auction of deceased officers' belongings continued including that of Captains Degacher and Younghusband. William Degacher was the younger brother of Lieutenant Colonel Henry James Degacher who was in command of the 2nd/24th Regiment. In the previous month when the officers of the 1st/24th were in the Mess at Durban one evening, they were commemorating the 30th anniversary of the Battle of Chillianwalla in 1848 when the Battalion was all but annihilated in India losing 21 officers and 503 dead and wounded soldiers. William Degacher proposed a toast 'that we may not get into such a mess and have better luck this time.' [18] Prophetic words indeed. Captain Reginald Younghusband commanded C Company at Isandlwana and is often reputed to have been one of the last officers to die during the battle.

Here for the first time we also learn of William Whitelocke Lloyd's skills as an accomplished artist. There were very few accredited correspondents covering the war and most of the famous paintings on the subject were done by artists who never actually visited South Africa. Consequently, they tended to depict romantic Victorian heroism rather than accurate battle scenes. Lloyd, however, was able to produce a lasting record which thankfully provides us with a far more realistic impression of the conditions under which the war was fought. Many of these have not yet been published, but others were used by magazines back in England to illustrate the many accounts being published about the war.

Saturday 8 February
Detachment CM on Corpl Keon 1/13th prosecuted moved up a lot of waggons and found a large laager for horses outside the entrance. Sale of kit belonging to Surgeon – – – Bought spurs boots and gaiters. Letter home to the Mother.

Sunday 9 February
Church parade as usual. Got leave off to arrange kits for sale got them ready and got an order for no sale and had to pack them up again. Col Degacher and a lot of Drift fellows came up and lunched.

Sunday Church parade was a regular feature of regimental life, despite individual religious inclinations, and would be conducted whenever possible. It would be held in a church if there was one, or in any available building. More often than not it would be outdoors at what was known as a Drumhead Service, where the drums would be piled up to form a makeshift altar and the Colours draped across them. On this particular Sunday, Wilfred was excused the parade to continue preparing officers' kit for sale, but on this occasion the sale was cancelled.

Despite the threat of invasion, Mess life would continue wherever possible and Colonel Henry Degacher, Commanding Officer of the 2nd/24th and elder brother of William who had been killed at Isandlwana, came up for lunch in the relative comfort of the Mess at Helpmekaar and to relieve the tension of living at Rorke's Drift.

Monday 10 February
One of the 13th in for insubordination and a DCM applied for. Acting Staff (regtt) in orders. Sold Degacher and Younghusbands kit. Black, Clery and some more up to buy. Clements and Brown (Dr) in hospital Smith Dorrien and Huntley also, laid up. Poney tried to cover a mare and got turned out.

Lieutenant Colonel C F Clery was the principal staff officer in Colonel Glyn's Column while Brevet Major Huntley 10th Foot (Royal Lincolnshire Regiment) was one of the transport officers. The unsanitary living conditions at both Rorke's Drift and Helpmekaar were beginning to take their toll and the number of officers and men going sick was beginning to increase.

Tuesday 11 February
Sent in application for Tyrell's C.M. forwarded to the Colonel for orders. Upcher went down to the drift to collect for yesterday's sales. Tried to get a servant for Browne the Dr had to tell off a man on fatigues yesterday's mail in no letters. Rode the poney for an hour for exercise. Sent Col Bray a nominal list of 1/13th draft not yet put through a course of musketry.

As there was a shortage of cavalry units during the early stages of the war, ad hoc units of mounted infantry were formed from soldiers who had an ability to ride for reconnaissance purposes. Lieutenant Edward Browne, 1st/24th commanded one such unit and was to go on to win the Victoria Cross in a later battle. In the meantime, Wilfred attempted to find him an orderly to look after his horse and equipment.

As in any campaign, it was important that the new drafts were tested on the quality of their weapon handling before being sent forward to join their respective units. Standards of individual marksmanship were not all that impressive (and not only on this campaign it has to be said) and the ratio of rounds fired to casualties inflicted is often very high.

Wednesday 12 February
Hard old day. Made out lists of Mostyn Anstey White Melville Daly and Hodson's kit for sale tomorrow. Parson Smith and Dunn Comst from drift. Application sent in for DCM on Army Hosp Corps man for stealing milk of sick officers. Collected some of the money for kits sold on Monday

Thursday 13 February
DCM on Tyrell 1/13th Sold some kits, Daly's Melvilles and part of White's, went very badly so did not sell all we had meant. 4th and 13th under orders for Utrecht starting tomorrow morning. Tyrell flogged on parade. Handed over documents of 13th to Hay of the 4 K.O. Regt.

Pte Tyrell 1st/13th Foot had been charged with insubordination and the DCM sentenced him to a public flogging. Of all the harsh punishments inflicted upon the British soldier over the previous 200 years, flogging was perhaps the most vicious and commonplace. For many years flogging was carried out with a rod but early in the 18th century this was replaced by the cat-o'-nine tails. In fact, this whipcord or leather whip usually had only six tails which were about two feet long and which were knotted (known as a blood knot) to cause even further agony. The severity of the offence would determine the number of lashes which could vary from as few as 25 up to a maximum of 1,500, with 300 to 500 being the most usual. In 1836, the Articles of War limited a GCM to a sentence of 200 lashes, a DCM to 150 and a RCM to 100.

Flogging nearly always took place in public with all available officers and soldiers paraded to witness the event as a form of deterrence. The prisoner would be stripped to the waist and bound upright to a suitable structure, either a purpose built frame or to the side of a wagon or even to a tree. Once the Commanding Officer, the Adjutant and the Medical Officer were present the flogging would begin, administered by drummers from the Regimental Band. They would relieve one another after 25 lashes and with up to four hours to deliver 1,000 lashes the agony of the victim is unimaginable. The medical officer was supposed to stop the punishment if he considered it excessive, but rarely did this happen. More often than not, if the prisoner started to collapse the doctor would merely bring him round so that the punishment could continue.

Surprisingly, the number of soldiers who died from flogging was very few indeed and most recovered from their ordeal fairly quickly but carried the scars for the rest of their lives. In 1868 flogging had allegedly ceased in the British Army but as Wilfred records it was clearly still taking place in 1879. It was finally abolished by an Act of Parliament in 1881. [19]

Friday 14 February
Shepstone left for P.M.Burg. 4th and 13th off by 7.30. O'Reilly AHC on orders to be tried tomorrow. Got in the money from fellows of the Mounted Infantry and Caribiniers under orders to leave tomorrow for Fort Pine. Made up the Canteen(Durban) Acts. About £126 in credit. AH Corps man who died last night buried by Lloyd this afternoon. Letter from Mrs Wynne Laager for Mtd Corps removed.

Present during the campaign were the Army Medical Department (AMD) and the Army Hospital Corps (AHC). The AMD consisted of both military and civilian medical officers who were attached to units throughout the various columns. The purpose of the AHC was to accompany the medical officers, to aid in tending the wounded and to remove them to the first available dressing station or Field hospital. For the central column this had been set up at Rorke's Drift and there was a Base hospital at Utrecht. AHC personnel were non-combatant but they were armed with revolvers for self defence. After Isandlwana, both these Corps were rapidly reinforced, often with only basic medical training, to make up the numbers.

Saturday 15 February
Letter to the Mother Bundle of papers from Wolfe which disappeared immediately O'Reilly AHC tried by DCM and acquitted. Col and Cleary from drift for lunch. Rode over to Burtons Camp and collected £ /11/5 from him due sales. Mtd Infantry and Carbiniers left for Fort Pine Smith Dorrien and Dr Brown left for Pine Town A new AMD man McCurrol joined Mess Berresford came back from Lady Smith. Convoy of 7 waggons in Conductor picked up several mails and parcels on the way.

Mail addressed to troops engaged in the Zulu Wars was circulated to the General Post Office (GPO) in London, from where it was despatched, along with the rest of the South African civilian mails, to Southampton or Dartmouth. The mails were carried on the weekly packet steamers to Cape Town owned by either of the two mail contactors operating that route; the Union Steam Ship Company, operating out of Southampton or the Castle Packets Company, based out of Dartmouth. The steamers took between 23–30 days to travel the 5,852 miles between Britain and Cape Town.

On arrival at Cape Town, the mails for Natal, including those of the expeditionary force, were extracted by the GPO and forwarded by boat to Durban. At Durban the GPO sent the mails forward to the expeditionary force under the postal arrangements agreed, prior to deployment, between the expedition's Deputy Quarter Master General and the local Colonial Postal authorities. Mail was carried forward by native bearers to the columns from the colonial post offices at Newcastle, Helpmekaar, Greytown and Stanger. Natives were used instead of express riders as the Postmaster General feared that the horsemen would overtax their mounts! UK bound mail from the force followed the same route but in reverse. With mail taking about 6 weeks to arrive from England, a person at home could expect to wait up to 3 months to receive a reply to a letter

Postage was payable on military mail. The soldiers paid 1d (less than 1p in present currency) in accordance with the postal concession first granted to troops in 1795. The officers were generally charged the normal postal rates between Britain and South Africa, which was about 6d (equivalent to 2½p) per half ounce. To qualify for the soldiers concessionary rate, the envelope that contained the letter had to be countersigned by the soldier's commanding officer. Soldiers were given an allowance of one inkbottle per three tents but with heavy usage this was soon depleted and therefore to supplement their allowance they made their own ink by mixing gunpowder and water. Mail censorship was not imposed until the Anglo-Boer war 20 years later. [20]

Sunday 16 February
Church parade by Major Dalrymple. Collected some more sale money Cashed a cheque for £20. Camp shifted. Hope and Dawson back from Ladysmith. A party up from the drift to take down the kit bags of the 2nd Battn and Officers luggage.

Monday 17 February
Board on losses of Camp equipment and kits on 18th and 22nd last month. Application made out for DCM on Askew. Logan up from the drift. Orderly Officer for the day. Lent Mr Dodd to Palmes for a ride.

Meanwhile, work continued on accounting for the losses of equipment at Isandlwana on the 22nd January. A Board of Officers is military terminology for a group of officers who would be assembled by the commanding officer to check and account for equipment, normally when there has been a significant loss. The procedure was laid down in the

Regulations for Field Forces in South Africa 1879 and Wilfred was part of such a Board.

Lieutenant Quentin Logan was a young subaltern officer in the 2nd/24th Foot. When Quartermaster Edward Bloomfield was killed at Isandlwana Logan took over this appointment on a temporary basis until a replacement could be found. The Quartermaster was responsible for all logistic support to the Battalion.

Tuesday 18 February
Application for DCM returned and corrected. Rode down to the drift with Lloyd over some wonderful country. Lunched with Thrupp. Saw the place and got home by 6.30pm. Note from Logan about the Band Boxes. About 10 waggons left for Ladysmith under Hope.

Now that the threat of another invasion by the Zulus was receding, this was the first chance that Wilfred would have had to visit Rorke's Drift himself and he took the opportunity of riding across the beautiful Natal countryside with his friend William Lloyd who would no doubt have sketched some of the magnificent views. He makes no mention of the defence of the mission station, but then his diary was never intended to be a record or commentary for the benefit of military historians at some later date. However, as a young man of 25 he can only have been in awe of all that had occurred in the previous fortnight.

Thrupp was a civilian surgeon attached to the battalion and he was in charge of No 1 Field Hospital in Colonel Glyn's Column. Health and hygiene were becoming important issues as sickness and fever spread and one of the senior medical officers was making a regular inspection at Rorke's Drift. Meanwhile, Colonel Glyn and Lieutenant Colonel Cornelius Francis Clery, principal staff officer to the central column came up to Helpmekaar from the Drift, no doubt for a break and a breath of fresh air.

Wednesday 19 February
Kraal for horses begun. Askew told off by Upcher. Col Glyn and Cleary up from the Drift. Reynolds from Ladysmith for Drift. S.M.O. inspecting. Cochrane to take command of the Basutos. Board in orders for regtt accounts to come off tomorrow.

Thursday 20 February
Claimed and got Field Allowance from the Board on White acts and sent in some claims. Com Gen Strickland and Richardson to inspect. S.M.O. to drift. Took evidence on 22nd ult. Col Degacher up from the drift. Big mail in Franklin 2nd Bat very ill, Clements removed into the Store Rainforth taking over the duties of paymaster Church passed through on his way to see

his wife who is ill.

Field Allowance was an additional payment made to soldiers when deployed from their barracks for any given period of time, usually on active service. It had to be applied for and Wilfred would have been responsible for claiming this on behalf of his Company. Meanwhile the senior commissariat officer was back again to check on the progress of resupplying the column and more evidence was being gathered about events on the 22nd January. Major Hugh Church would have been on his way to Durban or Pietermaritzburg where those families who had accompanied the Battalion to South Africa would have been housed.

Friday 21 February
Franklin died about 12 last night. On a Board on Contingent losses adjourned till tomorrow as that evidence was not ready. Took some more evidence on the 22nd. Franklin buried at 4.30. Tommy Walsh came in from Dundee with their wagon for supplies. Brought us some more butter.

Lieutenant Reginald William Franklin was a young subaltern officer in D Coy 2nd/24th Foot who had joined the Regiment in the previous year. He had been with the central column from the outset and had been present at the raid on Sihayo's Kraal just after the invasion began. He survived Isandlwana as he had been part of Lord Chelmsford's diversion to the Mangeni river, only to die from dysentery a month later at the age of 19.

Saturday 22 February
Note to Logan about Franklins poney and Browne about butter. Board on Bengough's losses sat at last. Col Glyn and Cleary up from the Drift. Cheque received by the latter for £190 from 90th Regt for distribution amongst the widows and orphans of the column. From Drift Moffat on his way to Ladysmith Reynolds and Thrupp who goes on with Minhils to P. M. Rode out a short way on the Dundee road to catch some wind.

As already mentioned, welfare provision for families who had lost their menfolk in action was almost non-existent, so the Battalions took it upon themselves to provide for them where they could. With such an unexpected disaster at Isandlwana, funds were at a premium and on this occasion the 90th Regiment made a much needed contribution

Sunday 23 February
No Church parade repairs of drains after last nights rains Orderly Officer. Letters to Mother Mrs Kingsley and old Wolfe. Cochrane to Drift and back ordered to join Col Russell

Monday 24 February
Wrestled a bit with Mess Acts. Mahoney went down to the Drift. Cochrane and his troupe left for Utrecht to join Col Russell's party. Went out for a ride with Commeline. Letter from the other one. Letters from Mother, Kit and Eve, Clements, Moffat, Wealans and Mitchell of the police left for Ladysmith Cooper and 13 others of the NNC through on their way to P.M.Burg. Shifted the mess from the store to a colonial marquee outside the fort and beds to one inside, some to tents outside. Papers from Wolfe letter from 13th Pay Office about missing certificate of draft under Degacher came out last Sept.

Tuesday 25 February
Letters to Mother, Kit and the other one. Galwey dropped in making a tour around the posts. Campbell police returned. Got some news with Rainforth. Michel J.D. from Greytown.

On a number of occasions throughout the diary, Wilfred mentions receiving a letter from 'the other one.' Kit (Catherine) and Eve (Evelyn) were the elder two of his three sisters, so it is possible that this was a family nickname for Mary, the third and much younger one. However, she was only 10 years old at the time so her capacity for letter writing would have been limited. Lieutenant C E Commeline was a member of 11 Battery, 7 Brigade Royal Artillery.

At the beginning of the war, the fort at Helpmekaar was a rectangular shape, surrounded by a ditch and an earth mound with one side adjacent to a wattle grove which provided some sort of windbreak on the high escarpment. Inside there were three iron buildings which were the officers quarters and the stores, with a number of marquees for the commissariat. [21] The soldiers were housed in the standard issue Bell tents. With the threat of another invasion receding, Heaton was directed to re-arrange the Mess accommodation for health reasons as sickness and fever was on the increase.

Captain Gallwey was the Adjutant of the 1st/13th Light Infantry. His battalion was attached to Colonel Wood's Column in the north but had a number of detachments along the border with Zululand for defensive purposes, so he was doing the rounds to visit them all. News travelled slowly between the various locations so Wilfred was able to catch up with what was happening elsewhere from Major Rainforth.

Wednesday 26 February
Rainforth and Phillips Upcher and Palmes out shooting no addition to the larder. Convoy of treasure per mule cart from P.M.Burg. Escorted by A.S.C. Sergt and two Officers

Given the seniority of its escort, the intriguing mention of treasure was probably money for the column being moved up the supply route to be secured at Helpmekaar.

Thursday 27 February
Signed Banking acts of Coy to date. Letter to Paymaster 80th about Jones Col Anmels servant. To Gen Depot and B Coy for nominal roll of men. Made up Mess bills to 28th Feverish. Police man suicided.

The spread of sickness was obviously beginning to catch up on Wilfred as he starts to feel feverish for the first time. He also records the suicide of a policeman. Whether this was an Imperial soldier or a local colonial is not clear and we can only imagine that the trauma of the war drove him to such a drastic end.

Friday 28 February
Muster Parade at 10am 1 man R.E. died last night Upcher early to Drift to go down the river as far as bodies of Melvill and Coghill buried. 2 funerals in afternoon Orderly Officer Letter from George Bucknill. Got the £10 for the Mess but sold to Commsrt from Dawson. Shaves all the morning about Zulus loping about. Some 17 natives of Flynn's from Sandspruit armed. Notice of liquor and stuff from Ladysmith.

There were more funerals to deal with and Upcher had the opportunity to visit the graves of Melvill and Coghill, despite rumours (or shaves as Wilfred describes them) of Zulus still in the vicinity.

CHAPTER 5

SETBACKS AND RECOVERY

Although Wilfred's diary records 1 March as St David's Day, the Welsh influence in the Regiment was not yet strong enough to celebrate the national day of Wales. However, he and Upcher did manage to take some time off for relaxation.

Saturday 1 March
The Colonel came up from the Drift with Staff for goods. Tongue passed through on his way to Ladysmith. for change of air Upcher and I went out about 6 miles along the Dundee road to look for buck he got a brace of shots. no result. A lot of sick from Dundee.

Sunday 2 March
Convoy in from PM Burg with Corpl Hurley who comes as O.R. Clerk in place of Sergt Wilson gone to the column office. Smith the Parson gave us service, (got leave off) He and Williams on their way to Ladysmith. Dobrie came up from Drift North Wales Chronicle from Mrs Addison.

O.R. is the Orderly Room, the administrative office within a battalion. George Smith, the padre of Rorke's Drift fame, would often take the Sunday service at Helpmekaar and on this occasion Wilfred had been given permission to miss it. Second Lieutenant Lionel Dobrie was an officer in F Company 2nd/24th Foot and had been with Chelmsford's column on 22 January. He resigned a few months later in May 1879 having decided that a military career was not to his liking after all. Meanwhile mail continued to arrive from home and Mrs Addison had sent him a copy of the local newspaper.

Dysentery and fever was spreading and eventually Wilfred became infected:

Monday 3 March
Hurley busy at squaring up the Orderly Room. Got off letters to Morshead for a coys Ballantyne and a couple of letters for Evelyn and Ernest. Guts back onto Chlorodine. 2 fellows from Drift for lunch. Had my bed shifted into my tent outside. Letter to Harford S.O. N.N.C. Drift about sums due for Pulleine's kit.

He tried to stay on duty but eventually had to report sick. There was no hospital as such so he isolated himself in a tent outside the Mess.

Tuesday 4 March
Much better of fever but diahorea just as bad. Prickley heat well out so went sick. Got another North Wales Chronicle from Mrs Addison wrote a letter for home mail. Fine thunderstorm and a minimal quantity of rain fell during the night.

By the next day he was feeling better but was not well enough to return to work.

Wednesday 5 March
Much better today prickly heat off legs not quite gone yet Letters by today's mail to Mother Evelyn and Ernest. Wrote also to old Wolfe. Beresford back again. Began to rain about 5:30 in the evening. Upcher brought me in some eggs and a fowl. One of the Natal Carbiniers died and was buried today.

Thursday 6 March
Rained hard all night. A note from Logan about stamps and leather. Letters to the Grand-Mother George Bucknill and Mrs Addison to thank for Chronicles. Wrote to Clements to enclose Mess Bills for himself, Brown and Huntley.

Given the rudimentary living conditions at both Rorke's Drift and Helpmekaar, the wet weather exacerbated the numbers going down with sickness and fever. Meanwhile Heaton kept up with Mess administration by sending out monthly Mess bills to those who had yet to pay up.

Friday 7 March
Showery night. Much better this morning coming off tomorrow probably. News of reinforcements from England. Beastly showery day. Got rid of a lot of kits from my tent.

The medicine began to take effect and within a few more days he was well enough to return to work.

Saturday 8 March
Upcher gone off to P.M.Burg with Col Harness. Bennett to the Cols Mess while Upcher is away. Off sick-list. Wrote to Smith–Dorien to send him his Mess Bill. Got some raisins for a cake and duff tomorrow. Showery day

Sunday 9 March
Rained hard all night. No Church Parade. Williams 2nd Bat came in from Ladysmith about 12.30 last night and Hope this morning settled up his

Mess Bills. Note and tobacco to Logan also 2/ stamps. Went out after lunch with Rainforth to see if we could shoot anything, he got one chiccup

Monday 10 March
McGann to Ladysmith with ambulance took Curling RA with him. Broke down about 6 miles out. Sold a lot of kits in the afternoon. Williams left for Drift with Cooper and Newman Moggs.

Lieutenant Henry Curling served with N Battery 5th Brigade Royal Artillery and had been present at Isandlwana. Although involved in the thick of the fighting he miraculously escaped and made his way back to Rorke's Drift and then to Helpmekaar. No doubt traumatized by his experiences his resistance was low and he caught enteric fever. He had to be hospitalized for a while which led to the rumour that he had suffered a nervous breakdown. [1]

Tuesday 11 March
Note to Cooper about the Cup he brought for us at P.M.Burg. Got leave for the Mess to sleep out in camp by Coys Symmonds up from the Drift. Note to Upcher on things in general. Wrote letters home Sent the poney to Palmes for afternoon. Newman Moggs up from Drift wanted to see our Colours recovered from the river to make a sketch of them.

To help stem the spread of infection, the Mess dispersed to sleep out in the open. Meanwhile, interest in the Queen's Colour recovered from the Buffalo River attracted the attention of a newspaper journalist who wanted to sketch it to include in his newspaper articles. Newman Moggs, or more correctly Charles Norris-Newman, was a garrulous but competent ex Imperial officer who was now serving as special correspondent for the *London Standard* and the only English journalist then in Natal. Known as 'Noggs,' he had attached himself to Lonsdale's staff.

Wednesday 12 March
Letters to the grandmother and mother. Tonque, Harford, Davies NNC passed through for Greytown and P.M.Burg. The Col and Major Cleary left for Ladysmith. Hope ditto. Rec'd sums owing to Pulleine's kit from NNC. Note to Logan about helmets for our Mess. Went out for a ride with Rainforth. Paid for the – – – – – we got from Shepstone at last.

Thursday 13 March
Beresford left for Rourke's Drift with Cooper who came up to lunch. Sent for nags could not be found were sent out with Police this morning. Got them later on and rode part of the way to the drift with Cooper.

Friday 14 March
Note to Upcher about Baccy etc. A lot of Butter got in the Canteen took some for Mess. Gen orders rec'dd. Rainsforth paymaster to regt. Rode out with Rainforth and he shot a teal had a pot at a Kaffir Crave but missed.

Given the poor quality of rations available, food was never far from Wilfred's mind and he made sure that some of the butter ration for the main canteen found its way to the Officers' Mess. There was also a general reorganization of appointments and Rainforth took over as Paymaster to replace Major Francis White, the oldest officer in the Battalion who had been killed at Isandlwana.

Saturday 15 March
Orderly Officer. Letter from Wolfe. Logan up from the Drift for lunch. Col back from Ladysmith and dined with us. 1 coy of the 4th from Greytown under Capt Moore came in early Heard of arrival of 91st at Cape and surrender of Ohumu.

Ohumu as Wilfred incorrectly calls him was in fact Prince Hamu kaNzibe a senior Zulu chieftain who was at odds with King Cetshwayo over the Zulu approach to the war. Lord Chelmsford was aware of this division and tried to exploit it in an attempt to weaken the Zulu resolve for continuing the war. In the previous week Prince Hamu had defected, as opposed to surrendered, to the British side. [2]

Sunday 16 March
4th Coy off by 5am. Rainforth went down to Drift with Campbell NMP (Qr Mr) Sergt RA died. No parson for church parade read service. Colonel Degacher in from P.M.Burg. Letter from Mrs Kingsley

Monday 17 March
Shave in that Col Wood was engaged from sundown on Saturday to 4pm yesterday and hammered the Zulus. Col Degacher went on to Drift went for a ride by myself saw nothing. Dunne up from the Drift on sick list.

Throughout the following week, reports and rumours (shaves) came in about the activities of No 4 column. At the beginning of the invasion, Colonel Wood's column saw relatively little action, apart from observing considerable enemy activity in the Zunguin and Hlobane mountain range area, stronghold of the abaQulusi clan, who were fiercely loyal to the Zulu king. When the news of Isandlwana came through, Wood set up a strongly entrenched camp at Kambula, to the west of Hlobane mountain, while he awaited further instructions from Lord Chelmsford. The first report on a prolonged engagement was clearly exaggerated.

Tuesday 18 March
Big mail in from Ladysmith mostly papers letter from Smith Dorrien. No news from Woods Column. Lloyd put on sick list.

However, the report on the events at the Ntombe Drift on the 12th March were more accurate.

Wednesday 19 March
Lloyd under orders for Greytown with Dalrymple. Letter home to Kit started off. One to Smith Dorrien, sent his kit off to him in the ambulances under Busby who left today. Orderly Offices some liquor and other things at up the stone. Shave that a Capt and 68 men 90th cut off while on escort duty to Col Wood last Wednesday. Moffats servant and poney went in to Ladysmith. Glover left for P.M.Burg 14 days leave

Wilfred refers to the 90th Foot, but it was in fact the 80th, or South Staffordshire Regiment.

Escorting supply wagons from the eastern Transvaal, Captain Moriaty, 80th Foot set up camp on 11 March on the northern banks of the drift at the Ntombe river, with a small force under Lieutenant Harward on the southern side. Once again the wagons were not laagered and there was no forward screen of picquets. Orders were given for the camp to be closed up but these seem to have been ignored. At about 4a.m. on 12 March, Zulus assaulted an unsuspecting camp inflicting over 60 casualties on the British force. Given the experience of Isandlwana, this was a classic case of complacency and sheer tactical ignorance. Although Colour Sergeant Booth was awarded the VC for his actions that day, this was an ignominious defeat which should never have occurred, had basic tactical principles of a secure laager in all-round defence been applied.

Thursday 20 March
Our Camp shifted over to the Men's. Discharge board held on Elliot and Payne sent home for invaliding. Went out for a ride with Rainforth to try and meet Upcher. Symmonds, Harvey and Curll up from the Drift, the latter for some days for change. The Col and Cleary rode over to Dundee found 2/24th fellows there and brought them in. Upcher and Harness came back later. Shave giving more particulars of Col Wood's fight, also that Pearson had one same day. Upcher reports Capt Williams Buffs dead also Cocker of Active and Puggy White wounded.

Meanwhile his friend Lloyd succumbed to the fever which was endemic throughout the camp and it was decided that he should be sent back down the line to Greytown to recuperate. Also, the diary for 21 March makes an interesting observation:

FOR QUEEN AND COUNTRY 65

Friday 21 March
Dalrymple and Lloyd left by mule and ambulance for Greytown. Former left a horse in my charge. Letters from the mother, Kit and Mary. 3 papers from Wolfe. The Col got a letter from Col Wood dated 18th making no mention either of his engagement on the 15th and 16th or the reported disaster on the 12th. Rode with Rainforth part of the way to Rourke's Drift with Simmonds and Harvey.

The engagements on the 15th and 16th refers to Wood's and Buller's expedition to extract the uHamu clan, who were in hiding in northern Zululand as a consequence of their leader, Prince Hamu and half brother of King Cetshwayo, defecting to the British. The reported disaster on the 12th is no doubt the debacle at Ntombe Drift. The Colonel who got the letter is probably Colonel Richard Glyn and as this was correspondence between two column commanders, Wood was under no obligation to make an official report to Glyn. Also at the time of writing, neither incident was considered significant enough to warrant detailed explanation.

Saturday 22 March
Some cases of drink in camp result of Lee's stock of liquor. Beastly wet. Letter from mother, Kit and Kenneth dated 12th Feb one from Wolfe. Canteen stores in from Stills Dundee. Letters to Clements and Mrs Kingsley. Disaster of the 12th true. Rode out with Jones and Cummerford to choose site of new camp.

Sunday 23 March
Orderly officer. Orders out for 1 Coy and remainder of Column to shift to new camp on Vermach's farm. Not carried out as they could not see him to get the leave!! New civil surgeon Johnstone turned up. Note to Messrs Reid and Actutt to clear acct forward for Mess box of Koff's soups sent out for Coghill.

In an attempt to improve living conditions it was decided to relocate part of the column to Vermach's Farm which was just below Helpmekaar and a few miles above Rorke's Drift. However it seems that someone had forgotten the small but important detail of asking the owner, a local colonial settler, beforehand!

Monday 24 March
English mail in. Letters from mother, father and Kit. Papers from Mrs Addison. Rode with Cleary Rainforth and Fowler to Umsingu McKensie Special for Standard came in on his way to Wood's Column. Com General came in after Mess

Notice of Variation

Please read through this notice carefully and keep it in a safe place for future reference.

HSBC
The world's local bank

We are making some changes to our General Terms, Current Accounts Terms, Savings Accounts Terms and applicable price lists (the "Terms").

We are also removing the identity theft assistance benefit from certain of our current accounts, see below for further details.

We are making changes to the Terms because of changes in law, regulation and industry guidance, because of changes to our systems and procedures or to the services we provide, and in some cases to make the Terms clearer or because the changes are favourable to you.

We have explained the changes we are making to the Terms below. Clause references are to the clause numbering in the current version of the Terms, unless stated otherwise; and where we have quoted parts of the Terms, we have done so in italics.

We are also making some other minor changes to clauses and formatting in the Terms (including updating cross-references and clause numbers to reflect the changes we are making). Because of the nature of these changes and because they will not affect the meaning of the Terms, we have not included them below.

The changes to the Terms will take effect from **1 December 2011**. If you are happy with the changes you don't need to do anything, so unless we hear from you we will assume you accept them. If you decide not to accept the changes, please inform us on our usual contact numbers before 1 December 2011. However, if you do so, unfortunately this will mean closing your account. Of course, there will be no charge for this, or for closing your account for any other reason before this date.

If you would like a full copy of the new Terms (including your price list), they are available at www.hsbc.co.uk/termsandconditions or you can ask in any of our branches or call us on 0800 783 4984.

Future Notices of Variation

Please note that, in the future, we will start sending out more Notices of Variation (including those which relate to changes in our overdraft service) by personal email or secure emessage within Personal Internet Banking.

For emails, we will use the latest email address you have supplied to us. It is therefore very important that you keep us up to date with your current email address and advise us promptly if you change it. If you think we may not have your correct email address, please notify us as soon as possible.

You can access our Personal Internet Banking service by logging on at **www.hsbc.co.uk**. If we send you a secure emessage this will be shown within "My Messages" within our Personal Internet Banking service.

As mentioned above, in the future, we may use secure emessage to notify you about changes to our overdraft service and, when you next use our Personal Internet Banking service, you will be regarded as having agreed to this. We will only send secure emessages to customers who have registered for Personal Internet Banking. If you want to register please visit **www.hsbc.co.uk** or ask in any of our branches or call us on our usual numbers

Summary of Main Changes

Changes to General Terms – Introduction and Section 1

1. We have changed the definition of PIB because we now offer certain pages from our Personal Internet Banking service in a format that is easier to view on a mobile telephone screen. The revised definition is set out below:

"PIB" means our Personal Internet Banking service. Whilst we may offer facilities through which you may access some but not all of your PIB services, references and requirements within the Terms to the Personal Internet Banking service are to the full service which is available by logging on at **hsbc.co.uk**

2. The Personal Internet Banking section has changed as we may upgrade our security procedures from time to time. The revised clause 3 is set out in full below:

Personal Internet Banking

Depending upon the account you have you may be able to make some payments through PIB by logging on, using your user ID and providing other security information that is personal to you that we request. We may notify you from time to time of changes in the security information we may require for accessing PIB. When you have provided your payment instructions, you will be asked to confirm those instructions. This will be your agreement for us to make the payment.

3

3. Clauses 9.2 and 9.3 which contain important security information have been extended to cover your use of any security devices, such as the HSBC Secure Key which is being sent to all customers who regularly use Personal Internet Banking.

4. We have clarified when we will make payments from your account in clauses 10.1 to 10.3 of the General Terms. These clauses are set out in full below:

10 1. We will make/authorise a payment from your account if you authorise it in any of the ways set out in this section 1 of the General Terms, and:

• there are sufficient cleared funds in your account; or

• the payment is covered by an overdraft that we have agreed following a formal or informal request from you for an overdraft or an increase to an existing overdraft limit (please see clause 3 of the Current Accounts Terms, and clause 15 of the Current Accounts Terms if you have Bank Account Pay Monthly, for more details).

10.2. Where the payment is to be made in the future, you must make sure that you have met the conditions in clause 10.1 at the start of the day the payment is due to be made (i.e. 00.00am).

10.3. If you do not meet the requirements set out in clause 10.2, we may still make the payment if, before 15.30 on the day the payment is due to be made, you pay in sufficient funds, and call us on the applicable number set out before section 1 of these General Terms to confirm that this has been done.

5. We have clarified how you agree to an exchange rate that applies to a payment you request.

We have inserted a new clause 11.1 and both revised and re-numbered the existing clause 11.1.1 (which will now be clause 11.2.1). These clauses are set out in full below:

11.1. General

The exchange rates we use are variable exchange rates which are changing constantly throughout the day (for example, to reflect movements in foreign exchange markets). The exchange rate applied to your payments will appear on your statement.

11.2.1 The exchange rate we will apply to payments you make involving a currency exchange, other than future dated payments, is the rate we provide or make available to you (including in our branches and on the telephone) when you request the payment, and which you agree by going ahead with the payment or by confirming the rate specifically. The exchange rate we apply to future dated payments will be the HSBC exchange rate applicable at the time your payment is processed. You can call us to find out rates.

6. We have clarified in clause 11.3.2 where you can find particulars of the charges that apply in respect of foreign currency payments into your account. A new sentence now states that details of the charges are in the price list that is applicable to your account.

7. Payments

7.1. We have made changes to the descriptions of some of the payments which can be made into and out of your account including bill payments, EFTs, Priority Payments, SEPA payments, WorldPay payments, standing orders and direct debits. The most significant changes have been made to the descriptions of bill payments and direct debits (which has been expanded to include SEPA direct debits) and the revised descriptions are set out in full below. We have also included below a description of Currency Account Transfers which can be made from some accounts. These are also referred to in clause 15.

Changes to Part A

1.2. Bill Payments – sterling payments (other than Priority Payments or Electronic Fund Transfers) from your account directly to the account of another person or organisation in the UK, Channel Islands and Isle of Man. Most bill payments will be processed using the faster payments service; we call these "faster bill payments".

1.4. Currency Account Transfers – payments between UK accounts you have with us in the same name, including joint accounts which you hold with someone else, that either involve a currency exchange or are made in a currency other than sterling.

1.10. Direct Debits – regular payments to a business or other organisation from your account, which may vary by amount or date. Each individual payment is requested from us by the business/organisation. Direct debits are sterling payments from sterling accounts, unless they are SEPA direct debits. A SEPA direct debit is a Euro payment to a business or other organisation in a SEPA country and is made from a Euro account. SEPA direct debits cannot be made from accounts held at branches in the Channel Islands and Isle of Man.

7.2. We have changed the information you need to provide when you make an EFT so it is the same as that required for bill payments and internal transfers. Clause 2 has been amended accordingly.

7.3. We have made various changes to the Payments Table in clause 15.1 of the Terms. These changes have been made primarily to reflect the requirements of the Payments Services Regulations 2009 which provide that, from January 2012, all UK payments which are made in sterling and payments made in euro within the EEA must be credited to the recipient's bank by the end of the working day following the time we receive the payment instruction from you (subject to applicable cut-off times). We are implementing these changes from 01 December 2011.

Where a payment type is not mentioned below it has not changed.

Bill Payments

The general cut-off time for giving instructions to us for bill payments which are not faster bill payments has moved forward to 3.45pm from 8pm.

The maximum execution time is now;

- immediate for all bill payments to other accounts you hold with us; and
- the same day for other bill payments (except for bill payments to HSBC Bank International branch accounts which will continue to take 3 working days).

Priority Payments

There are no longer general cut-off times for payments made through PIB, TBS and branch. However, currency cut-off times still apply.

SEPA payments

The maximum execution time for a payment to be made has been reduced from 2 working days to the next working day.

WorldPay payments

These can now also be requested by post and the maximum execution time has been reduced from 2 working days to the next working day for payments made within the EEA and in an EEA currency.

Global Transfers

The maximum execution time for the payment to be made is now the same day rather than the next working day.

Please refer to the table below for the details relating to currency account transfers and changes to standing order payments.

Payment Type	How you can request a payment	General cut-off time for giving instructions to us	Maximum execution time	Can you arrange a payment to be sent on a future date?
Currency Account Transfers	TBS Branch	Currency cut-off times apply	Next working day except Moroccan Dirham accounts which may be up to 2 working days	Yes if requested by branch or post. You can cancel the payment by calling TBS before 3.30pm the day before the payment is to be made, or going into a branch by the end of the working day before the payment is due to be made.
Standing Orders	PIB TBS Branch Post	PIB and TBS – 2 working days before first payment Branch and post – end of working day before first payment	• Immediate for standing orders to other accounts with us (up to 2 hours to a credit card account with us); • 3 working days for standing orders to HSBC Bank International branch accounts • same day for any other standing orders	Yes and you can cancel a future payment via: PIB, TBS, EB or in branch. You must cancel in branch by the end of the working day before the payment is to be made or via TBS/PIB before 11pm the day before payment is to be made

Standing orders cannot now be returned unpaid and so we have deleted clause 15.3 from the Terms. Clause 15.4 will also now be clause 15.3.

7.4. Direct Debits

We have set out below new clauses that relate to SEPA direct debits.

16.1. To set up a direct debit you must complete a direct debit instruction form with the recipient. This may be done in writing, over the phone or via the internet, unless it is for a SEPA direct debit in which case it must be done in writing.

16.2. The recipient will normally lodge the direct debit instruction electronically onto your account but may occasionally send the original direct debit instruction you completed to us (all SEPA direct debit instructions will be lodged electronically). When each payment request is sent to us we will check that the reference for that payment matches the reference on the direct debit instruction and will then make the payment from your account.

16.3. You can withdraw your agreement for:

16.3.1. SEPA direct debit payments, by telling us via branch or TBS before midday on the day the payment is due to be made, or by post provided that we receive your letter at the start of the working day before the payment is due to be made; and

16.3.2. any other direct debit payments, by telling us via branch, TBS or PIB before the end of the day before that payment is due to be made by us.

You should also tell the recipient that you have cancelled the direct debit instruction.

16.4. You can also tell us via branch or TBS to:

- *cancel all SEPA direct debit instructions;*
- *stop all SEPA direct debit instructions to a specific recipient; and*
- *pay SEPA direct debits to specified recipients only.*

16.5. The payment will be deducted from your account and received by the recipient's bank on the direct debit due date, provided that we receive the request to make the payment from the recipient, or the recipient's bank, by 10.30pm two working days before the due date.

16.6. Within five working days of the day a SEPA direct debit is deducted from your account, in a limited number of circumstances (please ask us for details), we may recall it from the recipient's bank and re-credit it to your account.

26.3. Refunding SEPA direct debits

You can ask us to refund the amount of a SEPA direct debit to your account within eight weeks of the date the payment was deducted from your account. You must provide us with details of the date the payment was deducted from your account, the amount of the payment, and the name of the recipient. It will be your responsibility to resolve any dispute about this refund directly with the recipient.

Clause 26.2.4 has been changed to make it clear that the Direct Debit Guarantee Scheme does not apply to SEPA direct debits.

7.5. Automatic Transfers

You can no longer change the transfer date for automatic transfers using PIB. However, you can still call us. Clause 15.4.3 (now clause 15.3.3) has been changed to reflect this.

7.6. Debit Card Payments

Changes have been made to the Terms to reflect the fact that we will start issuing contactless debit cards, at our discretion, from 01 December 2011. The clauses which have changed are set out below:

17.1. You can pay for goods and services using your debit card in the UK, the Channel Islands, the Isle of Man and abroad at retailers who accept VISA. A "cashback" service may also sometimes be available. You can set up recurring payments to be made from a VISA debit card. We may issue, at our discretion, debit cards with a contactless function which can be used at retailers who accept VISA debit card payments. Debit cards with a contactless function will have a transaction limit, which we will tell you about when you receive your card from us. We may change this limit by telling you in accordance with the requirements in clause 29.4.1 of these General Terms.

17.3. Before we will make a payment from your account:

17.3.1. for transactions in person, we will require you to:

- *enter details of your PIN into a keypad; or*
- *provide a signature; or*
- *If you use a contactless function on your card, hold the card near the contactless device provided by the retailer (you may be asked to also either enter your PIN into a keypad or provide a signature);*

17.3.2. for other transactions, we will require certain personal details and the three digit card security number on the back of your card.

We have also clarified the wording that explains how currency conversions are made when debit card payments are made in a foreign currency. The new clause 17.7 is set out below:

17.7. The exchange rate that applies to any foreign currency debit card payments (including cash withdrawals) is the wholesale market rate used by VISA applying on the day the conversion is made plus our foreign exchange charge, which is currently 2.75% of the applicable VISA wholesale rate. We will make the conversion and deduct the payment from your account once we receive details of the payment from VISA, at the latest the next working day. Details of the current wholesale market rates can be obtained by calling us on the usual telephone numbers, set out in the table before section 1 of the General Terms.

7.7. Cash Payments in

Clause 19.5 has been clarified.

7.8. Cheques

Following the removal of the UK Domestic Cheque Guarantee Card Scheme on 30 June 2011, a number of changes have been made to the terms namely clauses 21.1.2, and 21.4.1 have been amended and clauses 21.1.9 and 21.4.2-21.4.5 have been deleted.

7.9. Bank Drafts

Clause 21.6.2 relating to bank drafts has been clarified.

8. Clause 22 has been clarified to make it clear that a joint account cannot be converted to a sole account even if all joint account parties agree.

9. We have amended the frequency at which we send out statements on dormant accounts. The new clause 24.2 is set out below:

24.2. We will send you statements at least annually for any current account that you do not use for 6 months or more, and for any other account covered by these Terms that you do not use for two years or more.

10. We have clarified how our fraud prevention measures may affect how we deal with payments you request us to make. We have inserted a new clause 25.2 and amended the first sentence of the existing clause 25.2 (now clause 25.4) and details are set out below:

25.2. As part of these fraud prevention measures, we may need to speak with you to re-confirm some payments, e.g. high value payments, or we may need to ask you for additional security information. We will tell you when this is the case. If we need to speak with you but cannot do so for any reason, we will only make the payment if we believe it is genuine. Our fraud prevention measures may lead to the payment being delayed. This will not prevent you from later disputing you authorised the transaction.

25.4. We, or any other member of the HSBC Group, may take whatever action we consider appropriate to meet any obligations, either in the UK or elsewhere in the world, relating to the prevention of fraud, money laundering, terrorist activity, bribery, corruption, tax evasion and the provision of financial and other services to persons who may be subject to economic or trade sanctions.

11. We have clarified the information that some recipient banks may use when they allocate payments and the new clause 26.1.3 is set out below:

26.1.3. For payments to another bank account, we will make sure payments are sent to the recipient's bank. It is the recipient's bank's responsibility to make sure the payment is added to the bank account of the recipient. Some recipient banks will only use the BIC address, sort code or national bank code and the account number or IBAN when doing this.

12. We have clarified how we deal with unauthorised transactions and revised clauses 26.4.1 (now 26.5.1) and 26.4.2 (now 26.5.2) are set out below:

26.5.1. Subject to clauses 26.5.2 to 26.5.4 and 26.6, we will be responsible for any unauthorised transactions that you tell us about in accordance with clause 26.4 (if, on reasonable grounds, we suspect fraud or that you have been grossly negligent, we will investigate the transaction). Where we are responsible, we will immediately refund the amount of the unauthorised transaction and any resulting interest and charges. We will have no further liability to you. If we later become aware of evidence that shows we are not responsible for the transaction, we will recover an amount equal to the refund from your account.

26.5.2 You will be responsible for all losses if you act fraudulently or if you allowed another person to use your card, security details (including PINs, security numbers, passwords or other details which allow you to use PIB and TBS) or your account.

13. We have clarified the details we will take into account when processing payments into your account and a new clause 26.8.1 is set out below:

26.8.1. We will only process payments into your account using the BIC address, sort code or national bank code and the account number or IBAN provided.

14. We have amended the section that relates to changing interest rates that apply to your accounts, primarily to allow us to introduce "tracker" rates. The new clauses are set out below:

28.1. Changing interest rates that apply to money you have borrowed from us

28.1.1. If the interest rate that applies to money you borrow from us on your account is based on a reference rate (for example, our base rate or the Bank of England base rate) unless either clause 28.1.3 or 28.1.4 applies:

- *we will change your interest rate within one day of any change to the reference rate. We will not give you specific notice of these changes, but the new rate will be shown on your next statement; and*

- *we may change the amount by which your interest rate is set above or below the reference rate and/or provide that it is to cease to be based on the reference rate by providing you with notice in accordance with clause 29.4.*

28.1.2. If the interest rate that applies to money you borrow from us on your account is not based on a reference rate, unless clause 28.1.3 or 28.1.4 applies, we may change it in the following ways:

- *if the change is not favourable to you by telling you personally at least seven days in advance of making the change. We will also put a notice on our Rates and Charges Notices in our branches and in the national press within three working days of making the change; and*

- *if the change is favourable to you, by putting a notice on our Rates and Charges Notices in our branches and in the national press within three working days of making the change.*

28.1.3. In addition to the reasons set out in clause 30, interest rates we apply to money you borrow from us may be set and/or varied by us following our assessment of your ability to meet your financial commitments (which will include considering your credit history and information held about you by credit reference agencies as well as how you conduct your account once it has been opened).

28.2. Changing interest rates that apply to money you have with us in your account

28.2.1. If the interest rate that applies to money you have with us in your account is based on a reference rate (for example the Bank of England base rate):

- *we will change your interest rate within one day of any change to the reference rate. We will not give you specific notice of these changes, but the new rate will be shown on your next statement; and*

- *we may change the amount by which your interest rate is set above or below the reference rate and/or provide that it is to cease to be based on the reference rate by providing you with notice in accordance with clause 29.4.*

28.2.2. If the interest rate that applies to money you have with us in your account is not based on a reference rate, or is to cease to be based on a reference rate we may change it in the following ways:

- *if the change is favourable to you, either by, within 31 days of the change, telling you about it personally or by, within three working days of the change, putting notices in the national press and on our Rates and Charges Notices in our branches; and*

- *if the change is not favourable to you, by telling you about it personally at least two months in advance of making the change.*

15. We have slightly amended the clauses which relate to changing terms and conditions and benefits to make it clearer and the new clauses are set out below:

Other changes to the Terms and benefits

29.3.4. for overdraft information and to increase the charges that apply to money you borrow from us (other than interest rates that apply to money you borrow from us on your account), by giving you at least 30 days' advance personal notice;

29.3.5. for reductions in the charges which apply to money you borrow from us by giving you personal notice before we make the change.

29.3.6 for any other change, by giving you at least two months' advance personal notice.

29.4. We may make any other changes to the Terms (including introducing new charges or changes to the basis on which we charge for operating/providing product(s)/service(s)) and changes to benefits available with any account in the following ways:

29.4.1. if the change in unfavourable, by giving you at least 30 days' advance personal notice;

29.4.2. for any other changes, either by, within 30 days of the change, telling you about it personally, or by, within three working days, putting notices in the national press and on our Rates and Charges Notices in our branches (where the change relates to the terms and conditions relating to money you borrow from us we will give you personal notice before the change is made).

16. We have clarified clause 30 by replacing all references to "reflect" with "respond to" and we have added the following new paragraph:

Where we make any change under this clause the change will be proportionate to the underlying reason for the change.

17. We have slightly changed clause 32.1 to clarify that it does not apply to changes in interest rates on amounts borrowed from us.

18. We have slightly changed clause 33.7 to clarify that it also applies if you close your account in accordance with clause 2.4 of the Current Accounts Terms (clause 2.4 of the Current Accounts Terms is set out on page 10).

19. Clause 33.10 has been changed to make it clear that this clause does not apply to any account you have with us during a fixed term.

Changes to Section 2

20. A new sentence has been added to the start of clause 34.5.3 for clarification as follows:

In order to prevent or detect fraud, the information provided in the application will be shared with fraud prevention agencies

21. Clause 43 has been renumbered 35 and has been amended to state that we will treat any account, other than a current account, as dormant if it has been inactive for at least 2 years.

22. The clauses that relate to the Unclaimed Assets Scheme have been clarified and the new clauses are set out below:

Unclaimed Assets Scheme

36.2. We participate in the Unclaimed Assets Scheme established under the Dormant Bank and Building Society Accounts Act 2008.

36.3. If you have an account with us, including an account that we have closed in accordance with these Terms but we have not been able to repay your money to you, and there has been no activity from you in relation to that account for at least the last 15 years, we may transfer your balance to the Unclaimed Assets Scheme at Reclaim Fund Limited ("RFL"). We will give you at least 30 days' notice before we transfer any of your money to RFL. RFL is a not-for-profit reclaim fund which is authorised and regulated by the Financial Services Authority.

36.4. Upon transfer of the money to RFL we will close your account in accordance with clause 33 of these Terms (unless it has already been closed).

36.5. You will still have the right to your money after it has been transferred to RFL. We will handle all repayment claims and so you should ask us (and not RFL) for information about having your money repaid to you.

36.6. Both we and RFL participate in the Financial Services Compensation Scheme ("FSCS"). The transfer of the money to RFL will not affect any entitlement you have to compensation under the FSCS.

23. We have inserted a new clause 37.7 which reminds customers that they may have an obligation to report their worldwide income to the tax authority of a country with which they are connected. The existing clause 37.7 is now clause 37.8. The new clause 37.7 reads:

Obligation to report income

If you are connected with a country (for example, because you have income or assets there, or are domiciled or resident there), you may be obliged by law to report your worldwide income to a tax authority in that country. You should take tax advice if you are in any doubt about your reporting obligations.

24. A revised clause 36.7 (now 37.8) has already been notified to customers of Jersey, Guernsey and Isle of Man branches and came into effect for those customers on 01 July 2011. Changes have been made

to reflect the fact that retention tax was abolished in Guernsey and the Isle of Man on 01 July 2011. In respect of customers of our Jersey branches, we will not pay interest subject to deduction of retention tax if they benefit from an exemption under Jersey tax legislation and provide us with the necessary documentation and clause 36.7 (now 37.8) has been updated to reflect this.

25. We have amended the clause which sets out our right of "set-off" to make it clearer and the new clause 39 is set out below:

Our right of "set-off"

39.1. If:

* *any accounts you hold with us are in credit; and*

* *you have failed to pay us any amount which you owe on any other accounts you hold with us anywhere (including any card accounts and those in different currencies)*

we may use the money you hold with us to reduce or repay the amount which you owe us.

This is called our right of "set-off".

39.2. We can use our right of set-off in respect of accounts which are in your sole name and accounts which are in joint names as follows:

Account in credit held in name of:	Right of set-off can be applied against amounts owed on accounts held by:
A	A
A	A and B
A and B	A and B
A and B	A
A and B	B

39.3. We can use our right of set-off in respect of amounts you owe other companies within the HSBC Group and set-off amounts other companies in the HSBC Group owe against amounts you owe us (unless we are prevented from doing so by law).

39.4. We will not use our right of set-off against any money which we hold in an account in your name which you have advised us is not yours. We will also not use our right of set-off against any money which we are required to hold by law in an account in your name for someone else.

39.5 If we decide to use our right of "set-off":

* *we will tell you why and when it will be done unless we reasonably believe that you will try*

and prevent us from obtaining repayment of the money which you owe us by exercising our right (in which case we will tell you promptly after we have exercised our right and the amount(s) we have debited from which account(s)); and

* *in doing so, we may (and you irrevocably authorise us to):*

– bring to an end any fixed deposit period applying to any of the accounts you hold with us and adjust any interest payable by us;

– convert to sterling any balance that is in a currency other than sterling at the exchange rate that applies at the time; and in doing so we will have no liability to you.

26. Clause 43 has been amended to make it clear that you must notify us promptly of any changes to your contact details, including your email address, telephone number(s) and postal address.

Changes to Section 3 – Money Market Terms

27. Our Money Market Terms and Conditions have been changed to clarify how you can give us instructions, and to detail payment information that applies to money market accounts. The revised clause 3, a new clause 4 and a new clause 7 are set out below, clause 5 has been deleted.

3. You may only give us instructions in relation to your Money Market account in the following ways:

* *calling us on **08456 060 600**;*

* *calling TBS;*

* *visiting a branch;*

* *writing to us at HSBC Bank plc, Global Markets Money Market, 8th Floor, Norwich House, Southampton SO15 1GX;*

* *to give instructions for making a payment to or from your Call or Notice deposits, via PIB.*

4. Payments into and out of your account will only be made on a working day, other than automatic transfers which may also be made on a non-working day. If you call us or visit a branch, the cut-off time for giving us instructions in relation to your Money Market account (including instructions for payments into and out of your account) is 5pm on a working day. The cut-off time for giving instructions via PIB is 6pm on a working day. If you give us an instruction after the cut-off time, we will treat it as having been received the next working day.

7. For all Money Market accounts, we will only repay your deposit in full by internal transfer to your Nominated Capital Account. Otherwise, you may instruct us to make the following payments into and out of your Call and Notice deposits:

• Standing orders – these can only be made into your Call and Notice deposits from your Nominated Capital Account.

• Automatic transfers – you can set these up from your Nominated Capital Account to add to your Call and Notice deposits, and from your Call deposit to add to your Nominated Capital Account.

• Internal transfers – you can make internal transfers to and from your Call and Notice deposits.

Changes to Section 4 – Fixed Rate Saver Bond

28. We have amended clause 1 to clarify that we may change the fee in accordance with clause 29.3 of the General Terms

Changes to Current Accounts Terms and Conditions

29. We have changed section 2 that applies to additional benefits on your account to make it clearer when and how these benefits can change. The new clauses are set out below:

2.2. We will tell you which benefits are available when you enquire about or apply for the appropriate current account. We may later change the benefits that are available. We will tell you about changes in accordance with clause 29.4 of the General Terms.

2.3. Under the terms and conditions that apply to any specific benefit you have with your account, the provider of the benefit (this could be us, any other member of the HSBC Group or a specifically selected third party) may be able to make changes to the terms and conditions and may be able to cancel/close the benefit. Please see the terms and conditions that apply to the benefit for this.

2.4. If such a provider makes an unfavourable change to the terms and conditions that apply to any benefit that you have, or cancels/closes such a benefit, you may close your account in the ways described in clause 33.1 of the General Terms at any time during the period of notice of the change or cancellation given to you by the provider (this will be the case even if you are in an initial fixed period). If you close your account, all benefits will be withdrawn, and if a monthly fee is payable, the monthly fee will stop being payable after the fee for the month in which you close your account has been deducted.

30. We have amended the payment types that cannot be made from foreign currency/international personal accounts. Bill payments, standing orders, debit card payments, SEPA payments and global transfers cannot be made from any foreign currency/international personal accounts. In addition, direct debits (including SEPA direct debits) cannot be made from foreign currency/international personal savings accounts.

You cannot make any payments from foreign currency/international personal savings accounts via PIB.

Changes to Savings Accounts Terms and Conditions

31. We have amended the account that your Regular Saver will convert to at maturity if you are a Premier customer to a Premier Savings Account and the revised clause 4.12 is set out below:

4.12. On the anniversary of the date your Regular Saver was opened your account will cease to be a Regular Saver. If you have one of the following accounts with us in the same name(s) as your Regular Saver, your money and any accrued interest will be transferred to that account:

• *Instant Access Savings;*

• *Flexible Saver account;*

• *HSBC Premier Savings Account;*

• *any account that we have replaced any of the above with.*

If you have more than one of the above accounts listed we will transfer your money to the account which pays the highest rate of interest.

If you do not hold any of the accounts set out above with us, your Regular Saver will convert to a new Flexible Saver account, or, if you are an HSBC Premier customer, to a new HSBC Premier Savings account (or any accounts that we have replaced them with) in the same name as your Regular Saver, and will be subject to the General Terms and these Savings Accounts Terms. It can take up to five working days to convert your Regular Saver to your new account. You will earn interest at the rate applicable to your new account until it is converted.

Removal of identity theft assistance from Bank Account, Bank Account Pay Monthly and Graduate Service

The Identity Theft Assistance feature, provided by PrivacyGuard®*, will be removed from the following accounts: Bank Account, Bank Account Pay Monthly and Graduate Bank Account with effect from 1st December 2011. Therefore, as of this date, the following features will no longer be available: online risk assessment tool, identity theft assistance telephone helpline and one free online credit report per year. For information on keeping your identity safe, please refer to our website **www.hsbc.co.uk/security-centre** for advice or visit your nearest HSBC branch.

If you have purchased a PrivacyGuard® policy directly from Affinion International Limited, it will not be affected by the withdrawal of this feature and you will continue to enjoy the benefits offered by the policy for as along as it remains in force.

* PrivacyGuard® is a trading name and registered trademark of Affinion International Limited. Registered in England under company number 1008797. Registered office: Charter Court, 50 Windsor Road, Slough, Berkshire SL1 2EJ

Price list changes

1. We have introduced a new Price List and Interest Rates document for International Personal account customers. Previously details of prices and interest rates for International Personal accounts were contained in the International Business Price List. None of our existing prices or interest rates have changed, the details have simply been transferred to a new document. If you require a copy of the new International Personal accounts price list please contact us on **0800 783 4984**.

2. The changes to clause 17.7 of Section 1 of the General Terms and Conditions mentioned above are replicated in the "Debit Card – Using your card abroad – General" section of the following Price Lists and Interest Rates documents:

HSBC Premier Price List
General Price List
HSBC Passport Price list
HSBC Amanah Price List
Student and Graduate Price List

3. Student Price List. The credit interest rate we pay first year students for balances up to £1,000 in a Student Bank Account will be changing. The rate will change from 2% AER variable to 1.5% above the Bank of England Base Rate from 01 December 2011.

hsbc.co.uk

Issued by HSBC Bank plc.
Customer Information: PO Box 757, Hemel Hempstead, Hertfordshire HP2 4SS

CA0045 06/11 Printed by Communisis ©HSBC Bank plc 2011. All Rights Reserved.

Tuesday 25 March
Sent money to Rourke's Drift for William's kit and to P.M. General Depot for Senior's pay. Got Dalrymple's horse shod, rode him out for a bit with Upcher in the afternoon. Shave that Catchem alivo has been poisoned. Police and carbineers moved down to Vermachs on Drift road.

Some of Wilfred's dry sense of humour shines through in the diary with this play on King Cetshwayo's name.

Wednesday 26 March
Money from Brown for banking £6 for Pte Geo Davis. Cheque from Gleig P.M. 1/13th No 52/37252. Clements back from Ladysmith.

Thursday 27 March
4 Cts Mtls one Dist 3 regtt took up all morning. Major Bromhead and Lloyd 2nd Battn from PM Burg. Gonny Bromhead from the Drift. A dresser fellow from Ladysmith on Moffat's poney.

Towards the end of the month, the two Bromhead brothers got together for the first time since 22 January. Major Charles Bromhead was the older of the two. Born in 1840, he had been a Brevet Major since 1874 and during the Zulu wars he was in command of detachments along the line of communication at Dundee, Landman's Drift and Koppie Allein. Gonville Bromhead, known as Gonny to his friends, was five years younger. He was a 34 year old Lieutenant when in command of B Coy, 2nd/24th Foot at Rorke's Drift and is often unfairly portrayed as a slow, rather dim-witted officer who was hard of hearing and for this reason he was given the unromantic task of guarding the mission station with its store and makeshift hospital. His appointment to secure Rorke's Drift was pure coincidence and his gallantry and leadership during the historic battle must surely dispel any such misgivings. For his conduct at Rorke's Drift he was mentioned in despatches, appointed Brevet Major and awarded the Victoria Cross. The Lloyd mentioned in this diary entry was in fact the namesake of William Lloyd, serving in the 2nd Battalion.

Friday 28 March
Bromhead to Drift. Lent Lloyd Dalrymple's horse to ride down as his own had a sore back.

Saturday 29 March
Rode down to drift with Clements and Upcher to get up other nags got wet coming in. Letter from White's brother Col 56th and one from Mrs Addison. Convoy in with deserter C.M. Prisoner Chester other escaped leaving P.M.Burg.

Sunday 30 March
Church parade as usual leave off. Made up Mess Acts. A laarger made about 3/4 of a mile from the camp. Had to shift the camp up to it in the afternoon.

As the son of a vicar, Wilfred would normally have attended Sunday worship on a regular basis, but on this occasion he was given leave to miss the service as he was busy moving elements of the overcrowded camp at Helpmekaar into a newly constructed laager on its outskirts.

Monday 31 March
Muster parade. Read out the late C.M's Dillon flogged. Curll and Dunne left for Ladysmith convoy of 4 ambulances. Cummerford in charge. Williams and Phipps came in from the drift to lunch. The Native Contingent to be stationed here. Turner brought up 3 waggon loads of goods from Greytown. The Colonel got a despatch from Col Wood reporting actions of 28, 29 and 30th*. Loss of 1'000 to enemy and 7 officers and about 80 men to us. D Coy slept in the fort had to go in with them and lost my dinner by it.*

By the end of the month, Colonel Wood had sent through an official despatch which relates to the actions at Hlobane and Kambula. Lord Chelmsford had spent the last month assembling a column to attempt the relief of Colonel Pearson at Eshowe and he tasked Colonel Wood to create a diversion to distract Zulu attention while he did so. He decided to launch a pincer attack against the abaQulusi on the Hlobane mountain, with Buller taking a strong force up the eastern trail, while Russell created a diversion at the western end. The attacks were to be composed almost entirely of colonial horsemen and native auxiliaries, including 200 Zulus who had defected to the British. The two-pronged attack was designed to be a surprise with an attempt to deceive the abaQulusi into believing the target for attack was further to the south-east. In Colonels Wood and Buller there were two competent and experienced field commanders, but the attack was ill-conceived from the outset, by attempting to set horsemen against a rocky mountain fortress. Wood referred to this vague plan as a reconnaissance in force. It was risky in the extreme; he stood to gain little and he was overstepping by far the generous freedom of movement that Chelmsford had granted him. [3]

It is extremely unlikely that the abaQulusi were deceived by Buller's feint to the south-east. They would have seen Russell's column heading to the west and as subsequent events were to prove, they were prepared for the attack when it came. They were also aware that the main Zulu army, which Chelmsford had assumed would be opposing him at Eshowe 100 miles away, was, completely unbeknown to Buller, camped only six miles away from Hlobane. The initial assaults were unopposed, but as the two columns attempted to meet in the centre of the plateau they found their way barred by a precipitous cliff. This was the consequence of insufficient intelligence and lack of detailed reconnaissance. About to be encircled by the abaQulusi there was panic and pandemonium amongst the columns. Responding to an ill-defined order, Russell moved away from the plateau, leaving Buller to descend the mountain unsupported. When the columns eventually made the safety of Kambula that night, they had suffered the loss of almost 100 officers and men. The fight had been a shambles and the Zulus remained in complete mastery of the field. Furthermore, the main Zulu army, buoyed up by this victory, was advancing upon the laager at Kambula.

By about mid-day on 29 March, the Zulu army, some 20,000 strong, had deployed into traditional formation a few miles from the British position. With only 2,000 men and two infantry battalions in the position, Colonel Wood was seemingly outnumbered, but he was reliant upon the effectiveness of controlled volley fire to avoid a repeat of Isandlwana. As the Zulu advance began, Wood noticed that the movement of the two horns was not balanced, so he provoked the right horn into attacking without supporting cover from the left, by initiating a charge by his mounted men. Despite a valiant effort on their part, the Zulu right horn could not sustain their assault and had to retire. Although it was not immediately apparent, the failure of this first attack largely decided the battle. Instead of attacking in overwhelming numbers on all sides, the Zulus were now committed to a series of uncoordinated attacks and Wood could face each challenge in turn. In particular, he could move the four guns left outside the laager to meet each fresh attack and the effect of their fire – particularly when firing canister at short range – was devastating. It also prevented the horns from linking up, thus negating the value of their superior numbers. Once it was apparent that the Zulu attacks were losing their intensity, Wood was able to launch a counter-attack with his mounted infantry and before long the retreat turned into a rout. As at Rorke's Drift, British casualties were light, but the Zulu army took a heavy toll. In contrast to the previous day, Kambula was a well controlled action, inflicting upon the Zulus a defeat from which they were not to recover. By the end of the day, the hardest fought battle of the Anglo-Zulu war and probably its defining moment, was over. [4]

April Fool's Day jokes are fairly universal and they were no exception at Helpmekaar.

Tuesday 1 April
Camp made April fools of at 3 am, by report of a tent on fire in the Artillery lines. Wrote to Lloyd, Cummerford enclosing Mess Bills for former, Curll and Dunne.

Wednesday 2 April
Orderly Officer. No mail in. Worked at Mess accounts. Very wet afternoon and night. Sent Lloyd 2/24th receipt for saddle and bridle he rode the grey horse down on.

Wilfred kept in touch on a regular basis with Lloyd while he was away at Greytown as he often refers to him in diary entries this month. Meanwhile, news of the aftermath of Kambula continued to come in.

Thursday 3 April
DCM on AHC man Monroe prosecuted. Beresford from Drift. News in from 2 Dutchmen who were at Kambula at attack say 2800 men already buried and harassed 7 miles from camp. Wet again. Clements started getting up . . . for next Wednesday. Note from Lloyd. Letter to Wolfe.

While the central column awaited reinforcements, there were some adjustments to the existing force levels and two of the Coys of 2nd/24th Foot were redeployed to Dundee where they were to be used for route protection and the guarding of forts.

Friday 4 April
Letters to the Father and Kit. The Colonel, Cleary, General and Jones to Dundee to choose a site for a post there. Major Dunbar Harvey and Trower from the Drift with two Coys 2/24th for Dundee. Rode out with Rainforth Johnstone down to Drift. Letter from Lloyd.

Saturday 5 April
2/24th left for Dundee at 8.30 also the Coy RE. Went out for a ride with Clem after lunch. Dr Brown, Essex, Hope and Wealans from Ladysmith. Col and Co back from Dundee. Rainforth got a letter from Brown giving account of attack on Kambula Camp. Letter from Mrs Smedley and Lloyd due.

Mess routine continued and although Lloyd was away at Greytown for some time while he recuperated from fever, he still had to pay his Mess bill.

Sunday 6 April
Church Parade. N.A.M. read the service. Lunched with the Col. Went with Clements to inspect stores in old hut near first camp and rode on to look for mushrooms found none. Letter from Lloyd enclosing cheque for Mess Bill. Jones back from Dundee rode out again with Cleary and Harness.

The Mess was busy the next day when the General, Lord Chelmsford, came in after dinner. As many officers as possible would have been present for what Wilfred describes as 'a big drink.' He was in fact referring to what can only have been a celebration of the relief of Eshowe and the defeat of a large Zulu force at the battle of Gingindlhovu on 2 April, when Chelmsford's column moved towards Eshowe to relieve Colonel Pearson. Although the infantry battalions were newly arrived and inexperienced reinforcements, Chelmsford had learnt his lesson and the position was entrenched and well defended, with Naval gatling guns deployed at the corners of the laager. Scouting parties warned of the Zulu approach and despite their usual fanatic bravery, they could make little impact upon the position. Within a few hours the battle was over and as at Kambula, the mounted infantry followed up with deadly effect. [5] The Zulus lost over 1,000 men while British casualties were in single figures, testimony once again to the inevitable and obvious superiority of rifle fire against spear and shield and salutary evidence of what could have been averted at Isandlwana if only the same principles of defence had been applied.

Monday 7 April
3 men for Drunk. Cleary and Col Harness back from Dundee. Wrote to Cummerford to ask him to pay Ladysmith Bills sending cheques for £31.15.0 and to Lloyd. Upcher Clements and Wealans to Drift. Letters from Spring Reid and Accutt and Wolfe. Mounted natives arrived in Camp. Papers from home and Mrs Addison. Col Black up from the Drift. Col General etc in after Mess. A big drink. Sergt Hurley drunk and confined.

Tuesday 8 April
Orderly Officer. Letters about men dead etc. D Coy and Hd Qtrs of regt under orders to shift to Dundee on Thursday. Williams and Phipps from the Drift former slept. News of sinking of Clyde. Papers from Wolfe and Mrs Addison.

Although the 1st/24th Foot had been all but annihilated at Isandlwana, this was not the first time such a disaster had occurred and the battalion was not to be disbanded. Every effort was made to gather reinforcements at home as quickly as possible and eventually about 600 new recruits – and they were just that – were despatched to South Africa on the *SS Clyde*. Misfortune was to strike the Battalion yet again when the ship ran aground off Dyers Island on 3 April and although all hands were landed safely this caused considerable delay in the Regiment forming up its battle strength once more. [6]

Wednesday 9 April
2 DCMs. Col Harness President. Col Degacher, Symmonds, Bannister from drift. 10 wagons taken out of the laarger. Garrison athletics in afternoon. D

Coy won tug of war. Challenge from R.A to pull for £10. A lot of natives foot and horse came in the morning and left again for the Drift. Police and Carbineers left for same 2pm.

Although they were busy preparing for the second invasion, Wednesday afternoon in the British army has long been a sports afternoon by tradition and South Africa was to be no exception. Meanwhile, a number of other local colonial militia units were passing through Helpmekaar and as Wilfred reports the next day some were involved in skirmishing raids across the border in an effort to discourage the Zulus from attempting any further assaults themselves. They would also have been scouting for new routes for the column to advance on shortly.

Thursday 10 April
Flogging parade Jones and Hellet. Note from Brown about cheque. Mounted men and patrols crossed from Drift to make a raid. Rode with Upcher to the head of the Berg to see what we could see and found the men returning to the ponts. Tongue in from Greytown.

A Berg is a hill feature and in this case it would have been a high point on the Helpmekaar escarpment.

Friday 11 April
Letters for Mother, Mary and Kenneth. Church Parade at 11am the Parson having returned. Palmes sent down to Ladysmith with Tyhlwid . . . from Wolfe. Rode with Upcher Rainforth Dawson and Clements to look for duck. Got one brace and a partridge on the Berg. Dr Allthorpe from Ladysmith with money from Cummerford and Dunne for Mess Bills. New ordnance man in to relieve Fowler. 3 waggon loads of Canteen stuff for 2nd Bttn. D Coy beat R.A. best of 3 tug of war.

Saturday 12 April
Took inventory of box of clothes etc belonging to Cavaye and Dyson. Got a case each of stout and beer for Mess from stores for 2nd Battn. Party out shooting on flat towards Ladysmith . . . broke down twice yesterday and a third convoy since left today. Letter from Mother, Kit and Aunt. Mr Cummerford with receipted bills for Ladysmith and two papers from the Father.

Sunday 13 April
Orderly Officer. Letters from Spring de Wolfendale and others. Harisson Weatherhead's G. C. Medal. Papers from Wolfe and Mrs Addison. Wrote to Lloyd and Weatherhead. Double Colonial allowance granted from 1/11/78.

Letters to Aunt Margaret. Ted Spring and Camarford acknowledging receipts from Ladysmith. Started letters home.

There was also good news when the Colonial Allowance – an additional payment to compensate for the expense of being overseas – was doubled and backdated by 6 months. Such an increase in allowance would have been very welcome, considering a Lieutenant was receiving about £16 per month in pay and a private soldier only £7 per month. Compare that with pay rates in 2003 of £2,130 and £1,170 per month respectively! [7]

Monday 14 April
Upcher, Rainforth and Clements to Rourke's Drift to go and set up stone over Melvill and Coghill. Staid in and finished G Coy side of laarger. Letter to Editor Natal Mercury for copies of Defence of Rourke's Drift. Jones from Drift dined with us. The party returned late found Melvill's watch etc in breeches pocket.

Now that the column was regaining control of the immediate area, it was considered safe for some of the regimental officers to visit Melvill's and Coghill's grave at Fugitives Drift. Initially they had only been buried under a cairn of stones but now they had the opportunity to bury them properly with a memorial stone. When the bodies were being re-interred, they found Melvill's watch in his breeches pocket which had apparently stopped at 2.20p.m.; presumably the time that he had entered the river on 22 January.

Tuesday 15 April
Note to Thrupp about Mess Bill due to regtl mess. Got some stores from 2/24th canteen lot. Went out with Rainforth to try and shoot something.

Wednesday 16 April
Went to Sandspruit with Col Black on a mealie Board Found the Col and Hd Qtrs of the Column gone to Dundee. Mess to be broken up. Col Black under orders for Dundee. Logan up from Ladysmith and Commeline from Dundee to take down Comst stores.

The momentum for the next attempt at the Zulu army was building up and Wilfred had been given instructions to pack up the Mess from its static location. Once the column was on the move again officers would live off the waggons in the field alongside their soldiers. Likewise, the commissariat stores were being folded up ready for the move. Meanwhile, the Battalion Headquarters along with Colonel Black were on their way to Dundee as the advance party.

Thursday 17 April
Letters to Mother and Kit. Flogging parade 7am. Artillery and Police shifted to Dundee. Col Black to Drift. Camp shifted nearer the fort. Company NNC Rourke's Drift to Kusinga. Orderly Officer 40 minutes doing night rounds.

Friday 18 April
Note to Dawson including Mess Bill. Tent nearly down in high wind last night. Bell boating party en route to P.M.Berg. Rode with Upcher and Commeline to see if we could see the 94th on the road, saw nothing. Poney bad head swollen up.

Saturday 19 April
Poney kept up on Bran mash. Rode out with Clem to see for . . . did not find him or see anything of the 94th.

Helpmekaar was a continual transit camp during this month. By the end of the week, Lieutenant Lloyd was back on his feet and had returned to the Coy after the best part of a month's sickness, while others left for Dundee.

Sunday 20 April
Church parade at 8.45am. Col Degacher from the Drift. Lloyd came in from Greytown. Commeline and his party left for Dundee also the General and Essex. Boyd Comsrt from Greytown with Lloyd. Orderly Officer. 94th passed at Tugela yesterday

Monday 21 April
Out shooting with Rainforth got nothing but a pair that had been brought down by a hawk. Bought saddle for £3.1.0 from estate of Gubbins NNC. Note from Dawson to pay his Mess Bill in stamps.

Tuesday 22 April
94th and 2 Coys 4th Regt came in. Breakfasted the Officers. Poney nearly well. Ordnance officer to Dundee. Took Dawson's hat which he left behind with me. Letters from Mrs Kingsley, Mrs Addison, Smith Dorrien and Harman's Bill. Gunner Brown, Sharp 4th and few others in after Mess . . .

Companies of the 94th and 4th Foot came through Helpmekaar causing much disturbance:

Wednesday 23 April
The 94th and 4th left early after making night hideous with about 30 sentries all's welling after every 1/4 hour. Gunner Brown staid and went

down to Drift with Upcher Clem and Self. Lunched with Williams and went up to top of Oscar Berg. Saw the waggons on the neck and a few zulus coming from the camp. Letters to Huntley to hurry up our stores, and to Bengough to ask for 4 man as post runners. Jennings back from Ladysmith.

Meanwhile, Wilfred made another visit to Rorke's Drift and went to the top of the Oskarberg feature from where he could clearly see some of the abandoned wagons at Isandlwana. He was probably accompanied by William Lloyd judging by a number of his paintings, which were drawn from this position. He could also see some Zulu movement, but this was more than likely local inhabitants scavenging the area. As Lloyd recounts in a letter to his sister Selina, not long after recovering from the fever:

'. . . *we can see the place where the massacre or fight rather took place from here but dare not cross the river as it would be almost certain death so our fellows are lying unburied just where they fell and with a good telescope one can see the skeletons dotted about. I daresay when we cross again to march into Zululand they will all be buried but by this time its impossible to tell officers from soldiers as in a very short time the vultures and white necked crows pick any dead thing clean. I have been into Zululand twice only for a few minutes or so as I had to swim the Buffalo however I've stood on the enemies country and shaken my fist at him so feel quite contented . . . before I come to the end perhaps you don't know this letter is carried by Kaffir runners to Ladysmith about 60 miles from here our nearest town. Such rum looking chaps you will see a sketch of one in my book some day. They carry a letter in the end of a split stick but this goes in a bag . . .*' [8]

His reference to a book probably refers to the album in which his original watercolours now reside, but little was he to know that both his paintings of Isandlwana from the Oskarberg through a telescope and his caricature of a native mail runner would eventually be preserved for posterity.

Thursday 24 April

Orderly Officer. Letters to Adjt 94th for Sarney's crime and to Warnford to find out about Weatherhead's kit and G.C. Medal. Poney taken off the sick list. Note to Symmonds about box jams and hides for rifles. Brown the Dr to Dundee also Upcher and Gunner Brown. Major Dastrell from Umsinga to Dundee lunched with us. Parson dined.

Friday 25 April

Letter to the mother posted yesterday. Note from Tongue for receipt of oat cakes answered to Mrs Addison, Smith Dorrien and Dawson. Parson Smith off to Dundee Mansel of the Police back from Ladysmith. P.M.Berg etc. Rode out a short way on the poney. Upcher back from Dundee. Clements bought a horse from the Cyrus.

Saturday 26 April
Reports this morning and last night of raids and intended ones across the Border by the Zulus. Letter to Mrs Kingsley and Palmes. Rode quietly over the Berg after lunch. Letters from Mother and Kit. Harry Lovett. Dawson.

Report still came in about Zulu movements, indicating the concern still felt by the shock waves from Isandlwana.

Sunday 27 April
Church Parade as usual. Read the Service. Letters to Dawson and Cochrane and Vesey Holt to transfer £10 recd for old Mess hut to Mess fund. Rode with Clements got a 1/2 dozen copies of Smith's account of Rourke's Drift 2 to Clem, one to Lloyd 1 Cr Sergt Tompkins 1 to hospital.

The official report on the defence of Rorke's Drift was written by Lieutenant John Chard, but a number of survivors did produce their own accounts, often in the form of letters to their wives and families at home in Britain. Sergeant George Smith wrote once such letter the day after the battle to his wife in Brecon and this eventually found its way into the *Brecon County Times* newspaper on 29 March 1879. [9] Copies of the paper would have then been sent back out to South Africa and it is most likely that this is the report to which Wilfred refers. Padre George Smith also wrote about the battle, but if Wilfred had been referring to the parson then he would have written of him in more reverential terms.

Monday 28 April
Orderly Officer. Regtl C.M on Desmond. Sent cheques to credit at Standard Bank list on lst page. Gave Upcher one on V Holt for £55 in exchange for a colonial one. Letter to Wolfe and D.C. R.Es P.M.Berg enquiring after Victor Yorke. Porter came up from the Drift with 1/2 Jones Coy en route for Dundee and dined with us.

Throughout all this, Wilfred was kept occupied by Mess activity.

Tuesday 29 April
Parade at 7.30 to see Desmond get his 50. Porter and party left after Breakfast. Paid £1 for White's matrass that I have had in use for a long time. Arranged some kit for shifting. Went to Macpherson for his account against

the Mess. Letters from Robinson Vause and Co about Smith's act of Rourke's Drift. Thrupp enclosing cheque for £4 in part payment of his Mess Bill. Reid and Accutt re case of soups. Natal Witness to claim for subs. Stephens at Dundee about his letters. Also Harrisons states etc. Major Dalrymple back from Greytown.

The *Natal Witness* was a local newspaper which reported on much of the invasion so far. The Officers' Mess was keen to maintain its creature comforts as much as possible so a subscription had been taken out and Wilfred had to make sure that this was settled up before they moved on again.

Wednesday 30 April
Dalrymple to Dundee. Muster 10.30 letters to Mother, Thrupp acknowledging receipt of his cheque, and Standard Bank enclosing same. Rode out of the Veldt. Made some pumpkins in a garden.

CHAPTER 6

THE SECOND INVASION

During the coming month, Lord Chelmsford's reinforcement programme was to take shape and he would soon be ready to launch his second invasion. His also reorganized his original columns into two Divisions to advance on Ulundi in a pincer-like movement. The 1st Division under Major General Crealock was to take the route of the former coastal column once more while the 2nd Division under Major General Newdigate was to approach Ulundi from a more westerly direction. The more direct route which the former central column had taken was abandoned for a number of logistical reasons, but in essence Lord Chelmsford wanted to avoid the area of Isandlwana, where the dead still lay scattered on the battlefield. In addition to these two Divisions, Colonel Evelyn Wood's former column was retained but re-designated the Flying Column, giving the impression of a separate command but actually it was an intergral part of the main striking force, to which Lord Chelmsford attached himself. Sadly for the 24th Foot, the two battalions were not to play a significant role in this part of the campaign, Chelmsford's logic being that they had suffered enough as it was. Colonel Glyn did not see it this way, however and wanted the opportunity to avenge his Regiment's losses, but this was not to be. Companies of the 1st/24th Foot were to be used as column escorts and the 2nd/24th Foot spent the remainder of the campaign guarding the various newly constructed forts along the line of communication. [1]

Thursday 1 May
Paper from the Father. Clements to Drift and back. Col Black up from Drift. Staid in for Rainforth. Stocked a patent Veldt writing case. Sold some of Hodson's kit to Lloyd, sent paper on to Harry Lovett.

Friday 2 May
Bill in from Witness v Mess for 20 copies fortnightly edition returned to be amended and ordered copy of tri-weekly edition for self. Major Dartnell through for Umsingas, News. Col to have a Brigade, Dunbar the Regt. Davis Drum Maj. to be relieved here by police next week. 4 Coys 2/24th Dundee 4 the Drift under Black.

In his somewhat disjointed shorthand, Wilfred was recording here some Regimental news. It had just been announced that Colonel Glyn was to command the 1st Brigade in General Newdigate's 2nd Division for the next phase of the war, consisting mainly of the 21st Foot (The Royal Scots Fusiliers) and the 58th Foot (The Northamptonshire Regiment) but interestingly not including his own Regiment. Major William Dunbar was to take over command of the 1st/24th Foot from Glyn, to be part of the 2nd Brigade under Colonel William Collingwood.

Meanwhile, Major Dartnell was moving through to Umsinga, which was to the south east of Helpmekaar as border protection in preparation for the advance. Wilfred was also keen to retain a copy of the Natal Witness to keep up with the news so he re-adjusted the order with the newspaper.

Saturday 3 May
Waggons in to load up the Mtd Infantry kit. Sent off a lot of our own to P.M.Berg. Poney loose among troup of mares. Chased the whole afternoon and caught only at dusk.

Sunday 4 May
Upcher and Clements went over to Dundee to meet the draft expected in today. Went down to the Drift with Jennings to see Symmonds found that the Black and Bannister had also gone to Dundee.

Monday 5 May
Letter from Manager of Standard Bank acknowledging receipt of Thrupps cheque for £4. Nothing about the others. To ditto from Brown including cheque for McCloughlin. Dartnell from Umsinga. Rode with Lloyd Upcher and Clements from Dundee. Police left this morning to relieve us. Mess stores oatmeal and Worcester from Ladysmith and note from Inman.

Tuesday 6 May
Note to Inman. Posted letter to Kit. Hospital broken up all patients but three and the marquee sent to Ladysmith. Police in from Dundee. Bengoughs lot from Umsinga. Drew £9.2.6 pay for Camp Police from Rainforth.

For almost four months, Wilfred had been static at Helpmekaar while the ebb and flow of the abortive first invasion took place around him. At last he was to be on the move.

Wednesday 7 May
Left Helpmakaar for Dundee outspanned for breakfast at Van Tonders, went on to bottom of last hill before Dundee and camped. A lot of drunk in camp and on line of March. Colours carried by Sergts. Bengoughs Battn that came

into Helpmakaar yesterday marched for Langman's Drift this morning and camped below us by night. Breakfasted with the police before leaving.

Despite the anticipation of some active service at last, the Officers' Mess was still a high priority for him.

Thursday 8 May
Got in to Dundee soon after 11. The Drafts pitched our camp and got some dinner ready for the Mess. Lunched and dined with the Colonel. Got a lot of papers from Wolfe and some from home. Letters from the Mother and Kit. Glenne got a copy of the Gazette Murshead and Paton came in from Maritzburg with treasure.

Treasure was a term that Wilfred would use to describe any home comforts such as butter, milk, fresh bread or even a good claret, which would make life in the field more bearable. The following day there was a change of Commanding Officer.

Friday 9 May
Major Dunbar takes over command of the Regt and Drafts and Cotton the Adjutancy. Note to Thrupp receipt for £4 for the Mess and accepting his bet of case of champagne that the war is not further advanced when he comes back to the colony.

Saturday 10 May
Orderly Officer. Did Orderly Room in Cotton's absence. Upcher and co had a big foraging party result 9 geese 8 ducks. Flogging parade. Jennings over from Helpmakaar. Dunbar saw regt in marching order in the morning. Letter from Manager Standard Bank acknowledging part 107 of cheques and cheque book.

Sunday 11 May
Smith Dorrien and Dunne in from Ladysmith. Church parade 10.30. Letters and cheques to Mathison Bros, Turner Bros Robinson and Vause Inman Reid and Acutt and Morning Standard. Also P Davis and Sons. Rode with Lloyd to some Kraals etc got butter and fowls.

Monday 12 May
C.O. Parade 10 am. KDGs came in Lancers on to the Drift (Lanemans). Got the poneys shoes shifted by KDGs and branded 24 on off rear side. Great scare about a Zulu Impi supposed to be going to ravage Newcastle District. Browne came over from Col Woods on 3 days leave. Letters from Mother, Kit, Wolfe and V. Holt.

The acute shortage of cavalry units during the first invasion had now been rectified with the arrival of the Kings Dragoon Guards and the 17th Lancers who would take up their traditional reconnaissance role during the next advance. Wilfred took advantage of their expertise by having the Regiment's horses branded with the Regimental number for identification purposes. The threat of a pre-emptive strike by the Zulus was still ever present but it did not materialize.

Tuesday 13 May
Battn Drill 10am. 6 Cts Martial. Afterwards letters to Granny, V. Holt and Co, also McPherson Ladysmith for stout or porter and Bill. Note from Tongue.

Wednesday 14 May
Punishment parade 7am. 4 men flogged at 10am. Curious skirmishing drill. 3 guests to dinner. Wrote to Tongue lofed in camp all afternoon.

While preparation for the next phase would have kept the majority out of mischief, there was still a need to impose discipline with yet another flogging parade. This time around Lord Chelmsford did not want to be caught out by insufficient notice of enemy dispositions, so skirmishing tactics were introduced which meant that the infantry companies would be deployed quickly to the flanks of the advancing column if necessary to counter any build up of Zulu forces against them. This was a new concept to most of the Imperial forces who were used to operating in the traditional hollow square and inevitably it caused confusion at first.

Thursday 15 May
CO parade 10am. 2 GC medals presented. Letters from Granny, Mother, Ernest and Hugh. Receipt of cheque from Inman Board on damaged arms lasted nearly all day. Coy 90th L. I. for escort duty. The Gazette Tongue and Co in orders.

Friday 16 May
Inspection parade. Orders received for Langemans drift. Cheque from Dawson for Field Allowance 1/31 March £3.17.6. Extra Duty 23 Jan to 31 March £11.18.0. Sent some to Standard Bank. Letter to Mother. Field Allowance for February in cash from Dawson.

At last the long awaited orders to begin the advance had been received and after four months at Helpmekaar, Wilfred was on the move again.

Saturday 17 May
Got off at 10 for 9 from Dundee was sent on ahead to finish out our camping ground at the Drift. Col Harness and R. A. gave us lunch after camp pitching which was fit to make an Apostle swear! A Coy sent out on picquet almost before they had camped. Clements came in rather done up.

After such a period of inactivity they were all clearly out of practice at pitching camp on the move and by the end of the day most of the Company were worn out to say the least! Here they stayed for the next 10 days while the final preparations were made for the second invasion. Lord Chelmsford was leaving nothing to chance this time and inspected the whole column personally. A picquet is a small guard force on the perimeter of a camp.

Sunday 18 May
Under arms at 5.15 for an hour and a half. Letters to Harry Lovett and Palmes from Uncle Arthur. Bathed and swam into the Transvaal with Dawson. Dunbar lunched and dined with us.

Monday 19 May
Same old morning parade. Orderly Officer. Regt C.M. Harvey over from Dundee also Hope with bad accounts of Palmes. Letters to Chamberlin and Uncle Arthur.

Tuesday 20 May
Flogging parade after morning turnout. Great coats condemned lots of requisitions of all sorts sent in. Went out foraging with Brander Colvill and Lumsden. Col Bray over from Utrecht. Report in that Catch em alivo wants to make his submission and that Dunn has gone to see him to make no difference in the advance of Ulundi. Papers from the Father and Wolfe. Tents first allowed for the support on outlying picquet.

Since his recent defeat at Kambula on 27 March, King Cetshwayo was looking for some way to bring this war to a close without further heavy loss to the Zulu nation. Over the next 6 weeks he was to make several attempts at negotiation, but Lord Chelmsford was interested in nothing but the total defeat of the Zulu army to avenge his humiliation at Isandlwana. John Dunn was a white settler who had lived all his life in Natal and who had a close association with the Zulu King. Known as 'Chief John Dunn' he had adopted Zulu custom and had a large number of Zulu wives. He had also been allocated a reserve in Natal and was keen to remain neutral throughout the war. However, as the campaign progressed he realized that his future lay in siding with the British and Lord Chelmsford was to use him as a go-between on several occasions. [2]

Wednesday 21 May
Picquet at 4.30pm.

Thursday 22 May
Voluntary services. Kept our picquet till 9.30 on account of fog. Rode out with Nicholson to forage and got none. Patrol back from Isandhlwana 'saw no nigs'. Letter from Mrs Kingsley and McPhersons account.

As a result of his usual understatement, there is hidden poignancy in his entry regarding patrols coming back from Isandlwana. Since 22 January the corpses of those killed that day had remained where they had fallen as the battlefield was for a long time in the hands of the enemy. As the months progressed and the Zulus withdrew from the area Lord Chelmsford was keen to recover whatever equipment was still serviceable, especially the waggons, for his next advance. On 21 May a strong force under Colonel Drury Lowe of the 17th Lancers returned to Isandlwana to salvage what they could and to bury some of the dead, but Colonel Glyn had pleaded that the bodies of the 24th Foot be left alone as the Regiment wanted to bury their own at the first available opportunity.

Friday 23 May
10am parade. Two hour drill casualty one man bayonetted in the leg. Started a letter home. Parade at 2pm for punishment.

Saturday 24 May
Kit inspection by CO 11.30. Rode out foraging with Clem nobbled by a farmer. Mule transport carts handed over to the Regt. Lord Chemlsford and staff from Utrecht.

Despite the impending advance, Wilfred was keen to find some sort of diversion so he and his friend Clements went out hunting, no doubt for some decent meat to supplement the rations. However, it seemed that a local farmer did not take kindly to their riding across his land! Some of the 40 waggons recovered from Isandlwana a few days earlier were allocated to the Regiment to carry their heavy equipment and Lord Chelmsford arrived to check on the Division's progress.

Sunday 25 May
Church parade as usual. Made out the Mess Bills with the help of Dawson. Falls and Johnson 80th. Major Bromhead, Harvey, Glennie, Mainwaring and co over to lunch. Grenfell Splutterdash Smith Dorrien in after mess in the evening. Sent cheques to pay up Mattinson Inman and McPherson.

Monday 26 May
Orderly Officer. Column parade in the morning for the General. Cavalry out skirmishing and all sorts of services Cochrane over from Col Woods. The Colonel from Dundee. Paton appointed Mil Sec if Col Lanyon wishes to decline. 2 Coys on outlying picquet as 58th go tomorrow takes F&G letter from Standard Bank receipt of £15.15.6 cheque by Dawson.

Although a very strong force had been assembled, there was still the fear that opposition would be encountered from the outset.

Tuesday 27 May
Came off picquet at the Disperse after morning parade. Phipps posted to this Battn returned to Drift on leave to get his kit collected. A lot of Mess accounts. 58th Regt and Harness's Battery left this morning me to follow tomorrow. Report that a lot of Zulu's are assembling to contest our entry with in country. Paton off to Transvaal. 2 Coys 2/24th Harvey and Glennie from Dundee. Curll tasked last night to take up Commsrt and Post duties. Sent £49 odd to Standard Bank. Got off letters to Kit and Ernest.

The next day, Wilfred was up early for the move to Kopje Allein, with the 2nd/24th Foot remaining behind as planned. Lloyd was transferred to C Company for a while and this is the last entry that he makes in his diary about Lloyd. As we know from his paintings, he was present throughout the remainder of the campaign and travelled back to England with the 1st Battalion after the war. One gets the impression from Lloyd's paintings that he was something of a free spirit with a considerable sense of humour. He also clearly had strong views on the conduct of the campaign and had written privately to various people expressing his opinions while he was on sick leave. Imagine his annoyance and frustration when he discovered that someone had leaked a letter of his to the Press at home in Ireland, as conveyed in this correspondence to his friend Mr Bulmer La Terriere of the 18th Hussars:

' . . . I have had one or two letters lately in which people have said that "they were glad to see my letter in the Irish papers." My hair stood on end simply and the combined locks etc parted; well it's all very well now I know who did it and I've written such a snorter, but seriously, I hate people putting private letters in print and I was awfully put out by having a disjointed rambling scrawl sent to be criticized and laughed at by everyone; a letter which was only intended to let my people know the various little items of the march after we were ordered to the front, and another and more serious thing is this. We, (the fellows belonging to the two companies), and a good many others, know certain things concerning Lord Chelmsford's actions on the 22nd Jan which if they were raised abroad, would simply dam him in the

eyes of the world and cause his recall in double quick time. So, if I had been foolish enough to let the cat out, even in a private letter, the publishing thereof would have caused, most likely, a most awful row. All I can say is I sincerely hope he won't command us and what I say is perfectly true; and that is that Col Durnford was partly to blame, in extending and so weakening his line against such enormous masses. But that Lord Chelmsford could have saved the camp, if he had had the sense of the youngest militiaman in the Service, and attended to men who knew what was happening that day and not shut his ears and relied on his own wretched knowledge of what was going on . . .' [3]

Wednesday 28 May
Rouse 5.45. Regt marched about 8.30. F&G companies on rear guard left about 11.30 and got in to Kopje Allen about 6.30. Men nothing to eat since early morning coffee good management! Lloyd sent on picquet with C Coy and First 2. Lanemans Drift left by all but the 2 24th.

The movement of a large military column is never easy and it was a fraught day by all accounts.

Thursday 29 May
Letter from Bennett about some things drawn from Ordnance on our way up country at P/M/Burg. Sent Trainer out to get some mealies from the Kraals for Mr Dodd. All turned out after lunch to improve the shelter trench run up last night. Sent a cheque for £20 to Standard Bank. P.M.B waggon laargers in course of construction all the afternoon. Shave that we move on Sunday.

Private J Trainer was one of the Rocket Battery under Captain Russell RA and had been attached to Colonel Durnford's Column. They had been called up to Isandlwana from Rorke's Drift on 22 January and arrived at about 10.30a.m., whereupon Durnford moved his troops forward from the camp, allegedly to support Lord Chelmsford who had move out earlier that day. In the ensuing battle, the Rocket Battery was overwhelmed and destroyed by the left horn of the advancing Zulu army, but Trainer and two other members of the Battery miraculously managed to escape, being three of only six white soldiers to survive the battle. Having retired along the Fugitives Trail, he eventually made his way back to Helpmekaar where he was attached to Wilfred's Company for the remainder of the war. Not being a trained infantryman, he was employed as Wilfred's groom and looked after his horse Mr Dodd. [4]

Friday 30 May
For night picquet today. Letters to Mrs Kingsley and Wolfe from Harry

Lovett and McPherson . . . 21st came in met Wilkie Collings. Bennett joins takes over A Coy. Sergt Dredge my Clr Sergt appointed to musketry.

Saturday 31 May
58th and 21st with Harness's Battery and part of the Cavalry crossed the river. Brown and Davies of the mounted Infantry over from Woods Camp. Rode part of the way back with them, with Brander and Tongue. Splutterdash rode over from the Drift and came in after dinner, rode back again in pitch dark and rainy night. Met Chichester an O.M. in the 21st.

By the end of the month, Lord Chelmsford was ready to avenge his humiliation at Isandlwana and the second invasion began with a number of diversionary moves along the border. Misfortune was to strike Lord Chelmsford yet again when Louis Napoleon, the exiled Prince Imperial of France, was killed on a poorly led and badly executed reconnaissance patrol. Louis was the son of the last French Emperor Napoleon III who had fled to England with his wife the Princess Eugénie in 1871 after the Franco-Prussian War, where they were hosted by Queen Victoria. Louis then later trained at the Royal Military Academy Woolwich and had been granted an honorary commission in the Royal Artillery. When news of the Zulu War reached England and much against Chelmsford's better judgement Louis managed to get out to South Africa to gain some operational experience as a result of Royal pressure at home. Attached to Chelmsford's column in an entirely unofficial capacity, he managed to get out on a patrol accompanied by Lieutenant Jalheel Brenton Carey, 98th Regiment of Foot (later the 2nd Battalion North Staffords) and a small escort of militia from Bettington's Horse. Later in the day they stopped for a break in a small donga, but failed to post any sentries. Suddenly they were ambushed by a Zulu war party, during which time Louis Napoleon and Troopers Abel and Rogers were killed. Lieutenant Carey was blamed for this disaster and was immediately tried by Court Martial for cowardice in not trying to save the Prince. He was found guilty though not sentenced and later on the findings were to be quashed. Carey was to carry the stigma of this blunder until 1883 when he died in Karachi of peritonitis. [5] While Louis was much to blame for his own demise quite frankly, the untimely death of the Prince Imperial was politically sensitive as far as the British Government was concerned.

On the other hand and embarrassing as it may have been, it did not affect Chelmsford's overall strategy and the advance continued as soon as possible. Progress was slow as the Division was turned into a strongly defended laager every night and many of the reinforcements were young, inexperienced recruits. Un-nerved by the disasters of the first invasion, there were numerous incidents of ill-disciplined shooting at imaginary Zulus during darkness, often inflicting casualties upon their own troops. Ironically, Chelmsford could have been more cavalier at this stage and advanced at a faster pace. The Zulu army was in disarray and now that he had regular cavalry under command, he had the means to determine enemy dispositions and movement well in advance, but he chose not to do so and caution prevailed.

Sunday 1 June
Left Kopje Allins en route for King's Kraal at last. Regt brigaded with the 94th (two Greens, Lincoln and Howards) moved off after many counter orders. Got 9 miles about laagered and threw-up an earthwork by about 7pm. Shave in that the Prince Imperial has been assegaied having gone out on a patrol of six men one other also killed. Receipt of £4.4 from Inman for last cheque. South African mail from Wolfe.

News travelled fast and within 24 hours the Prince's body had been recovered, his funeral conducted and arrangements made for his body to be sent home to England.

Monday 2 June
Party went out 7am to recover Prince's body. Wrote part of letters home to the Father and Mother. Also to Dawson for some tobacco and a pouch to replace the one lost last yesterday. Fine grass fire well put out. Funeral service held over the remains of the Prince. Photo taken of the ceremony by Kish. Body embalmed to be sent home.

The advance then continued as soon as it could although security was paramount as Lord Chelmsford was determined to reach Ulundi unscathed. Night picquets were bolstered up and foot patrols had mounted cavalry attached to them, while water collecting parties had armed escorts. Although Louis Napoleon's body was sent home to England, eventually to be buried at St Michael's Abbey Farnborough, those of Troopers Abel and Rogers who died with him were buried where they fell.

Tuesday 3 June
Left by 7.30am to a place near where the Prince was killed. Passed through a lot of crops and secured a good feed for the poney. On night picquet natures posted between our groups and groups of mounted ones attached to each picquet for patrolling. Saw Wood's camp about 2 miles off. All water parties sent out armed as one of Wood's was assegaied last night at the stream. Body of the guide of Carey's party found and buried very much mutilated.

Wednesday 4 June
Went a short march in the afternoon to Woods old camp of yesterday he having moved on. News in of an impi seen by Woods natives. Lancers under order to go for them tomorrow. Had to work very late doing up the laarger.

Thursday 5 June
Moved off as soon after the morning turnout as possible our brigade in advance. Dunbar in a very bad frame of mind. Laargered up before lunch. The Lancers returned from Woods Camp about 4.30 report their Adjutant shot dead 2 men and some horses wounded. Some men came in they said from Catchwayo to ask for terms of peace generally believed that they did not come from him but wanted to find out what the terms are he not having told them to the nation.

General Wood's Flying Column was being used as pathfinders during the advance and Wilfred makes numerous references to their progress over the next month. Meanwhile, King Cetshwayo continued to make efforts to negotiate peace and a delegation came into Lord Chelmsford's headquarters for this purpose. However, Wilfred had the impression that they were trying to gain information for themselves as they seemed unaware that Chelmsford wanted nothing but total surrender.

While the advance continued, Cetshwayo's emissaries were sent back with Chelmsford's terms for ending the war and it is possible that Wilfred is a little confused here. Chelmsford wanted the King to restore all the horses, oxen and arms captured since the war started and several Zulu regiments would have to suffer the indignity of publicly disarming. The messengers protested at the impracticability of these demands and apparently Lord Chelmsford relented by settling for the oxen actually at Ulundi, the two Artillery guns taken at Isandlwana and the surrender of only one regiment. The Adjutant of the 17th Lancers was Lieutenant F J Cockayne Frith who was killed in a skirmish with a Zulu war party while out patrolling at eZungeni hill on the banks of the Upoko River.

Friday 6 June
Four companies A, B, E and F ordered to hold themselves in readiness to go with General Wood to Conference Hill and Landtemans Drift. Report that the men who came in from Catchwayo have been sent back offering an ultimatum milder than the original with a present of an ox. Also 8 days armistice granted. A grand old night alarm any amount of ammunition wasted principally by the 58th* who started it. Result 1 Sergt and 3 men R.E. wounded. 1 horse killed 1 dog wounded 1 nigger assegaied and several tents cut to ribbons.*

Although the Division was strong and well defended, many of the newly arrived reinforcements were young recruits who had no experience of active service. Fired up no doubt by lurid tales of what had gone on during the first invasion and false alarm at night was to cause a degree of panic and Wilfred blames the 58th Foot (the Rutlandshire Regiment) for this particular episode.

Saturday 7 June
The rest of the column left early. We remained to off-load stores etc by the forts held by detachments 21st and gathering under Major Chard RE. Kept at it until 4.30 then marched into Woods Camp in time for practice alarm had to go as Orderly Officer to take orders. Found 4 dozen jams just arrived for me and sent to Wilson at Dundee for more stores. The answer sent to Cetshwayo is that when he returns Harness's guns we will talk of peace, that is according to Collingwood.

Wilfred's 25th birthday was on 7 June, but it is interesting that the day passes without any recognition or comment in his diary, apart from the receipt of a small birthday gift of some jam. Meanwhile, messages continued to be sent to King Cetshwayo. There was obviously much talk about King Cetshwayo's attempts to negotiate a peace and Wilfred had heard from Colonel Collingwood, commanding the 2nd Brigade, about the condition regarding the artillery pieces at Isandlwana, Lieutenant Colonel Harness having been the commanding officer of N Battery, 5th Brigade Royal Artillery.

Sunday 8 June
Reveille at 1.30am. Breakfast 2.30. Marched off 3.30. Halted for two hours at daylight. After next start all the men rode on the empty waggons. A & B Coys detailed to go with the horse and mule waggons to Landsmans Drift started before us. Outspanned for the night about 2.30pm about 2 miles from the Prince's Kraal.

Monday 9 June
Reveille 2. March 5am. Outspanned Itelezi hill, got on to Kopje Alleine. The two Companies E & F sent across the river to make an early start tomorrow. Dined with Harvey & Co. Found Phipps there on his way up. Posted letters to both the Father and Mother also to Still.

Tuesday 10 June
Turned out at 1am. Got off about 3.30 with 60 empty waggons a very cold night but the men rode from choice. Made Lanemans Drift about 1.30. Degacher in command there a lot of . . . on their way up to join us. Set to work all the afternoon by the great and good to superintend loading waggons.

Wednesday 11 June
The Company turned out at Reveille by Tongue after he had warned us last night that we should not have to do so. On fatigue by 2 hourly reliefs from 8am loading the waggons. Got orders to take my Company across the Drift to act as a guard on them when drawn up. Tongue gone into Dundee with the mule cart to fetch stores Lumsden ditto sent to Wilson to fetch down some of the stores by mule cart if possible. Great excitement among the leaders and drivers some of whom are trying to bolt. Orders to leave with first convoy to Lanemans Drift at 8am tomorrow.

Thursday 12 June
Got the Company waggons to the front of the convoy by 7.45. Rest did not get off by 10 and got mixed with the second convoy starting them. Outspanned half way for two hours and had dinner rest passed us while there. Orders for escort sections with first and last waggons. Own ammunition cart in centre with half the Coy and to keep the men together! Cart broke down and had to take the cases the last mile by hand. Got in just before first post.

The advance towards Ulundi was slow and laborious with strongly defended laagers by night and well protected columns during the day. As Wilfred wryly remarks, the soldiers did not want to be far from their reserves of ammunition.

Friday 13 June
Breakfast 8.30 left for Itelezi hill put in charge of the transport started after dinner at 11.30. Camped on the rise beyond our old camp by 4.30 false alarm as usual with Woods 5.15.

The pressure of a long campaign and hard marching was beginning to tell.

Saturday 14 June
Ordered as part of the Advance Guard to leave about 7.30. Tongue in a very sad frame of mind threatened to put Muirhead under arrest. Got into camp by 11. Tongue made a fine mess of laargering, and laid it on young Phipps strongly. Had a wash first for 2 days. Camp about 2 miles short of the Prince's Kraal, did not get any further on account of the heaviness of the road after the rain of last night and this morning.

Sunday 15 June
Sent with the 80th to occupy a stoney kop in rear of the camp while the waggons moved on. Wasted a lot of time during which we might have had dinners. Moved on to the left bank Itolozi by 3 o'clock went on picquet. False

alarm occasioned by return of Buller from a patrol with a few hundred head of cattle.

Colonel Redvers Buller, later to be awarded the Victoria Cross, commanded the mounted troops of Wood's Flying Column for the whole of their numerous and varied operations during the war. His troops were out constantly patrolling the flanks of the advancing Division and on this occasion came in with a herd of cattle captured from the Zulus, many of which would make their way eventually into the cooking pots.

Monday 16 June
Crossed over to our old camp ground saw Wilkie Collings who told one of Sturdy's illness and collared the case of jams for the Mess. Posted letter to Wilson of Dundee about stores.

Meanwhile, Wilfred kept his eye on Mess administration.

Tuesday 17 June
Trekked early and got into our camp at the Upoko river by lunchtime, found Wilsons bill that I wrote for yesterday and the stores he sent up. 2 home letters one from the other one, one from Dawson. 4 papers from home 5 from Wolfe and one Colonial also tobacco from Dawson lost my patent pen last night. Sent cheques to pay the Dundee Store man as also Macpherson at Ladysmith. Zulus to assemble at Kraal at new moon so shave goes.

Wednesday 18 June
Reveille and strike tents at 4am did not get off until about 8. Marched along the Upoko for 6 or 7 miles over the worst ground we have had yet, county becoming bushy, got in towards 4pm. Had to do part of the laargering work in the dark. Carey marched as a prisoner in rear of Rainforths Coy. Wood halted on a rise about 2 miles ahead of us.

Though unopposed by the Zulus at this stage, the route march was still very difficult and the laagers still had to be completed irrespective of time. Lieutenant Carey, who had led the ill-fated patrol with the Prince Imperial was still with the column awaiting disciplinary action.

The route that Lord Chelmsford had chosen for the second invasion deliberately avoided the battleground at Isandlwana for a number of reasons, but as Wilfred noted, they moved through or close to the nGwebeni valley from where the main Zulu army had launched its attack on that day.

Thursday 19 June
Moved about a mile and 1/2 to Woods camp of last night had to go on night picquet when we got in. 2 shots fired about 11.30pm and 235 men of the

Company bolted into the laarger 58th began it as before. Fort made by all available hands for the remainder of the 21st to stay in. Carey left here to be passed on to Durban and so home. His case to be laid before the Queen. This place the spot where the impi hid the night before Isandhlwana.

Once again, the poor old 58th Foot were guilty of starting a false alarm and it must have been an amusing sight to see so many men trying to seek the safety of the laager in the dark! Arrangements had now been made for Carey to return home to England where his case would be considered further, his reference to the Queen being more likely the judicial process which would follow the findings of his Court Martial. In fact, Napoleon's mother, Princess Eugénie, did ask the Queen to intervene as an act of clemency and the findings of the Court were overturned, allowing Carey to return to his Regiment.

Friday 20 June
Shifted about 7am to Woods Camp of last night about 4 miles on.

Saturday 21 June
Left camp about 9am. Coy in escort to Brownlow's convoy. Helped them through a few drifts etc. Came on a grand collection of cow dung and filled a few bags near the new camp. Got in about 4.30 and with Bertie's Coy. Pitched all the tents for the Regt who turned up about 7pm and then had to trench in the dark. Wood halted about a mile further on across a spruit.

Sunday 22 June
Wood left at 6.30.2 Coys 21st and one RE with him to make a fort. We turned out at his rouse and were disciplined for 3/4 of an hour. Heard the Black has been over the Isandhlwana and buried our dead. Recognised Wardell, Dyer and our Sergt Major among others. Division halts today. Church parade 8.45. Bullocks hardly a kick left in them.

Although Isandlwana occurred some 5 months previously, it had always been the wish of the 24th Regiment to bury their own battle dead and this began on 21 June. Wilfred mentions this in passing, but once again makes no particular comment about such a sensitive and poignant occasion. However, his diary was not intended for public consumption and to him this was sufficient to remind him of the great tragedy which had occurred that day. Meanwhile it was time for a day's break from marching and the oxen pulling the wagons were in desperate need of a rest.

As the Division got closer to Ulundi, battle plans began to take shape and the diary entries for the next seven days tell their own story.

Monday 23 June
Trekked some 5 miles to St Peter and Pauls. Joined Woods who are building a fort. F and G Coys up on waggon fatigue. Arrived late in camp, tents pitched for us. Anderson 80th dined with us. Finished up letter home for tomorrows mail. The men who bolted off picquet told off Regimentally by permission.

Tuesday 24 June
Letter to the Mother. Made a short march in advance guard, but had to use the drag ropes both up and down some very bad hills. F & G Coys left at one till all had passed and got in very late. Other pitched our tents for us.

Wednesday 25 June
Letters from home and Wolfe also a Cape Times 16th May from latter. Very bad roads, had to cut a brace of new ones on the side of a hill and then use drag ropes. F & G Coys on picquet had to get over 20 men to make up our number of files. 1st issue of grog. A tremendous row before we started this morning half the Regt wng by various Generals.

Thursday 26 June
Shifted about 2½ miles today ourselves in rear guard. RA Landers and natures shelled and burnt a large military Kraal no opposition. A new system of shelter trench digging brought in today. Warned for an early start tomorrow.

Friday 27 June
Marched 11 miles by staff measurement to Magni Bonium Laargered to Wood's right rear.

Saturday 28 June
Sent out wood cutting. Coys detached to go onto Ulundi A, C, E & G, Upcher to be left in charge of the waggons etc here. A Coy to go under me. F handed over to Farrer per temp. An alarm of an Impi about 2pm when Wood was shifting on, our laarger altered and everything in a great state of confusion. All tents struck. Wood halted and slept opposite our posts in the laarger.

Sunday 29 June
Went on picquet at 9am for 24 hours with orders to allow none of Catchwayos messengers to pass through without orders from Chelmsford. Laarger shifted about 1/4 mile in rear of Woods. No tents pitched for Coys going. Remainder camped near the waggons to be left behind. Left paper of instructions with Upcher.

Monday 30 June
A row on about my picquet sentries not fixing bayonets last night. Marched about 5 miles, very easy ground to work the trenches so had to make them rather high. Prince Imperial's sword sent in to Upcher, also information of 20,000 of an impi at Ulundi. Message sent that as a further test of Catchwayos sincerity in wishing for peace he must let us cross the Umvelosi unopposed. Had to send in a letter to explain about the bayonets.

The exchange of messages between Cetshwayo and the Division is outside the scope of this diary, but suffice to say that Chelmsford had little interest in anything but comprehensive defeat of the Zulus. As they approached Ulundi, Chelmsford did give the impression that he would delay his advance across the White Umvolosi River, but it probably suited him to do so anyway. He also received information about the size of the army being raised against him, but he was more than confident that he had sufficient strength to cope with this. As part of his earlier demand for weapons to be handed in, the Prince Imperial's sword was returned and Russell Upcher took it into safe custody (it was eventually conveyed to Louis' mother the Princess Eugénie). At this stage, Wilfred was more worried that his sentries had not fixed their bayonets while on duty so close to the enemy and he had to explain in writing to his Commanding Officer why such a lapse in discipline had occurred. Given his diligent nature and attention to detail this would have concerned him very much indeed.

By the beginning of July, the Division was in sight of Ulundi and ignoring last minute attempts at mediation by King Cetshwayo, Chelmsford was determined to lay the ghost of Isandlwana once and for all. Most of his successful actions so far were centred on a strong, entrenched laager position with heavy concentrations of rifle fire and mounted infantry in reserve to follow up when the Zulu assaults slackened. Also, casualties in each case were very low compared to Zulu losses. There is no doubt that this was a recipe for success and for this battle Chelmsford wanted to consolidate his strengths and at the same time create a mobile laager, in hollow square formation, to take the fight to the enemy. General Wood attempted to persuade him to keep to the tried and tested formula, but Chelmsford was determined to show that he was capable of beating the Zulus in the open. He was also desperate for the final victory to be his own before he was replaced. At home, both Parliament and the War Office had expressed their severe displeasure over the debacle of Isandlwana, but saw fit to leave Chelmsford in place for the time being. Eventually General Sir Garnet Wolseley was sent out to replace him, but arrived too late to take over for what was to be the closing battle.

By this stage, Wilfred had taken over command of A Company and they were getting close to Ulundi. Inevitably, nerves were starting to fray in some quarters.

Tuesday 1 July
Got off early and had a very hot march through the thorn country to the Umvelovsi. Saw two large bodies of zulus leaving the Kraal estimated at 12 to 15 thow. Laargered up smartly about 4pm. A Coy told off to the guns. A scare about 12 o'clock when all the natives sleeping outside the Abattis came tumbling in their buff and assegais causing tremendous flunk lots of men bolted under the waggons and into the laarger, rifles etc lost in some cases. A Coy stood fast bar Rassel who fired one shot. D Coy came in off picquet.

Wednesday 2 July
The Coy detailed for bush clearing to make a laarger close to Wood. At work from 8am to 6pm improving, cutting, repairing, blocking waggons etc new system of sleeping outside laarger with Abattis some 50yds. To the front scare started by Bengough's men one of who fired a shot at something.

Unfortunately for him, Wilfred was not to take part in the impending action itself and his Coy was allocated the less glamorous, but important, task of protecting the water parties:

Thursday 3 July
Told off for water picquet left 7am. ½ Coy 58th came down a couple of hours later to relieve us. Zulus from Krantz opposite began firing just as they arrived so we staid as reinforcement, one of their men wounded by first volley which drove them back into the bush where they reformed with some difficulty. Ordered to retire gradually fired a few shots, about couple of hours after the mounted men sent out and 9 Pds let drive one or two of them about 150 killed some 25 by our fire according to Leibenrood. Recalled about 5pm for a couple of hours laarger work bashing up the waggons

Wilfred's diary entry for 3 July does not convey the fact that there was a small but significant action that day which could have ended in disaster. As Lord Chelmsford went on to the offensive, he sent Colonel Redvers Buller forward to identify a place on the Mahlabathini plain for the coming battle. Small war parties of Zulu snipers in fact led Buller into a carefully laid trap and he was lucky to escape with only three dead and four wounded. During this skirmish, Lord William Beresford, Buller's staff officer, Captain D'Arcy and Sergeant O'Toole of the Frontier Light Horse were awarded the Victoria Cross for rescuing unhorsed troopers in the face of charging warriors. [6] Captain Leibenrood, 58th

Foot (The Rutlandshire Regiment) commanded the water picquet that day and was one of those wounded.

On the morning of 4 July, the largest force ever to be assembled for any of the battles of the Anglo-Zulu war moved into position on the edge of the Mahlabathini plain. In an attempt to find its weak spots, the Zulu army of some 20,000 warriors began to surround the rolling laager, but against 5,000 rifles, 12 artillery guns, two gatlings and a rocket battery there was no contest. Mounted troops under Colonel Buller provoked the Zulus into an attack and although they bravely charged to within about 25 metres of the British position, they faltered under its heavy fire and their reserves gave no support. Within the space of two hours the attacks petered out and Chelmsford launched his cavalry for a final rout of the retreating Zulu army. Very soon it was all over and as the final humiliation the Royal homestead at Ulundi was put to the torch.

Once again, British casualties were minimal compared to over 1,500 Zulu dead and although Chelmsford claimed this battle as a great victory, the reality is more likely an anti-climax. The back of the Zulu army had been broken and the war was over at last, but Ulundi could hardly be described as a tactical triumph when such a large, impregnable force had been deployed against the remnants of a native army, which had been inexorably worn down since the start of the campaign. Wilfred remembers the day as follows:

Friday 4 July
Bellairs left in command of our Coys and details left behind in laarger. 4 half Coys of ours sent out at reveille to relieve picquets. The column started across soon after daylight firing began soon after 8am very heavy from about 8.40 to 9.15 when they broke and were pursued by the cavalry Mounted Infantry Basutos and shells from the guns which made very good practice. A big Kraal on fire prevented our seeing the fight. Ulundi itself fired about 11am. The column returned about 4.30pm. 1 Offr Lancers killed, about 50 offrs and men killed and wounded (9 killed). Phipps, Milne and Adjt 94th among the latter.

Once again, Wilfred's account of the day contains little of the associated drama or any comment on the overwhelming defeat suffered by the Zulus. There is always great relief at the end of a campaign or battle not only in the victory but also in the realization of personal survival, yet there is no expression here of this quite natural emotion. As this has been a trend throughout the diary one can only conclude that he was by nature a rather unemotional and detached young man, his diary entries in many ways reflecting his own personality, even if they were intended for his own use. Lloyd on the other hand had been able to capture the atmosphere of the whole campaign through the medium of his paintings displaying both a sensitive nature and a sense of humour, which comes across so often in his watercolours.

No sooner was the battle over than the Division began to withdraw to Entonjaneni, or Magnibonium as Wilfred refers to it.

Saturday 5 July
Left about 6am for Magni Bonium as Advance Guard outspanned at old camp for about 2 hours. Being Orderly Officer had to take water parties about a mile and ½ and march fatigues to camp. Went on picquet with the Coy.

Sunday 6 July
A day of rest. Did no fatigues or parades till 5.30 in the evening. Had a good tub and got off letters to the Mother and the other one.

Here the Division stayed for the next five days, due to appalling weather, but once it improved the withdrawal began again. In the meantime, Lord Chelmsford and his staff wasted no time in leaving altogether, now that he had effectively been replaced by General Wolseley who was on his way to take over as soon as he could. Though he was never to command troops in action again, on his return to England Lord Chelmsford was received by the Queen and made a Knight Grand Cross of the Order of the Bath (KCB) and promoted to the rank of Lieutenant General in 1882. In 1884 he became Lieutenant of the Tower of London until 1889, by which time he had been promoted to General. In 1905 at the age of 78 he died suddenly in the middle of a billiards match at the United Services Club in London.

Monday 7 July
Rained very heavily early in the morning. Reveille parade in the tents. Did some sewing after breakfast. Comparison of Defaulters Books 2.30 Inspection of boots for greasing. Started a letter to Wolfe. Went over to Woods camp to see Harry Lovett found that he had been sick in hospital since the 3rd with fever. Sent him my Kaross. Phipps very chirpy. Leibenrood in considerable pain. Padre very likely to have a leg taken off. Chelmsford resigned he and staff going home, also Wood on sick certificate. Heavy rain and wind all day.

So bad was the weather that the morning muster parade had to be held in the soldiers tents, which given their small size would have been most awkward to administer and no doubt became a farce. As far as the soldiers are concerned, if a parade cannot be held properly then it is not worth holding at all. His friend (and possibly his cousin as we will see later on) Harry Lovett was a young Second Lieutenant in the 13th Foot (Somerset Light Infantry) who had missed the final battle at Ulundi as he had been struck down by fever. Wilfred kindly lent him his kaross, which is a coat made from animal skins. Lieutenant Arthur Phipps, who had been Colonel Glyn's staff officer, was severely wounded at Ulundi but was clearly making a good recovery, while Leibenrood was still in some pain.

Tuesday 8 July
Halted today. Wood cutting parties out. Weather cleared. Wrote to Dundee for stores, to the Grandmother and Wolfe. Letters from Father, Mother, Kit and Chumni Palmes. Lovett got enteric. Padres leg to be saved if possible.

Wednesday 9 July
Weather much better but still threatening. Woods column left for Kwamagwasa. on water guard wrote to the Father, Palmes and Birke started one to Kit.

Meanwhile, Wilfred was concerned for the padre who had been injured at Ulundi, but unfortunately it is not clear who this might have been. Concerned as he would have been for anyone sick or injured, as the son of a vicar himself the wounded padre may have affected him more than most, hence the diary entries.

Thursday 10 July
Went back to F Coy. Marched about 9 miles to our old camp ground. On night picquet. Sick doing well except Padre, great fears for him.

Friday 11 July
Left behind the Regt which went in Advance Guard and had to follow up. Kept back by Montgomery to put the waggons through a drift. Kept a long time at the top of a steep hill and outspanned below where we made the roads by about 3.30pm.

Saturday 12 July
Trekked about 8 miles to Upoko camp of 21st June. Told off as Coy on hospital fatigue to strike and pitch their camp. D Coy to return tomorrow for Fort Evelyn to relieve the Coy 58th there. 4 papers from home.

Sunday 13 July
Made up the Mess Bills. Church Parade. Suttler in from Fort Marshall gave him an order for the Mess. D Coy went back to Fort Evelyn. B and C probably to be left at Fort Newdigate. Haircut. Patients in hospital all doing as

well as can be expected. Harry Lovett asleep whenever I went to see him. One man 58th wounded in groin died today, buried in the morning. Fatigue parties off mending the drifts.

Now that the Division was starting to make its way back to Natal, the Battalion could reorganize its Companies once more. Forts Marshall, Evelyn and Newdigate were all based along the route through Zululand, guarded now by Companies from the Battalion and through which they would all be passing at some stage over the next few weeks. There was still however a need to secure them even though the main fighting was now over.

Monday 14 July
Marched at 6.45 for Ibabanango spruit. Spent a couple of hours getting the waggons up the hill. Got in early found the store waggon with the mess order well in before us. Padre operated on today and died some time after of palpitation of the heart. A new dodge of preventing grass fires on by digging a trench round the camp. Shave in that Catchwayo has been murdered and Ohamu proclaimed King instead.

Sadly the padre died of heart failure after his operation and was buried on site.

One of General Wolseley's first tasks was to find and capture the King who was not actually at Ulundi during the final battle. An intensive search took place and eventually on 28 August King Cetshwayo was found at the remote kwaDwasa homestead in the Ngome forest by a detachment of the Kings Dragoon Guards, led by Major Richard Marter. (7) Despite rumours about his murder and that Prince Hamu had replaced him as King, he was in fact taken to the coast and then by sea to Capetown where he was to remain in exile for the next few years while his future was determined.

Tuesday 15 July
Marched as advanced party did a hill and turned up in rear guard. Padre buried at Fort Marshall. Found Watkins waggon there, ordered more stores. Got into Upoko about 1.30. Night picquet Bengough FO. Mail in no letters.

Wednesday 16 July
Got most of the Mess bills paid and handed over about £23 to Watkins for stores. Got a horse for Harry Lovett and got him to work. writing a letter home. Division halted. Expeditions to Isandhlwana and for shooting. Coy for wood cutting came in on account of some firing heard in the distance. Firing found to be by the shooting party. Upcher brought in a guinea fowl dikop and hare.

While the Division took a short break, Wilfred had the opportunity to sort out the Mess administration once again so that the officers could get back to some of their creature comforts. There was a chance for some of the officers to visit Isandlwana now that it was in safe hands, although there was still a nervous edge to the Companies when they heard unexpected shots being fired, fearing some sort of attack by Zulus who may not have surrendered. However, all was well on this occasion.

Thursday 17 July
D & C Coys told off to go to Fort Newdigate with 21st and hospital. A Coy strike hospital tents E & F wood cutting again. Started letters home. The column to go down same way as we came. Road by Isandhlwana badly reported on. Very bad state Rourkes Drift to Helmakaar and also through the thorns.

Friday 18 July
Letter to the Mother. Hospital off to make 4 miles beyond Ft Newdigate tonight. Races fixed for tomorrow. Lysons in last night, says 3 Regts to be left in each colony. A letter to Dawson asking for pay sheets pay lists, ledger book and cigarette papers. Wrote to Wheeler & Coy Dundee for more stores. Hospital and Coys off to Fort Newdigate. Heard that the first lot of stores from Dundee are on the way up. Signed up two months of the Company's accounts.

Saturday 19 July
On a funeral party. Orderly Officer and for picquet. The Upoko races commence at 12 noon. Lt Couter Transport Dept tried my poney not good enough to enter. Went off splendidly. Basuto race grand sport.

Now that the war was to all intents and purposes over, the officers could get back to some of the recreational sports they traditionally enjoyed. Horse riding and hunting were two such activities and the Officers Mess decided to hold an impromptu Point-to-Point meeting, aptly called the Upoko Races. Wilfred could not take part himself as he was the duty officer for the day, so he loaned his horse to Lieutenant Couter, but unfortunately it was not good enough to enter.

Sunday 20 July
Church Parade as usual, being 'off picquet' did not go. Started a letter to Ernest about his coming into the Service. Wrote letters to the Mother, Uncle John and Ernest. Moore and Connolly & Co joined. Fitzgibbon a civilian attached.

Monday 21 July
Made one of a party got up by Parson Smith to go to Isandhlwana borrowed a capital poney from Watkins the suttler. Found little or nothing there worth bringing away, but got a better idea of the fight. Nearly all the bodies buried now, a few black men lying about. Spent a couple of hours there and got back by 5pm. Had a shave when we started that ½ Battn of each 24th to escort a convoy to Magnibonium, but Col came in during dinner with telegram counter ordering and ordering us to assemble at Pine Town previous to going home.

The return route took them close to Isandlwana once more and at last both Wilfred and his friend Lloyd had the opportunity to visit the battlefield for themselves in a party led by Padre George Smith. This gave him a much greater insight into what had gone on and it was a relief to know that all the bodies of the 24th Foot were now buried, or more accurately placed in shallow graves topped with cairns of stones which were later to be painted white. The body of Lieutenant Edgar Oliphant Anstey was later exhumed by his brother Captain Thomas Anstey of the Royal Engineers and returned to England to be interred near the family plot in St John's Churchyard, Woking. He is thought to be the only member of the 24th Regiment killed at Isandlwana to be buried in Britain.

Yet another rumour was started to the effect that many of them would be escorting a convoy back up the route to Ulundi, but this was countered by Colonel Glyn that evening in the Mess tent, who confirmed that they would all going back to Pinetown in Natal prior to travelling home.

Tuesday 22 July
Shifted camp about a mile and ½ to ridge near where Frith was killed. Orders out for Bennets Coy to rejoin from Ft Evelyn leaving tomorrow. Assembly sounded 4.30 for new laarger posts. Trainer reported for . . . the poney.

Wednesday 23 July
Cattle laarger shifted ground prepared for men's sports to come off tomorrow. For picquet. Some zulus came in. Assembly sounded to keep the men out of the way.

Thursday 24 July
On fire picquet DCM at 10am. Sports 11 and after dinner. Won tug of war. Bennets Coy came in from Fort Evelyn. Shave at Fort Newdigate that 2nd Battn to go down to Pine Town with us.

DCMs resumed once more as did sports afternoons. There was also a rumour that their sister Battalion was to accompany them to Pinetown, but in fact they travelled separately and were to stay on in South Africa for a while longer.

Friday 25 July
Orderly Officer. DCM at 10. Letters from Mother and Kenneth. 2 papers from Wolfe. Sent order by Clem the Paymaster for £7 to Standard Bank and cheque to pay for Witness.

Saturday 26 July
On Commissariat Guard. Two Coys 2/24th *Bromhead, Harvey, Mainwaring, Curll and O'Donnell came in with convoy of 100 waggons. 94*th *and Coy Engineers left to establish a new post between Conference Hill and Magnibonium. Latest shave that we go on Tuesday.*

By now, the Battalion had received orders to march to Durban for embarkation back to England.

Sunday 27 July
Shave that Regt starts tomorrow. Upcher, Rainforth and self to go straight down with Col Glynn to go at Accounts. Carrington arranged to leave 94th *Regt to go back to Magnibonium with 58*th*. Note from Dawson to say he placed allowances to mid of June to credit in Standard Bank. Returned receipts. Picquet.*

Monday 28 July
Left Upoko and fetched Princes Kraal. Letter from Wolfe. Shave that I go home to the Depot with Brander. Left B & C Coys at Fort Newdigate to follow on when relieved. Major Winsloe 21st *joined Mess. Carrington left for Magnibonium. Clem to do Adjutant and Connolly C. M.*

Once again, the rumour factory was at work with Wilfred hearing, correctly this time, that he was to be posted to the Depot at Brecon. Captain William Brander, 12 years older than Wilfred, had already been the Depot Adjutant at Brecon and had travelled out to Natal as part of the reinforcements for the Regiment a few months ago. He was Mentioned in Despatches for 'skill and judgement in selecting a landing place and camping ground at the wreck of the steamship Clyde on 4 April 1879.' [8] On returning to Brecon he was to resume the appointment of Adjutant again. Major (Brevet Lieutenant Colonel) R W C Winsloe 21st Foot (Royal Scots Fusiliers) had been severely wounded in the chest at Ulundi and was moving back with the 24th Foot on rehabilitation.

Tuesday 29 July
Left Princes Kraal made Itelezi. Handed mess over to Clements. Williams and Worledge rode over from Kopje Alleine to see us. Harness sent back with his Battery. Met B & C relief on the march.

Wednesday 30 July
Letter to the Mother. For picquet tonight. Made Kopje Alleine. Lunched with the Detachment there.

Thursday 31 July
Rode on ahead of the Regt to see about mess stores up. I found all right at Landtmans Drift sold a lot of them to other messes. Had a bathe in the river. Gonny dined with us.

Having left the main Mess in the hands of Clements for a while, Wilfred went on ahead to Landmans Drift to meet up with the Mess supplies he had ordered from Dundee. Everything was in order and he was able to sell off surplus stores to some other unit Messes. He also took the opportunity of having a good bathe in the river and that evening his friend Gonville Bromhead VC joined them for dinner.

CHAPTER 7

Returning Home

The first two weeks of August saw Wilfred and the Battalion making their way back along the line of communication towards Durban. As they got closer to civilization, the officers were able to pick up on their social life once more, while the soldiers continued to make the best of what they had.

Friday 1 August
Left Landtemans Drift and got in to Dundee before lunch. Rode over to the Fort. Settled up with Wheeler & Co. Dined with Bannister.

Saturday 2 August
Marched 6.45 to old camp between H.M.Kaar and Dundee. Outspanned for Breakfasts and Dinners got in to camp for the night one tree hill about 6pm. Got a lot of papers from Wolfe. Found out stores of our missing when we left Dundee and answered another, lost slaughter cattle sent Connolly back for more. Drum Major absent when we marched off.

James Henry Connolly transferred into the Regiment from the 30th Foot (East Lancashire Regiment) in April 1879, coming out to South Africa as part of the reinforcement programme. He was sent off to get replacements for the slaughter cattle – that which was destined for the cooking pots – but did not return until the next day, having had trouble with his own horse.

Sunday 3 August
Started about 8am. Found the Police under Campbell and Mansel at Helpmakaar also drafts for 2/24th under Cavaye. Coy Mr Hutton 52nd etc. Outspanned for lunch. Trekked on at 2pm to . . . Mission Umsinga. Cavaye and Evans 23rd came to dinner. Connolly turned up from Dundee excuse broken down horse.

Monday 4 August
Started 11am. Made one trek to old camp of 20th January in the hour. Orderly Officer today. Made up the Mess Bills.

Tuesday 5 August
Trekked at 4.15am. Outspanned at the Tugela all waggons across by 12.

Bathed got some stores from a wagon of Turners on its way to the front. Bertie came in from Rourkes Drift and dined.

Wednesday 6 August
Trekked at 4am. Outspanned at the top of the hill for breakfasts. Camped at the Mooi where we arrived at 11.30. Bertie went on to P.M.Burg with Major Dartnell of the Police.

Thursday 7 August
Trekked at 4am to Burrups where we outspanned for breakfasts and dinners. Went on again right in to Greytown leaving one waggon behind. Dined at Mrs Plants. A Coys tents not up men had to sleep under the waggons all more or less drunk in consequence. Heavy rain all afternoon got wet through, tent nearly blown down wet blankets in consequence.

By now the Battalion had reached Greytown and the weather had turned bad once again. A Company had not got their tents up in time so spent a wet night under the waggons, turning to drink for solace! For the officers however, the social round continued and Heaton had dinner at Mrs Plants' house, one of the local settler families he had met on arrival earlier in the year.

Friday 8 August
Rain all morning again. Looked for the blacksmith, could not find him. Ordered some stores from Turners, Men drunk all over the village. Last waggon came in this morning. 17 bullocks lost yesterday. Dined at Mrs Plants. Found the tent broken into when I was away and a lot of Lumsden's stores . . .

This was not one of Wilfred's better days. Discipline was becoming a problem now that the soldiers had little to focus on and they were no doubt making up for lost time when drink would not have been available to them. Also, with the officers away socializing as often as they could, their tents were fair game for pilfering as they were not difficult to break into.

Saturday 9 August
Only about 60 prisoners brought up this morning started at 2pm and outspanned for the night near Umvoli bridge. Holt came into Mess. Crpl Parry told off for C.M. Poney very bad after the wet told him off for 2 days leading.

Sunday 10 August
Started at 7 and marched about 7 miles for finners. Corpl McGuire brought

up and reduced. Went on at 2pm to Stirks spruit. Got a lot of grand eggs.

Monday 11 August
Marched to the far side of the Town Hill that Birtie camped on a piece of very dirty ground. Did some C.Ms at the dinner outspan. Carried the Queens Colour.

As the Battalion marched in and out of new locations it would do so with the Band playing and the Colours paraded. The Queen's Colour recovered after Isandlwana was now a revered icon and Wilfred took pleasure in carrying it when he could.

Tuesday 12 August
Left at 8 and got into camp at Fort Napier by 3pm. Dined at the Royal with . . . Gardiner.

Wednesday 13 August
Staid in P.M.Burg. Kit inspections sales of non effectives etc going on all day. Lunched with Palmes at the Club and dined there to Kennedy with Palmes and Michel.

Thursday 14 August
Got leave to follow the Regt out of P.M.Burg and settle up by Bank acct etc. Col Glynn took over command. Palmes and Rainforth rejoined. Found that Mrs Rugaton has been in town a couple of days unable to visit her.

Now that Colonel Glyn had relinquished command of his operational Brigade responsibilities he took over command of his Battalion once more. Palmes and Rainforth also rejoined in preparation for the journey home.

Friday 15 August
Trekked to Lazenbys for the night out spanning at Camperdown. Note to Armitage about his cheque.

Saturday 16 August
Outspanned at Halfway house lunched there. Met Major Hipe on his way down country. Tried the Drum Major for Drunk and reduced him. Camped near Foxhill.

Drum Majors are traditionally great characters within a Battalion. Always marching at the head of the Band and Drums on parade he was often seen as an ambassador for the esprit de corps of a Regiment and he was usually selected for his military bearing and appearance. He was usually an older soldier and would stay in this appointment for some time as good Drum Majors were few and far between. It was not everyone's cup of tea however and now and then he might go off the rails as was the case with this one. He had obviously tested the patience of his Company Commander and his punishment was to be reduced in rank, but more than likely he would have stayed in the appointment. A few days later, the Battalion was back in Pinetown, some 14 miles from Durban after an absence of about seven months.

Sunday 17 August
Left at 7am got in early to Pinetown. Breakfasted with the Buffs. Went out afterwards and bought liquor and vegetables for the Mess. Letters from the Mother and Kit. Finished one to the former. Dined with Wylde of the Buffs.

Monday 18 August
Tried for leave to Durban not to go until return of accoutrements etc completed. Sold Mr Dodd for £20 to Wylde. Went out into the town for Mess things. Upcher came up and brought a case of phiz. Wet evening.

The Officers' Mess was quickly set up and Wilfred sold his horse, Mr Dodd, as he would not be needing it much longer.

Tuesday 19 August
Mrs Upcher, Gordon and Miss Reynolds came up to lunch and staid to hear the Buffs band. Found Trainer drunk in my tent. Shopped him and got Manley out of the Coy to do my work. Had some of the Buffs to dinner.

As mentioned earlier, Private Trainer had been allocated to Wilfred as his groom and orderly, so he would have spent much of his time in and around his tent. On this occasion drink had obviously got the better of him and for Wilfred to have 'shopped' him implies that he had not been formally punished, but had probably been given some extra fatigues to perform as a timely warning that next time the matter would be taken much more seriously.

The next 10 days were spent on Company administration in preparation for the journey home. Wilfred continued to enjoy the social round as a typical diary entry explains:

Wednesday 20 August
Went into Durban to sell my saddle revolver and odds and ends. Called on the Addisons dined at the Club and went to a dance at Grundy's. Slept at the Club. Harrisons Company arrived from St Johns.

Capt Harrison had commanded H Company which had been deployed to St Johns River on the northern border with the Transvaal throughout the war where they saw little or no action at all.

Thursday 21 August
Lunched with Mrs Gordon and Mrs Upcher. Did some shopping and came out by the 5pm train. Moffat came down to join.

Friday 22 August
Tried Sergt Hurley and Corpl W Jones by C.M. Settled some Mess business and ordered a lot of liquor.

Saturday 23 August
Kit inspection at 12 noon. Letters from the Mother and Kit. Tongue and the two other Companies came in.

Sunday 24 August
Ch Parade at 8.15. Orderly Room at 10. On account of the number of prisoners in the Gd tents. Browne and Davis of the Buffs came in with the remounted men.

Orderly Room at 10 means that because of the large number of soldiers being held in detention, formal disciplinary proceedings had to take place to deal with them appropriately. It would be unusual for this to take place on a Sunday, hence Wilfred's comment on the matter.

Monday 25 August
On a Board in the Buffs Camp at 11. Postponed and self relieved on account of the length it is likely to take. Dunbar got orders to remain with the 2nd Battn.

Just before the Battalion left Durban, an important ceremony took place.

Tuesday 26 August
Parade at 7.30 for the presentation of VCs to Browne and Reynolds. B Coy and heavy baggage sent down to the point by 6.30 train. Went down to Durban by the 2 train and did a trifle of work. Secured some photos and good phiz for Mess in exchange for . . .

A Brigade parade assembled to witness the award of the Victoria Cross to Surgeon Major Reynolds, Army Hospital Corps, for his actions at Rorke's Drift and to Lieutenant Edward Browne, 24th Foot, for his conspicuous bravery in saving the life of a mounted infantry soldier at Kambula, on 29 March. While Wilfred does not mention it in his diary, Private Henry Hook was presented with his VC by General Wolseley at Rorke's Drift on 3 August. This was a particularly significant occasion as it is highly unusual for such a medal to be presented at the actual location where the award was won in the first place. The other medals were presented at a later stage in various locations. Corporal William Allen, Private Frederick Hitch and Private William Jones received their medals from Her Majesty Queen Victoria (albeit on different dates) towards the end of the year, Lieutenant Bromhead and Private Robert Jones were presented with their medals by General Wolseley at Utrecht in the Transvaal before leaving South Africa, while Private John Williams (who had changed his name from Fielding when he joined the Army) was decorated in Gibraltar in March 1880, over a year after the event, by Major General Anderson. [1]

The following day, after four and a half unbroken years service in South Africa, Wilfred embarked on the SS *Egypt* with the $1^{st}/24^{th}$ Foot for the long journey home, while the $2^{nd}/24^{th}$ Foot remained in South Africa for a while, pending their next posting to Gibraltar, so ending the time that these two battalions had spent together.

Wednesday 27 August
Coys taken down to the point in detail last to start E & F who left at 1.30pm. Got all on board and started during dinner. Russelbrook ordered ashore. Mrs Addison came off for a passage refused at the last moment by the Captain. Share cabin with Clements and Spring found light baggage all correct barring the case.

It is not clear who Russelbrook or Mrs Addison were, but in both cases they were not going to sail with the ship on this occasion.

Thursday 28 August
Parade in the morning for Doctor and Muster Messes all shifted passed a Union ship on the way to Natal and one of Donald Curries coasters on a down trip.

Friday 29 August
Passed a few sailing vessels very near one which gave us a cheer.

Saturday 30 August
Got in at Simons Bay about 10. Got leave ashore till the ship sails. Heard of the capture of Catch-em-alivo. Went off in the Port Captains boat and caught the 12 train to Capetown. Put up at the Royal. Went to the . . . etc after Dinner. Met a cracter from the Diamond fields.

Although they had not sailed far, the ship was to dock at Simons Bay for a few days during which time Wilfred took the opportunity to head off for Capetown to catch up with some friends. News was travelling quickly for a change as King Cetshwayo had indeed been captured, but only two days previously. For the next two years Cetshwayo was held in exile in Capetown and in July 1882 he was allowed to travel to England to put his case for repatriation to Queen Victoria. In January 1883 he was granted permission to return to Zululand, which by this time had been broken up into 13 impotent chiefdoms. Cetshwayo had limited authority only and he died a broken man in February 1884 apparently from heart failure, although some allege that he was poisoned. [2]

The 'cracter,' or more accurately the character, from the Diamond fields is a reference to the time that Wilfred spent at Kimberley about three years ago prior to the ninth frontier war

Sunday 31 August
Went out to the Mounts by midday train for lunch. Staid on there. Went to Claremount Church in the evening got some flowers off poor Deanes grave and met Milton.

Lieutenant Richard Deane it will be recalled drowned in a swimming accident on 31 January 1877, despite Wilfred's gallant attempts to resuscitate him. They were close friends and Wilfred wanted to pay his last respects, not knowing if he would ever return to Capetown again. In fact he was to return to South Africa 25 years later after the Boer War, but it is not known if he made the journey to Capetown once more. [3]

Monday 1 September
Called on Mrs Merriman had to make a bolt for the train back and came a sure cruncher on the line. Lawn tennis party at the Club. Van der Byls and a dance at the Castle in the evening did not go to the last.

With the ship due to sail the next day, Wilfred could not afford to be late even if his efforts to catch the last train were extremely painful! Milking every social moment that he could, there was tennis to be played and a dinner dance at the Castle Hotel before reluctantly making his way back on board again.

Tuesday 2 September
Left Rondebosch by the 6.45 train. Breakfasted at Coggills and got on board by 10. The Col and family came off soon after and ship started soon after one.

Once Colonel Glyn and his family were on board, the SS Egypt set sail once again.

Wednesday 3 September
Passed the Fenton which left Cape for England yesterday. Sugden in charge of G Coy. Self transferred to H.

Made 217 miles from Cape point light.

With the Battalion now no longer on active service the Commanding Officer could make some administrative changes to command appointments. William Sugden was moved to G Company and Wilfred was transferred to H Company.

Thursday 4 September
On watch 12 to 4am. Some fine rolling which rather did for some of the ladies.

(486) Made 269 miles.

While Wilfred records that he was on watch, this would have been more as the duty officer rather than as a Naval watchkeeper, an appointment for which he was clearly not qualified. The sea was quite rough that night which upset some of the more gentle stomachs by the sound of things!

Friday 5 September
Same as yesterday. Disposed of the remainder of the Mess stock to the steward and shared out the surplus phiz. Had a morning in the baggage room found my tin uniform case all right. Tub smashed.

(767) Made 251 miles.

The tub to which he refers was a portable bath which got damaged somewhere along the way, either by constant handling during the war or as a result of the rough sea in the last few days. With his customary eye for detail, Wilfred also recorded the nautical mileage covered per day which he would have got from the log book on the Bridge.

Saturday 6 September
Board on the books on board for the troops. Self in orders for librarian to be struck off duty.

(1859) Made 292 miles.

This is an interesting little entry. As a compulsive diarist and prolific letter writer, Wilfred had a great interest in books of all kinds, evidence of which can be seen in the large personal library at *Plas Heaton* today. On this occasion he made sure that he was appointed the ship's librarian for the journey home which very conveniently ensured that he was taken off the duty roster for the duration!

Sunday 7 September
Church parade on the Quarter Deck.

(. . .) Made 266 miles.

Monday 8 September
Made out the Mess Bills for July and August rate about 9/6 per diem for last month.

(1589) Made 264 miles.

Tuesday 9 September
Orderly Officer for Rourstron to pay back one he did for me at Simons Bay.

(1853) Made 264 miles.

So that he could get out and about when at Simons Bay, Wilfred had exchanged a duty officer with Lieutenant Rourstron, but now it was payback time.

Wednesday 10 September
Did some Board of Adjustment work with Upcher in the morning.

(2136) Days run 263 miles.

Thursday 11 September
Cleared off a lot of old letters and receipts from writing case.

(2461) Days run 265 miles.

Friday 12 September
Signed up a lot of Company Accounts.

(2667) Run 266.

Saturday 13 September
Finished the ledgers. A grand midnight steeple chase meeting.

(2921) Run 264. 1st night slept on deck wind having gone round to port side.

To keep themselves occupied, the officers would make up their own entertainment and on this occasion they designed an impromptu steeple chase course, less horses obviously, no doubt using the Mess furniture as makeshift jumps. As they were sailing northwards into the tropics the weather was starting to get hotter and they would sleep on deck whenever they could as the cabins got very stuffy.

Sunday 14 September
Church parade as usual. Afternoon in saloon tub. Run only 248 miles. Stokers choked off by heat (3169).

Monday 15 September
Finished off the small books. Run 265 (3434)

Tuesday 16 September
Very hot bad headache. Egyptian Rollers entertainment a great success. Run 243 miles. Took some medicine and slept below a regular vapoor bath nearly 200°. (3477)

Wednesday 17 September
Ran 240 miles asleep got up on the drop of anchor at St Vincent . . . (3917).

After sailing almost 4,000 miles, the ship came into port at Cape St Vincent, Portugal where they stayed for a few days to replenish.

Thursday 18 September
Came into St Vincent about 9am. News of capture of Catchwayo gone home via Zanzibar and out here before us. The Serapis in on the way to Natal to take up the 58th and Lancers. Sent us a lot of papers. False report of death of Rushe's brother in America. Australian mail vessel and one of Union both outwards came in to coal. Also a White Star homeward. (4005).

There was the usual run ashore and the opportunity for a cricket match.

Friday 19 September
A lot of fellows ashore for a cricket match. Spring brought me off a few nuts etc. Upcher and Bennett for shooting. Dance on board the Australian she coaled up all night. Union boat cleared out.

Saturday 20 September
Australian sailed at day break. More cricket ashore, our team beaten again. Some of the telegraph men came off and dined with the Colonel and Captain on deck. Mrs Morshead very seedy. Reynolds and Bourne looking after her.

The next day they set sail with Mrs Chiquita Emily Charlotte Morshead, wife of Captain Arthur Anderson Morshead, 1st/24th Foot, in a poor condition, the sea journey no doubt having affected her during the latter stages of her pregnancy. Wives and children were able to accompany their husbands on overseas postings, but the facilities provided for them were quite rudimentary. Part of a barrack room would be quartered off for their accommodation (which is why Service houses today are still referred to as Quarters) and when the two battalions began the invasion, the families remained behind at Greytown and Pietermaritzburg and some were even as far away as Capetown.

Sunday 21 September
No church parade. Left about 11am. Mrs Morshead very ill child stillborn.

Monday 22 September 879
Run 207 miles. Mrs Morshead died.

Tuesday 23 September
Run 215 miles. Mrs M buried. Col Glynn read the service (422).

There were complications with the birth of their daughter Rosalie and sadly, Mrs Morshead died the next day and only 10 days from getting home. Both were buried at sea and Colonel Glyn took the service. [4]

The journey home was not without its problems and one of the ship's screws was damaged. News was also received about the 2nd Battalion's next posting to Gibraltar which, unknown to him at the time, Wilfred would be posted to in two years time.

Wednesday 24 September
Ran 210 miles. Had an 11 o'clock tub in the saloon. Another piece reported to be off the screw. 2nd Battn reported ordered to Gib. Major Winsloe paid his Mess Bill. (632).

Major Winsloe, 21st Foot, who was being invalided home, still had to pay his Mess bill which Wilfred would have scrupulously prepared!

Thursday 25 September
Upcher paid Mess Bill. Ran 193 miles. Got up some sail in the afternoon. (826)

Friday 26 September
Wind changed sail taken in again. Passed several sailing vessels. Sighted Madeira about breakfast time. Lost it about 4pm. Run (203) (1029)

Saturday 27 September
Calm. Run (207) (1236)

Sunday 28 September
Church parade as usual sea like a billiard table. Met a West coast mail (223) (1459).

The weather in the Bay of Biscay was traditionally rough, but it did not stop the young officers enjoying themselves with some high jinks after dinner!

Monday 29 September
Ran 229 miles into the Bay. Found it rolling. Great ructions on deck after dinner passing men in through the smoking room windows. Took Moffat's Mess Bill.

Tuesday 30 September
Muster parade at 10am. Met a lot of steamers in the morning. All books to be returned to the library. Had an afternoon among them. Ran 282 miles (1920).

With only a few days to go, the ship had to be tidied up and all library books returned. Ever the book-worm, Wilfred enjoyed an uninterrupted afternoon browsing amongst them all.

CHAPTER 8

ON EXTENDED LEAVE

The homecoming of a troopship from overseas was always an emotional moment, particularly as some of those on board had not seen the shores of England for almost four years and so many of the 1st/24th Foot had been left behind forever on the battlefield of Isandlwana. On the morning of 2 October 1879, 37 days after leaving South Africa and a journey of almost 6,000 miles, the SS *Egypt* and the 1st/24th Foot arrived at Portsmouth harbour and although the ship had sailed up the Solent in the early hours of the morning, the decks would have been packed with soldiers straining for their first glimpse of home once more.

Wednesday 1 October
At the books and games all morning. Board on them at 2pm. Letters to Major Dunbar and home. Run 233 miles. To do 178 miles. (2153)

Thursday 2 October
On watch 12am. Saw start light at 12. Pilot on board 5.30 alongside the wharf by 10am. Inspected by the Duke. Uncle Arthur down to meet me. Disembarked 2pm. Marched to Gosport addresses flags etc Letter to Mother dined at Coy the Regt.

HRH The Duke of Cambridge, Commander in Chief, Armed Forces, came on board to inspect the Battalion and see the renowned Colours (which Mrs Glyn had made a gallant effort to repair during the journey home) prior to the Battalion disembarking that afternoon. Then they marched to Gosport where a civic reception had been arranged. The next day there was another round of inspections and speeches when the Duke of Cambridge expressed himself well satisfied with the fine appearance of the battalion, despite the ragged state of their clothing. Wilfred found this all a bit ' soapy ' – another indication of his reserved nature, perhaps.

Friday 3 October
Orderly Officer. Sorted out the baggage of deceased officers. Uncle Arthur came over in the morning. Clean shave cut myself all over the shop. The Duke inspected us at 5pm. Made a very soapy speech. Letters to Major Dunbar and Ernest. Dined at the India Arms.

The possessions of those officers – and although he does not mention it, the soldiers too – were brought home to be claimed by the next of kin and Wilfred took it upon himself to sort this out on their behalf. He also had the opportunity for a decent shave, but made a mess of it by all accounts!

Saturday 4 October
Parade at 11am. Mess meeting afterwards. Letter from the Mother. Most of the fellows on leave. Birth of son and heir to J.G.O. Letter from Evelyn.

On several occasions over the next two months Wilfred makes reference to someone by the initials J.G.O. only. Unfortunately it has not been possible to find out who this person was, but it is assumed to be a male relative or friend as they spend quite some time together during his forthcoming leave.

Sunday 5 October
Church parade at 10.45 in the recreation room. Went over to Southsea pier in the evening.

Monday 6 October
Got a note from Mrs Bateson that ought to have arrived Saturday night. Mrs Smedley bothering around in Barracks did not get out till late. Went to call on Mrs B. Dined at the officers horse and booked in at the Blue bills.

Mrs Smedley was the widow of Sergeant John Smedley who had been the Regimental Master Tailor and who had been killed at Isandlwana. She had come to collect her husband's effects which clearly took Wilfred some time to sort out, before calling on Mrs Bateson and then out to dinner.

Tuesday 7 October
Had a great hunt for a letter to Vesey Holt. Telegram the mother coming down tomorrow.

Wednesday 8 October
At work about the men's furloughs. Dined at an hotel at Portsea. Letter from Uncle John to send cheque for £20. Staid late and slept in Portsmouth. Clothes from Flight.

Furlough means a leave of absence from military duty and Wilfred had to work out the detail for his Company. The period of leave would vary from a weekend pass to anything up to six weeks and on this occasion they were all being granted an extended leave to compensate for the time they had been away from home. The soldiers would be paid in advance and a record kept of their leave addresses so that there was at least a point of contact if any did not return when the furlough expired; a common occurrence then as it sometimes still is today! They would also be fitted out in some civilian clothing, akin to the famous demob suits after the Second World War, so that they went away from the Barracks reasonably well dressed.

Thursday 9 October
Furloughs again and paying out. Letter from the Mother. Can't make out whether she is coming or not. Boots down from Stokes. Letters to Mother, Uncle John, V Holt & Co. Met old Causeland.

Dinner in the Officers' Mess was usually a fairly formal occasion at a set time with the Mess members expected to be dressed in a suit or military Mess Dress uniform. However, it was not compulsory to dine in and quite often the young officers in particular would prefer to dine out at a club or hotel where they could entertain their wives or girlfriends, ladies not being able to enter the Officers' Mess unless by express permission of the Commanding Officer and only then on very special occasions. This strict Victorian protocol continued in many Regiments well into the middle of the 20th century, but today the Officers' Mess is far more relaxed and egalitarian.

Friday 10 October
On a District C. M. until about 3. Called on the Batesons and got late for Mess dinner. Dined at the Star. Went across the water. Orders down for Browne and me to go to the Depot.

Wilfred and Lieutenant Edward Browne VC were being posted to the newly established Regimental Depot at Brecon in South Wales. Outside the natural coal belt of the Valleys, Brecon was – and still is today – a small agricultural market town nestling against the northern slopes of the Brecon Beacons and on the junctions of the rivers Usk and Honddu, from where it gets its Welsh name of Aberhonddu, meaning the mouth of the River Honddu. For many years travel to and from this fairly remote area was by horse drawn coach, but the industrial revolution saw the opening of the Brecon and Merthyr Tydfil Junction Railway in May 1863. The benefits were twofold; the rapidly increasing population of the South Wales coalfields and iron and steelworks rejoiced in cheaper agricultural products from the Breconshire hinterland (including Welsh lamb) while coal, lime and manufactured goods became more economically available among the northern towns and farmsteads. In due course another unforeseen amenity manifested itself, in the shape of tourism. [1]

Saturday 11 October
Prosecuted on a Regt CM for Clements. Spent all the afternoon trying to fit clothing on furlough men.

Sunday 12 October
Leave off church parade. Called on the Batesons and dined at the Pier Hotel with Palmes.

Monday 13 October
Harrison off to Depot. Last of men for furlough got away. Ordered a new trunk. Sent heavy baggage and a lot of non-effective kit away. Dined at Mess.

Tuesday 14 October
Cleared up all over the town. Saw Causeland in town again. Every one clearing out for leave.

Wednesday 15 October
Left from Gosport road for the Depot with Browne. Got down to Brecon about 10 and put up at the Castle.

Situated on the Watton close to the town centre, the Barracks in Brecon opened in 1873. With the advent of the new railway line which came up from Merthyr over the eastern shoulder of the Brecon Beacons (but sadly to become a victim of the Beeching cuts in 1962) access to the town was now much easier but it still took a full day's journey to get there from Gosport, having to change trains several times on the way. Accommodation in the Officers' Mess was limited and as they arrived late in the evening it was more convenient for them to stay at the Castle Hotel, which forms part of the original town wall defences. His heavy baggage had gone on ahead by freight train but still took four days to get there.

Thursday 16 October
Went up early and turned Curtess out of bed. Lofed about all day no difficulty about leave. Browne left by afternoon train for Scotland.

Apart from unpacking his kit, there was little for Wilfred to do at the Barracks, so the Depot Commanding Officer let him go on his well deserved period of leave one day earlier.

Friday 17 October
Baggage in early. Col Cotton let me go off in anticipation of leave. Managed to get off by 1.10 train to Shrewsbury. Where met Keith and staid the night.

Saturday 18 October
Left 12.10 after shopping a lot at Steads. Lunched at the Chester refreshment room. Saw Aunt Margaret Mary and Daisy before leaving Shrewsbury. Mrs Grantham did not turn up. Saw Aunt Rachel at Rhyl. Met at the station by the Father. Kit Hugh and Gilbert great goings on in the village guns bonfires speeches by Bennett illuminations and Deputation from the village. Mrs Wynne came down to meet me.

On 18 October he arrived home at the vicarage at Bettws yn Rhos in North Wales to much joyous celebration. Although living in only a small parish the Heaton family was very well known in the wider community and the whole village turned out to greet their hero on his return from what had become the famous Zulu war. His sister Kit and brothers Hugh and Gilbert were instrumental in organizing a homecoming to remember and no doubt the party went on well into the night. The rest of the month was to be very leisurely as he relaxed and unwound with most of the time spent either at home or socializing with friends.

Sunday 19 October
English service in the morning said away afternoon. Called up at Ffarm turned over my kit and wrote this up for last week or more.

His comment on the English Service, a Said Eucharist in the morning, refers to the fact that Welsh was very much the first language in North Wales at the time and the Services would vary between the two languages on Sundays. He would normally have gone to Church again in the afternoon, but it was important enough to him to record that he was away in the afternoon that day and did not attend. He also took the opportunity to bring his diary up to date as life had been quite hectic since coming home again.

Monday 20 October
Drove over to Gwrych with the mother and Kit. The Lewis's of Llanfair and Oldfields came to tea.

The next few weeks of his diary reflect the fact that the social round was very much part and parcel of the landed gentry at the time. *Ffarm, Coed Coch, Gwrych* and *Havordunos* (recently destroyed by fire) were the country homes of his relatives and friends, where meeting regularly for lunch, afternoon tea or dinner in the evening was quite normal, as was calling on neighbours for drinks. A gentleman would carry a number of calling cards (about the size of a credit card) on which his name and address would be printed and these would be left on the hall table of the homes he had visited so that the hosts could call on him in return at a later stage.

Tuesday 21 October
Went over to Rhyl with the Father. Saw cousin Joe Lovett, Uncle and Aunts Charles. Fred, Rachel and Ellen. Dined at Coed Coch.

If Joe Lovett was his cousin, then it is possible that Second Lieutenant Harry Lovett, 13th Foot, mentioned in his diary entry on 7 July, was also a relative of his, but he makes no reference to the fact at the time. From his perspective of course, there was no reason to do so as he never intended that his diary would be published for public consumption.

Wednesday 22 October
Father and Mother to confirmation at Llanddulas. Letter from Sillery. Billiards with J.G.O at Ffarm. Forwarded to Clements letter from Dr Hughes and one for Hunter. Walked with Kitty to call on Mr and Mrs Roberts. Brynflunich

Thursday 23 October
Went to Coed Coch to lunch with Kitty. Drove on to Havordunos with the Father and Mother to dine. Met Bishops, Mr and Mrs Roberts Parson and Morgan also. Slept there. Sent off . . . watch to his father.

Friday 24 October
Found Kit out hunting with Mr Wynne. Hounds having met at C.C. Letter from Margaret Lovett. Letters to Margaret Lovett. Mrs Joe Lovett. Ernest send tomorrow.

Saturday 25 October
Got at destroying a lot of old letters. Aunts Rachel and Ellen Heaton over from Rhyl. Uncle Charles sent £2–2- for photos. Dined at Coed Coch. Letter to Armstrong about change in plans.

What these change of plans were is not made clear. It could either have been to do with his social activities or possibly a further extension to his leave as the next day he wrote to Colour Sergeant Wadley, 24th Regiment, presumably the Orderly Room Sergeant at Brecon, on this matter. Also, being a prolific letter writer there was clearly a large number that he did not consider worth keeping so he had them destroyed; a great pity for us in hindsight as they may have contributed much to study of the social dimension of his life and times.

Sunday 26 October
Welsh Service in the morning. Letters to Cr Sergt Wadley and Austin about my leave. Also Dalby and Cooper making appointments.

Monday 27 October
Billiards with J.G.O. in the morning. Drove the grandmother afternoon. Mrs Thompson came in to tea.

Tuesday 28 October
Left at 7 with Kit for Abergele lunched at Rugby. Got to Hanslope Lodge about 3. Went down to stay with a farmer name Farnborough.

Wednesday 29 October
Breakfasted with Farnborough again at the Lodge. Wedding went off very well at Hanslope Church. About 30 to Breakfast. Walked to call on a Mrs Wiseman afterwards.

With his sister Kit he had been invited to a wedding at Hanslope, a small village just north of Newport Pagnall, although he does not tell us who was actually getting married. It was a small affair judging by the numbers who sat down to the wedding breakfast, but as most of the guest rooms at the Lodge were taken up by other people he and Kit stayed nearby with a farmer friend.

Thursday 30 October
Called on the Watts of the Park in the morning with Duer and Lingard Monk and walked with the girls in the afternoon. Ball at Newport Pagnall.

It seems as if the wedding festivities continued somewhat as there were two Balls to attend in the local area, which went on into the small hours by the sound of it!

Friday 31 October
Got to bed about 5.30 lofed around walked with Dawkins and Duer in the afternoon. Went 13 miles with them. Kit and Frederica Watts to a Ball given by a Mrs Hoare.

Saturday 1 November
To bed about 4am. Left about 11. Kit average tired no grub to be got at the Railway station. Reached Westminster about 3pm. Had to go out to buy some shirts having no clean ones left. Went down to Paddington station to fetch a new greatcoat.

It is no surprise that his sister Kit was 'average tired' after several late nights and having travelled this far from North Wales they had decided to spend a few days in London where they arrived in the mid afternoon. The next day they went to Church twice, once to Westminster Abbey in the morning (a long service by the sound of it) and then to another service at the Church in Margaret Street which is just off Oxford Circus. After that it was on to his cousin's house for tea. For the aristocracy it was quite usual to have a house in London and a residence in the country.

Sunday 2 November
Church in the Abbey in the morning a service some miles long went for a walk in St James Park afterwards. Called on Mrs Puzzi with Kit and went to church in Margaret Street. Cousin Henry had two of the boys in to tea.

Monday 3 November
Went after breakfast to secure tickets for the Merchant of Venice at the Lyceum. Had a short time in the stores buying things. Went with Kit and Evelyn to lunch at Ecclestone Square. Walked back and went to the Aquarium with Eve. All three and Cousin Mary to Lyceum.

His sister Evelyn had joined them in London for the weekend and they all decided to take in a show, deciding upon The Merchant of Venice which was running at the Lyceum Theatre. Wilfred put her on the train home from Victoria Station the next day and then went on to sort out a few domestic matters including some personalized stationery. There were also some more friends and relatives to visit during the week.

Tuesday 4 November
Saw Eve off at Victoria. Found Aunt Fan when I came back. Walked with her to the Langhams to see Uncle Arthur and wife had not arrived. Met Aunt Em and Little Bell. Went to see about writing paper at Rodrigues also . . . at Aide's left watches at Whites in Cockspur Street. Took Kit to Clapton saw Uncle Tom . . . and Mrs Duval. George Buckmill and Frank Crawley to dinner. Also one of the Furns

Wednesday 5 November
Went down to Norwood with Kit. Called on some Crawleys and lunched with Aunt Fan. Got back to Westminster in time to drive up to Hampstead with Constance Powell. There to stay.

Thursday 6 November
Went with Kit and Constance over to Buckhurst Hill to lunch. Home for dinner. Nellie back from Cromer.

Friday 7 November
In to town after breakfast. Saw Gardiner. Lunched Criterion bought tub Photoed hair cut etc. Went to Strand Theatre with Kitty and Constance to see Madamme Favart.

After lunch at the Criterion, an exclusive Gentlemen's Club to which he would not have been permitted to take his sister, he then went on to purchase a tub, which was a portable bath. This was to be delivered to his home in North Wales in due course. En-suite plumbing had yet to become common place and in many a home a bath was taken in a tin tub in front of the fire in the kitchen with hot water being poured in from the stove. In Wilfred's case, the tub would have been more sophisticated, perhaps in decorated enamel, installed in a separate bathroom and it is assumed that the hot water was delivered by the house staff.

That evening they had one more trip to the theatre, this time to see Madame Favart at the Strand Theatre before beginning the journey home the next day, stopping off for lunch at Oxford on the way.

Saturday 8 November
Left by the train from Paddington. Lunched with Jack Buckhill at Oxford. Came on by the afternoon train to Lendginton.

Sunday 9 November
Couple of Services. Went to see Hester Davis an old Bettws servant.

Monday 10 November
A couple of Parsons over to lunch one Willie Craven. Walked part of the way home with one of them. Several people to high tea had a great job with a pair of ducks.

Tuesday 11 November
Drove into Shrewsbury lunched at Col Edgehills. Went to an evening feed at a certain Turners.

Wednesday 12 November
Called on a few people in the morning. Left by an afternoon train for Belmont.

Thursday 13 November
Went into Oswestry with Harry house hunting found none. Dancing lesson in the evening. Cousin Heaton returned from shooting near Conway.

It is interesting to note that house hunting was as difficult then as it can be today; also the fact that Wilfred was taking dancing lessons as well. To be able to dance properly was a great social asset, given the number of such functions that he would usually attend and it was the ideal manner in which to make the acquaintance of eligible young ladies who were otherwise closely chaperoned.

Friday 14 November
Oswestry again with Cousin Heaton and Harry. Photoed by Mr Tardy and lunched at the Souquet Villes.

Formal portraits were very fashionable in the Victorian era, but photography was not that well advanced at the time so it would be quite usual to go to a professional photographer to have this done.

Saturday 15 November
Walked over to Chirk in the morning and call at Fernhill in the afternoon.

Sunday 16 November
Church at Wellington with Harry lunched at Fernhill walked home and had a smoke with Major Leadbitter who called after Church.

Monday 17 November
Walked to Ebnal Lodge in the morning took out Dick who had a fit. Caught the 1.6 train and fetched Abergele at 3.45. Drove home Queen in the small trap.

It is not clear who Dick might have been, but it is assumed that he was a relative or friend who was confined to a nursing home. Queen however was the name of one of his horses who pulled the trap he used to get home to Bettws from the station at Abergele.

Tuesday 18 November
Letters to OC F Coy 1/24th Browne about leave, Ellis Price, Uncle John Heaton, Rodrigues with cheque for £3 for Stationery. Millard cheque for £4–11–6 for tub. Flight to send in account. Smith Chester silk socks. Called on Mrs Oldfield and went after lunch to Coed Coch with the Mother and Kit.

The Battalion was never far from his mind, however and he took this opportunity to catch up on some administration. He also settled up his bills with the stationer and for the bath he bought in London a fortnight previously.

Wednesday 19 November
Letters to Armstrong to stay here on his way home from London. Ernest about concert. Coltman about books. Drove the mother over to lunch at Havordunos.

FOR QUEEN AND COUNTRY 125

Thursday 20 November
Went to Plas Heaton to lunch with Kit. Met Mr Tidmanner a geologist. Mrs Salisbury and Mrs Guise, Misses Lewis and another from Coed Coch at the station and the Misses Batison. Uncle Llewelyn asked me to go and stay Saturday next to Tuesday. Lettr from Curtess and a couple of receipted Bills from Rodrigues and Millard.

Friday 21 November
Met at Coed Coch. Kitty went out with Mr Wynne. Letter to Curtess about Champagne. Flight to pay part Bill. Stokes to pay Bill. Billiards at Ffarm in the afternoon. Wrote Smith and Son for socks. Dined at C.C. take J.G.O with me.

Saturday 22 November
Went over to St Asaph to stay with Uncle Llewelyn at Bryn Polyn. Miss Knowles, Miss Mainwaring, and Miss Dawn came over to spend the afternoon.

Sunday 23 November
Very wet day went to Henllan Church in the afternoon with Uncle Ll and put in to Garn afterwards.

Garn is the name of the country house belonging to his Uncle Arthur and which is just outside the village of Henllan, close to *Plas Heaton*. Being a particularly unpleasant day, he and his uncle Llewellyn went to tea there after church.

Monday 24 November
Went with Aunt Amy to call on the Caleys of Llanerch, the Birches, Blews, Mainwarings, Griffiths, Chambers and Plas Heaton. Only Blews and Aunt Em in.

Tuesday 25 November
Went driving with Uncle Ll to the meet at the Travellers Inn above Mostyn and saw a lot driving about the lanes. Dined at the Deanery.

By driving, Wilfred is referring to a pony and trap. Given the narrow lanes in that area it was probably quite entertaining.

Wednesday 26 November
Came to Rhyl by 3 trains from St Asaph. Called at Uncle Freds. Uncle and Aunt Arthur came over from Garn to stay till Saturday.

Thursday 27 November
Wrote letters to Brander Curtess, Halliday, Moore and Ernest and Margaret Lovett. Walked down to Llanddulas with Uncle A.

Friday 28 November
Hounds met at Llanfair, walked up the hill above Garthewin with Uncle A and saw a lot of them. Went up to tea at Coed Coch in the evening. Wrote to Maclardy to order photos.

The countryside of Denbighshire lends itself well to hunting and Wilfred would have ridden out to hounds quite regularly. On this occasion he was just a spectator with his uncle Arthur and one can only guess what his reaction would have been to the present bitter divisions in the country over its future.

Saturday 29 November
Uncle Arthur and Aunt Fanny went to stay at Bryn Pullyn. Took some of us down to Abergele the Father being there on a tax commission. Went to see Margaret our old nurse.

Being a local magistrate, Wilfred's father would have sat in as an arbitrator on tax disputes and inquiries and the family took advantage of a day trip to the coast at Abergele while he was working there to see one of the family nurses. Members of the staff often became very close to the household and were always well looked after when they retired.

Sunday 30 November
Same as any other Sunday at home.

Monday 1 December
Drove to Llandulas with Granny and Kit to call on the Misses Chambers home for lunch played some Billiards at Ffarm after.

Tuesday 2 December
Some Billiards. Walked with J.G.O to call at Garthewin after lunch and down to Abergele for a concert. Supped at Mrs Phillips and walked home by ¼ past 12.

Wednesday 3 December
Letters to Uncle Charles and Fred, Breander, Lincoln and Bennett and Coleman. From V Holt & Co Uncle Fred, Aidie's receipt and photos from Faulkeners. Drove Kit and Granny to Llandulas to call on the Misses Chambers.

Thursday 4 December
Drove with Kitty to Dolwen in time for lunch, went up to skate on Galltfaenan pool afterwards and drove home by 8.

Friday 5 December
2 Llandulas Chambers and Miss Davis daughter of Jenkin came over from Llandulas to scate at Coed Coch, found the ice covered over with a couple of inches of water.

Saturday 6 December
Gilbert and Arthur Lovett over from Tudor Owens went up to Coed Coch and found some splendid ice joined by the Miss Batesons.

Sunday 7 December
English service in the afternoon gave Mrs Wynne an arm to the Gwyndy gate. Went down to the pool and found whole in very fair order.

On the face of it, much of what Wilfred did during his extended leave period might sound somewhat mundane, compared with the extensive travelling that a young bachelor might do today on his time off. Apart from a week in London he spent much of the time at home in North Wales, but he had just spent a good four years away from home so this was the ideal opportunity to restore his personal contacts. Social interaction was an important part of his way of life and he would have derived as much pleasure from this as others might have done travelling abroad.

Monday 8 December
Borrowed a pair of skates from JGO to take to C.C. this afternoon. Went to skate on the Coed Coch pool after lunch. Lord Cochrane's sisters turned up for an hour. Kit and I dined there, she slept I changed and walked home.

Tuesday 9 December
Miss Loughton (Tip) came over from Garthewin to spend the day and slept. Went up to skate found a lot of water on the ice.

Wednesday 10 December
Miss Loughton went back. Old Llewis Llanfair buried walked part of the way there with the father. All went out for a turn after Dinner. Thaw set in.

Thursday 11 December
Cheque from Dunbar for Mess Bill. Wrote to him, Clements, V Holt & Co

and Trust The Batesons came to lunch walked part of the way home with them Rooked JGO out of 1/-

Friday 12 December
Off by the 10.30 train. Mother and Miss Loughton came as far as Chester. Got to Marlborough about 9.30.

Saturday 13 December
Hunted for skates no success. Lunched in Hall. Went down to the Butts and RO extinguished by Ernest. Dined in Common room with Richardson.

Sunday 14 December
Had the boys down to breakfast and then Chapel thrice. Bright preached in the morning. Had supper and a talk with Busby.

By the middle of the month, leave was over and it was time to go back to work.

Monday 15 December
Left 8.20 for Brecon where arrived 5.30. Room all ready.

Tuesday 16 December
Took over a lot of accounts from Brander and drove in the afternoon with him to call on the James' and Morgan's.

Wednesday 17 December
Got leave off the marching out parade and did some work in the morning. Played Billiards at the Castle in the afternoon.

Life was not particularly busy at the Depot in Brecon at this time of the year and as the Christmas round of social activities was beginning at home, by the weekend he was back in Denbighshire for a Ball:

Thursday 18 December
Got up at 6 breakfast ½ past and left by 7.15 train. Tried to fetch Denbigh via Wrexham and told had to stay 5 hours at Hope J. Got in about 8 dined and dressed at the Bull and drove home to Garn with the Griffiths. Made acquaintance with Lady Guise at the Ball.

Friday 19 December
Went up to Galltfaenan in the morning and to Khinmel from Garn drove home nice squash of six in the village fly.

Galltfaenan was another country house just outside Henllan and the village fly was a horse drawn carriage which they packed to capacity on the way home.

Saturday 20 December
Very bad with a cold and did not go anywhere.

Sunday 21 December
Took leave of church for cold. Mrs Wynne came in to say goodbye and promise introductions for Brecon.

Having gone down with a cold over the weekend, most of the time was spent at home. Mrs Wynne called in to give the details of some more social contacts in and around Brecon to make his stay there as comfortable as possible.

Monday 22 December
Left with Granny by 10.30 train. Lost mid Wales train from Oswestry had to come round Hereford way lost last train there and had to put up at the Green Dragon.

Tuesday 23 December
Got away by 9.20 train to Brecon in time for inspection of recruits for 5th and 30th Regts. Did an afternoons work in the Orderly Room.

Although Christmas was upon them, there was still work to be done. Not all recruits trained at the Depot were for the 24th Regiment and on this occasion men were being sent off to the 5th Foot (Northumberland Fusiliers) and 30th Foot (Lancashire Regiment).

Wednesday 24 December
At work all day getting documents ready for the 1st Battn.

Thursday 25 December
Took the men to Church in the morning. Went to some ponds near for skating which was very bad. Dined with a Mr Overton.

Unfortunately for him, Christmas was to be a rather mundane affair, spent on duty in Brecon. Quite naturally he would have gone to church on Christmas Day and he took the soldiers in the Barracks to St Mary's Church in the centre of the town which is only a short distance from the Barracks. This was – and still is – the parish church of Brecon. What is now Brecon Cathedral did not receive its elevated status until 1923; before that it was the Priory Church of St John.

Friday 26 December
Called on Mrs Browne in the afternoon and stayed a bit in the Castle Billiard room. Wrote letters to Major Dyson, General Cavaye, Halliday etc dined with Cyril Flower the Liberal candidate for next election.

There was no Hunt for him to follow this year so after some billiards at the Castle Hotel he decided to write to Major Dyson and General Cavaye whose sons Edward and Charles respectively had been killed at Isandlwana. Lieutenant Francis Halliday was a young friend of his who had come out to South Africa as part of the reinforcement party. Cyril Flower, later Lord Battersea, was successful at the next election and became the Member of Parliament for the Borough of Brecon from 1880 to 1885. Much revered in the Borough there is a stained glass window dedicated to his memory in St Keynes Chapel in Brecon Cathedral. Some 30 years older than Wilfred it is interesting that they should have dinner together on Boxing Day; no doubt one of the introductions put his way by Mrs Wynne the previous week.

Saturday 27 December
Called Mrs Calrow. Very wet day.

Sunday 28 December
Went to Church. Too wet to go out in the afternoon.

Monday 29 December
Called on the Overtons with Sugrue. Ordered some things in the town. Went up to the Castle.

Tuesday 30 December
Had some Billiards. Dined at Twighams with the Major. Harrison came back from leave.

Wednesday 31 December
Caldwell up to town early. Saw Sugrue off to Ireland. Dinner a miserable farce. Austen and the Colonel down from leave by last train.

While New Year's Eve was not as exciting as he would have liked it to have been, the year of 1879 which had started on the sun drenched beaches of Durban and finished at home on the rain swept hills of the Brecon Beacons was one of the most dramatic in Wilfred's life. In later years, as we are about to find out, he was to see active service in Burma with the 2nd Bn South Wales Borderers (as the 24th Foot became in 1881), get married to Florence Church in India, and then return to South Africa at the end of the Boer War as a Colonel on the Reserve in command of one of the newly formed Garrison Regiments. He was also to provide valuable reserve service during the First World War, but the experiences of the Zulu Wars left an indelible impression upon him, being a year he would not forget for the rest of his life.

For the Zulu nation, 1879 was a catastrophic year. A totally unjust war had been instigated against them to further a British policy of confederation, to subdue the Zulus in order to repress apparent widespread black resistance to expanding white domination and to prevent the Zulu blocking British progress and ultimate expansion. There was also personal prestige to be gained for the High Commissioner and for Lord Chelmsford, and it would eventually free Zulu manpower resources for labour hungry European commercialism. The disaster at Isandlwana was a totally unexpected setback, but thereafter the defeat of the mighty Zulu army was inevitable. Following their success at Ulundi, the British Government had abandoned Zululand as fast as it could and attempted to rid itself of any responsibility by dividing the nation into 13 separate and impotent chiefdoms. In 1887 Zululand was declared British territory and 10 years later it was annexed to Natal. [2]

As far as the Zulus themselves were concerned, a once proud and mighty nation was humiliated and turned in on itself to fight a bitter and ignominious civil war. As the discovery of gold followed that of diamonds, the Zulus eventually joined the other indigenous tribes in the much needed supply of cheap labour. This only served to widen the gap between black and white, leading to the ugly period of apartheid and the divisions that still exist between tribal factions in South Africa today. Most significantly, confederation, the prime catalyst for the whole invasion, was never achieved.

13 School of Musketry, Hythe Kent 1880 Wilfred (with drooping moustache) is seated on the left of the third row looking directly at the camera and just below the left elbow of the officer standing with his arms folded. (Royal Welsh Museum collection)

14. Line Laying Course, School of Military Engineering, Chatham Kent 1880. Wilfred is seated second from the right, looking away from the camera. (Line laying was for communication purposes, with the advent of the electronic field telephone). (Royal Welsh Museum)

15. The Heaton brothers in 1897. Rear L – R: Ernest, Wilfred (then age 43) and Bernard. Front L – R: Gilbert and Kenneth. Bernard was the last survivor who died in 1959. (Richard Heaton's collection)

16. Colonel Wilfred Heaton, as a reserve officer in 1911 at the age of 57, from a family oil painting. (Author's collection)

17. Mrs Florence Heaton, from a family portrait, painted in 1911 at the age of 41. (Author's collection)

18. The parish church at Henllan, where Wilfred was a warden for some years and where many of the Heaton family are buried. (Author's collection)

19. (Foreground centre). The final resting place of Wilfred and Florence Heaton, Henllan parish church cemetery. (Author's collection)

CHAPTER 9

THE LATER YEARS

While it is possible that he may have missed the breathless pace of life associated with active service, the next 15 months were to be a period of relative stability for Wilfred. Stationed at the Barracks in Brecon, he was involved in the training of drafts for the battalions and he had the opportunity to travel home to North Wales on a more regular basis to visit his family and friends. There was also his own training to consider. The Army Instruction Manual was in the process of being changed, whereby all Regimental instructors and Sergeant Instructors of Musketry were to be abolished. [1] In future the musketry instruction of the recruit and trained soldiers would be carried out by the officers commanding troops assisted by their subaltern officers, so Wilfred attended a course at the School of Musketry at Hythe, Kent. This he successfully accomplished with a 1st Class pass and he subsequently attended a course in military engineering at Chatham. Then, on 4 September 1880 at the age of 26 and after 6 years service he was promoted to the rank of Captain. (With a touch of journalistic licence no doubt, his obituary was to record that ' – *at the age of 24 . . . (he) was gazetted to the rank of Captain and at that time was the youngest Captain in the British Army.'*) [2]

The following year was to see a significant change in the Regimental title as part of the Cardwell Reforms. On 1 July 1881, the Regiment received orders that the time honoured numerical titles of the infantry of the line were to be discontinued officially and that all regiments were to be known henceforth by territorial titles only. [3] Battalions were to be amalgamated by pairs, some into forced marriages with a strange partner, but fortunately the 24th Foot already had two battalions and so they became the South Wales Borderers, the title coming from one of the militia battalions under command of the Brigade Depot since 1873. However, by common practice and precedent, the Regiment still continued to use the familiar title of the 24th, but all links with Warwickshire were finally abandoned, save for a Regimental March, 'The Warwickshire Lads' which continues to be played on occasions. By this time, Colonel Glyn had handed over command of the Battalion to Lieutenant Colonel William Dunbar and by 1882 had been promoted to the rank of Major General, having commanded the Brigade Depot at Brecon. He became an honorary Lieutenant General in 1887 and in 1898 was appointed to be the Colonel of the Regiment. He died in 1900 at the age of 69.

Having stayed on in South Africa for a while after the Zulu Wars, primarily because of transportation problems, the 2nd Battalion eventually made their way to their next posting of Gibraltar. As part of the regimental re-adjustment, Wilfred was cross posted to 2 SWB which he joined in Gibraltar on 25 April 1882, where he had first joined the Regiment 7 years previously. By coincidence, the following day was to see his friend William Whitelocke Lloyd resign his commission, having decided that he no longer wished to pursue a military career. Lloyd returned to Ireland for a while, where he married Catherine Anna Mona Brougham on 25 June 1885. Over the next 5 years they were to have 2 children, a daughter and a son, and William continued his painting in a professional capacity, working for some time as an artist with the Peninsular and Orient Steamship Company.

On 6 August 1882, Wilfred was on parade for the presentation of new Colours to replace those lost at Isandlwana. The Queen had intended to present them herself, but it was not possible to send a Colour Party back to England for this purpose. On her behalf the Governor of Gibraltar, Lord Napier of Magdala, made the presentation with the Colours proudly bearing the silver wreath of immortelles at the head of the pike, a unique honour bestowed upon the Regiment by Her Majesty to commemorate the immortal defence of Rorke's Drift and all those members of the Regiment who had lost their lives at Isandlwana and during the Zulu Wars. During this time, the Battalion was under orders for its next period of active service and one week later set sail for the East Indies, arriving at Bombay on 1 September 1882. Initially intended for the Afghan frontier, there was a change in the operational situation and the Battalion was diverted to Secunderabad, where they stayed until December 1883. In February 1884, the Battalion moved to Madras. While there, Wilfred took a detachment of 150 men for duty on the Andaman Islands, where the 2nd/24th Foot had been awarded five Victoria Crosses in 1867, while another Coy was detached to Malliapuram on the Malabar coast, where it was involved in suppressing an uprising among the Moplahs, Mahomedan fanatics. [4] It was during this time, on 25 November 1885, that Wilfred was promoted once again, this time to the rank of Major. He was now 31 years old and had seen 11 years service, the majority of which had been spent overseas.

By the summer of 1886, 2 SWB was back on active service again, this time in Upper Burma. Since the accession of King Theebaw in 1878, relations between England and Burma had grown strained. With an uncanny similarity to the situation in South Africa prior to the Zulu wars, the King was issued an ultimatum, which he rejected and an invasion followed.

This was rapidly successful, but with the King overthrown and the country annexed, it now had to be conquered. When 2 SWB reached Rangoon in May 1886, the insurrection was in full swing. The first company, under Wilfred's old friend Major Clement, was the first to deploy and six weeks later Wilfred followed up with his company. For the next two and a half years, the Battalion was involved in low level terrorist warfare, during which they lost one officer and nearly 60 NCOs and men, mostly it has to be said by disease. In June 1888, Colonel Upcher (Wilfred's former company commander in Zululand) left the Battalion to retire on half pay and as his replacement, Lieutenant Colonel C J Bromhead was not due to arrive until the end of the year, Wilfred had the distinction of commanding the Battalion for six months, over-seeing the end of operations and the re-deployment back to India. The Battalion was not sorry to quit Burma for Calcutta, where it landed on 14 November 1888 prior to proceeding up country to Bareilly. For this period of active service, Wilfred was awarded the Burma campaign medal, with the date bars of 1885– 87 and 1887–89.

For the next three years the Battalion was to enjoy a period of stability in India and it was during this time that Wilfred was to experience a special change to his own personal circumstances. Enjoying a good social life with the expatriate population, he soon met Florence Church, the young 19 year old daughter of William Thomas Church, who worked for the Indian Civil Service and who came from Coleraine in Northern Ireland. Florence was obviously swept off her feet by this 35 year old bachelor major and on 8 July 1889 they were married at the aptly named Church of St John in the Wilderness at Bareilly. [5] Attended by his brother officers and friends, the service was conducted by the Rev W J Burdett, chaplain of Rorkee, who officiated for the chaplain at Bareilly and the official witnesses were Florence's father and Wilfred's younger sister Evelyn Jones Bateman (she had married Herbert Jones Bateman two years earlier) to whom he was very close. His parents unfortunately were too old to make the long journey from England. During this period, the Battalion spent time in both Bareilly and Rhaniket in the North West Province and it was while the families were moving up country to Rhaniket for the cooler summer weather that Wilfred and Florence's first child, Wilfred John was born on the 5th June 1890, two days before his own father's birthday. Florence was travelling on horseback when she went into labour, which may account for the fact that Wilfred John was born with curvature of the spine, with which he was to be afflicted for the rest of his life. [6]

At the end of 1890, the Battalion moved to Allahabad, where, on 31 January 1891, Lieutenant Colonel C J Bromhead handed over command to Lieutenant Colonel William Penn Symons. Hardly had he done so than his brother Gonville, who had also been serving with the Battalion, died of typhoid fever on 7 February at the age of 46. The following telegraph was received from the Commander in Chief on this sad occasion.

> *Please let all ranks of the South Wales Borderers know how much the Chief sympathizes with them in the loss of Maj Bromhead VC, who behaved with such conspicuous gallantry at Rorke's Drift and so well supported the reputation of his distinguished Regiment.* [7]

Gonville Bromhead never married, so the descendants of this famous hero are through his brother Charles.

The sadness of the year was to continue for Wilfred and Florence following the birth of their daughter Florence Catherine on Wednesday 1 July 1891 at Allahabad. It is not clear whether there were complications at the birth, or if she contracted fever, but tragically she died three weeks later on 22 July. She was buried the following day in the military cemetery at Allahabad, where her name is inscribed on the Regimental memorial.

The Battalion remained in India until October 1892 when it moved to Aden for a year's posting. Earlier in the year however, Wilfred and Florence had returned to England. Florence was pregnant once more, but she was not enjoying good health and with the pressures of an invalid son and the loss of their daughter, time at home in a better temperate climate was considered a more compassionate posting. [8] Also, Wilfred's father, the Reverend Hugh Edward Heaton, had died on 19 December 1891, so there were important family matters to attend to, now that he had inherited the estate at *Plas Heaton*. This home posting was justified by the safe delivery of their third child, Hugh Edward, named in memory of his grandfather, on Thursday 7 July 1892 at *Plas Heaton*. [9] Hugh was baptized the following month in the parish church at Henllan and one of his godfathers was Colonel Edward Browne VC, who had been with Wilfred during the Zulu wars. Wilfred would have been employed on a staff appointment of some nature until his Battalion returned from Aden in November 1893. The next two years were spent at Portsmouth Command and then in November 1895, 2 SWB took up residence in Badajoz Barracks, Aldershot.

While at home for the birth of his son in the summer of 1892, Wilfred made an interesting discovery. Tucked away in the drawer of a desk was a parcel wrapped in brown paper which was marked 'Flag remains found at *Plas Heaton* 1865' and which was thought to be a portion of the Colours of one of the battalions of the Royal Scots Regiment. Understanding only too well the importance and significance of

Regimental Colours, Wilfred wrote to the commanding officer of the 2nd Bn The Royal Scots, Lieutenant Colonel Frederick de Lamare Morison, telling him of his discovery. He very quickly received a reply in which the commanding officer told him that when he had first joined the Battalion at Manchester in 1861, a Colonel Heaton who lived near there, seemed to have been a very popular man in the Regiment, often dining at the Mess. He asked the senior officers to his place to shoot and perhaps he may have had the Colours given to him. [10] The officer in question is likely to have been Wilfred's uncle, Lieutenant Colonel John Richard Heaton, who was serving with the 37th Foot, or Royal Hampshire Regiment, at the time. Unfortunately, little light can be thrown on this story and it is highly unlikely that the officers of the Royal Scots would have given away part of their Colours, however hospitable. It is more likely to have been part of a banner from a bagpipe, fanfare trumpet or music stand, which would have looked quite similar. There is also the remotest possibility that it could have been a remnant of the 1843 Colours of the 37th Foot, which were replaced, by coincidence, in 1865 and this was a case of mistaken identity; this theory cannot be verified, unfortunately. Anyway, Wilfred despatched the remnants to the Royal Scots and there the matter ended.

It was during his tour of duty in Aldershot with the 2nd Battalion that Wilfred's career as a regular officer came to its end and on 30 September 1896 he was retired on half pay as a Lieutenant Colonel. The system of retirement on half pay was a manning control mechanism which enabled the army to stand down officers for whom there was no longer full employment, or to provide vacancies for more junior officers to achieve promotion. Being on half pay meant he could be called back to the Colours (ie. reinstated as a regular officer) if the manning situation so required it. This process has now been replaced by the award of a permanent pension, subject to age, on retirement and a fixed period of time on the reserve of officers, normally up to the age of 55. At the age of 42, Wilfred was still quite young and the elevation to Lieutenant Colonel was not only a reward for his valuable service to date, but recognition of the rank in which he could be employed if he had to be recalled at a later date. As was the custom, Wilfred was dined-out by the Officers' Mess and he presented an impressive mantle-piece clock in a mahogany case to mark his retirement. Made by Herbert Blockley of St James's, London, there is a brass plate on the front which reads ' – *Presented to the Officers 2nd SW Borderers by Major W Heaton 1896.*' As an amusing aside, Wilfred received an apologetic letter from the Commanding Officer, in which he berated the officers serving at the Depot in Brecon, whose farewell telegram to be read out at the Dinner in Aldershot arrived too late! [11] The clock has survived and now sits, appropriately, on the mantle piece in what is known as the 24th Room in the Officers' Mess of the Headquarters 160 (Wales) Brigade in the Barracks at Brecon where his career had started 129 years ago.

Although he had officially retired and there was the estate farm at *Plas Heaton* to manage, he had not given up on the aspiration to continue military service in some form or other. He had lobbied his commanding officer for a militia command appointment and in 1901 his wish came true. The Boer War in South Africa had identified the need for additional troops for security duties in garrison towns to take the pressure off the regular battalions and on 27 August 1901 he was appointed to command the 4th Battalion The Royal Garrison Regiment which had formed up at Warley. Wilfred nearly missed this golden opportunity as he had been involved in an accident of some nature, the details of which are not clear, but sufficient for the War Office to write ' – *I trust that your smash up will not keep you away from duty beyond a fortnight.*' [12] Fortunately all was well and he joined the Battalion on 13 September 1901.

The Battalion strength was about 400 initially, made up primarily of reservist soldiers called back to the Colours and it rose to a peak of just over 1,000 a year later. After a short period in Aldershot, the Battalion embarked at the Royal Albert Docks, London in May 1902 for service in Malta where they were to spend the next two years. Families were able to accompany the Battalion, but Florence Heaton remained at *Plas Heaton* and Wilfred would return home on leave from time to time. Whilst in Malta, he was promoted to the rank of Colonel in the Reserve of Officers on 18 October 1902 and in April 1903 he had the distinction of parading the Battalion for the visit of His Majesty King Edward VII on his visit to the island. The summer of 1904 then saw Wilfred back in South Africa once more where his Regiment had responsibility for security of the Harrismith District. He remained as commanding officer until 10 February 1905 when he left on retirement. In his farewell message, he thanked all ranks for their good conduct and cheerful performance of duties, which he said had made his term of command a pleasure. He wished them all good luck and success in the future and hoped that they would have occasion to look back with pride on their time in the Regiment. Not long after his retirement the Regiment began disbanding, its role no longer being required. [13]

It was now some 25 years since the Zulu wars, but the memories were still with Wilfred and he wanted a Zulu shield and assegai as a keepsake of that memorable time. In his two visits to South Africa he had not been able to acquire one so in 1905 he made contact with Harriett Stokes who he had met while at Harrismith and who lived at Kwamagwaza,

Melmoth, Zululand. While she was unable to find one from the 1879 period, she did manage to get one used in the subsequent Zulu troubles. From the battle of Ulundi and the abortive British political settlement of September 1879, to the final collapse of Zulu resistance to British rule, in September 1888, the Zulu nation had been embroiled in civil war. In 1902, the Zululand Lands Delimitation Commission was set up to demarcate sufficient land for native locations and to set aside the rest for grants to whites. (14) The continuing unrest, exacerbated by this commission and which culminated in the Bambatha rebellion in 1906, affected the local white settlers, thus limiting their freedom of movement. Wilfred had sent the money for his shield in advance, but there was a considerable delay in despatching the goods. Before long however, Harriett made contact.

> *Dear Col Heaton,*
> *You will be bothered about the cheque and the war shield. Forgive me, this late Zulu rising took place almost at our gates and we were thrust into laagers etc, all the South African routine – and then the Bishop of Zululand sent me home.* (15)

Despite the upheaval and pressures in Zululand at the time, the shield and assegai eventually arrived. For many years they were to reside at *Plas Heaton*, but more recently they were donated to the South Wales Borderers Museum in Brecon by his grandson, Mr Richard Heaton.

After his tour with the Royal Garrison Regiment, there was a brief respite from military duties and Wilfred was able to turn his attention to his responsibilities at home. He was both a Justice of the Peace and Deputy Lieutenant for the county of Denbigh and he seldom missed any such meeting. There was also the inevitable matter of Church politics to contend with. *Plas Heaton* sits equidistant between the villages of Henllan and Trefnant, although the former has been more closely associated with the estate and many of the Heaton family are buried at the church there. On one occasion, the vicar of Henllan, the Rev H Humphreys wrote to Wilfred to ask politely, but pointedly, why he was attending the Sunday morning service at Trefnant and not at Henllan, which he thought was more appropriate for the local squire. Wilfred pointed out that he had long attended the service at Trefnant with both his father, who had been a vicar in the area and his uncle, because the service was in English. (16) The first language at the time in North Wales was Welsh and as the staff at *Plas Heaton* were predominantly English, they could not follow the service at Henllan. All was to resolve itself amicably however and in later years, Wilfred became the vicar's warden at Henllan.

As the storm clouds of the First World War began to gather, the martial spirit in Wilfred called for a return to uniform once again. He was almost 60 by this stage and his request for overseas service with the Colonial Office was sympathetically turned down, but he was made of sterner stuff than that, and he came back to the Reserve as part of the postal censorship unit. It was the responsibility of regimental officers to censor their soldiers' mail to ensure that there were no references to troop dispositions or operational plans and so on, but in addition there was a military organization which was responsible for censorship in general. Quite separate from the Royal Engineers postal section, there were a number of Base Army Post Offices (BAPOs) and it was to one of these that Wilfred was attached. He would randomly check soldiers' mail to ensure regimental officers were doing their job and he would liaise with the civilian postal authority to ensure that any military mail posted in civilian boxes would be handed over to the BAPOs. A number of these were set up in France, but Wilfred worked out of London and while there he had the distinction of a visit by HM King George V in November 1917, who commented most kindly on the work being done.[17]

It was while working with the censorship unit that he met with a serious accident. One night in 1918, while crossing a road in London he slipped and fell heavily. He was found unconscious and taken to the Queen Alexandra's Hospital for Officers suffering from concussion and was diagnosed as having fractured his skull.[18] Much against his wishes, he was unable to return to work and finally had to accept full retirement. However, his energy did not desert him and as would be expected from a man of his standing in the local community, he was the president of the Vale of Clwyd tennis club, a commissioner of taxes (as his father had been before him), a Governor of Howell's School in Denbigh, and a member of the Denbighshire Infirmary Committee. Also, during its existence, he was a prominent member of the Denbigh and District Habitation of the Primrose League and he took part in the development of the Vale of Clwyd toy industry, which his sister Mary had founded.

Despite all this, he paid a price for his heavy fall and his health was not the same again. In September 1921 he was enjoying a holiday at the Beechwood Hotel, Harrogate in Yorkshire when he was taken ill with gastro-enteritis. His wife Florence and his son Hugh were sent for and he seemed to make some improvement, but a few days later in the early hours of Thursday 29 September 1921, almost 25 years to the day that he retired from 2 SWB, he died suddenly from a heart attack.[19] The funeral took place on the afternoon of Monday 3 October at Henllan Church, preceded by a short service at *Plas Heaton*, conducted by his brother the Rev Gilbert Heaton. The coffin, made of plain oak and bearing the inscription ' – *Wilfred Heaton, Colonel, died September 29th, 1921*' was brought into the church on a bier borne by the estate workmen and was covered by the Union Flag with his sword resting on the top. The church was full to capacity with his many friends, former Regimental colleagues and representatives from the various organizations with which he had been involved. Unfortunately, his eldest son Wilfred John was unable to attend as he was working with the Colonial Service in Accra on the Gold Coast and could not get back in time for the service.

He was buried in a simple grave in the cemetery at Henllan and when his wife died 12 years later she was interred with him. The inscription upon their gravestone reads:

> *To the dear memory of*
> *Wilfred of Plas Heaton,*
> *late Colonel 24th Regiment,*
> *who died 29th September 1921 aged 67*
> *and of Florence his wife*
> *who died 20th June 1933, aged 63.*
> *Until daybreak and the shadows flee away.*

So passed away one of the Regiment's most loyal and hardworking officers who had always held true to the ideals and standards upon which the reputation of the 24th Regiment of Foot and the South Wales Borderers was built. He had been present during the most momentous year in the Regiment's illustrious history and his diary of 1879 is a valuable record for posterity in that respect. He served three Monarchs of his country for well beyond the normal age of retirement and it was only ill health that prevented him from serving for longer.

He was also instrumental, by virtue of his own Welsh background, in helping to establish the strong national identity and flair of the Regiment today.

Epilogue

In the 300 years of glorious history of the 24th Regiment of Foot, now the Royal Regiment of Wales, there have been many noble and memorable events. However there is one date that comes easiest to mind in the memory of its serving and former members – the 22nd January 1879. In the space of 24 hours, the Regiment had suffered one of its heaviest ever defeats at the hands of a native army equipped only with shields and spears; nine officers and soldiers had been awarded the Victoria Cross, this country's highest possible accolade for bravery in the face of conflict; two officers had given their lives in an attempt to save the Queen's Colour and in the heroic defence of Rorke's Drift the Regiment had ensured immortality in the annals of British military history. It comes as no surprise therefore that the Regiment has perpetuated this honour and glory by commemorating this hallowed date each year in many different ways, even when on active service. There have been military parades, tattoos, concerts, dinners, exhibitions and of course Church services where in moments of quiet reflection those who gave their lives are respectfully remembered.

On Sunday 18 January 2004, the Brecon Branch of the Regimental Comrades Association marked the 125th anniversary of the Battle of Isandlwana and the Immortal Defence of Rorke's Drift with a commemorative service in Brecon Cathedral. Despite the wintry conditions, the Dean of Brecon, the Very Reverend John Davies welcomed a very large congregation consisting of representatives of other Branches of the Regimental Association from across South Wales, civic leaders, serving and former members of the Regiment and many families and friends. The Regimental Band of the Royal Welsh Regiment sounded a moving fanfare as the Branch Standards processed into the Cathedral and were laid up at the Altar by the Dean for the duration of the Service. During the Service, the Colonel of the Regiment Major General Christopher Elliott CVO CBE made the following tribute:

> 'Next Thursday, on the 22nd of January, we recognize one of the most significant dates in our proud and noble Regimental history – the 125th anniversary of the Battle of Isandlwana and the Immortal Defence of Rorke's

Drift. On that date I, along with the Regimental Secretary, will represent the Regiment at the commemorative events of the Battlefields in Natal. While the origins and causes of the Anglo-Zulu Wars are no doubt questionable there is no question at all about the acts of bravery and heroism of the 24th Regiment of Foot on the 22nd January 1879, to whom all credit is due and to whom we pay tribute during this annual commemorative Service.

The act of war is never glorious and we can only imagine the horror of the Battle of Isandlwana, when all but six men of the 1st Battalion the 24th Regiment of Foot lost their lives in that unexpected assault by the mighty Zulu army of King Cetshwayo. Individual bravery however was seldom in doubt, even when the outcome of Isandlwana was inevitable and the tenacity, resourcefulness and courage displayed by the defenders of Rorke's Drift later that day, against seemingly impossible odds, epitomizes all that was best in our Regimental forebears, of whom we are so proud.

This outstanding courage was recognized by the award of seven VCs, this country's highest possible accolade for bravery, to B Company of the 2nd Battalion the 24th Regiment of Foot and by the subsequent award of the Victoria Cross to Lieutenants Melvill and Coghill who gave their lives in their attempt to save the Queen's Colour of the 1st Battalion during the Battle of Isandlwana. We pay tribute also to the 20,000 brave Zulu warriors who took such heavy casualties during the fighting of that day. Although they suffered greatly after the war of 1879, it is one of the most enduring and redeeming facts that the Zulu nation does not bear a grudge nor any animosity towards the British people. As an expression of that reconciliation the 121st South African Infantry Battalion, made up predominantly from the Zulu people, is affiliated to the Regiment today.

After the war, Her Majesty Queen Victoria asked to see the Colours of the 24th Regiment of Foot at Osborne House on the Isle of Wight on their return to the United Kingdom. She placed a floral wreath of Immortelles upon the Queen's Colour and decreed that this should be carried for evermore by the Regiment, in honour of all those who had given their lives during the Zulu Wars and to commemorate the immortal defence of Rorke's Drift. This distinction is unique throughout the British Army and it is one which we acknowledge with respect and appreciation.

Today Isandlwana stands quiet and empty save for the memorials and the cairns of white stones which mark the graves of our Regimental forebears, while Rorke's Drift has become a small village community. However both sites still proudly preserve the memory of that historic day with great dignity. In the same way Brecon Cathedral is guardian of the noble heritage of the 24th Regiment of Foot witnessed by those Regimental Colours and the Wreath of Immortelles now laid up here in the Havard Chapel and the many *brass and marble memorial tablets on the Cathedral walls. The main east window behind the Altar was installed soon after the Zulu wars in a joint project between the Regiment and the town of Brecon as a tribute to all those who had lost their lives in that conflict.*

This heritage continues today and The Royal Regiment of Wales is proud of its close links with Brecon and is honoured to be able to commemorate this unique event each year in this Cathedral by kind permission of the Dean.

I am also privileged to be able to welcome to the Service today Mr Douglas Bourne, grandson of that most famous Colour Sergeant Bourne who fought with such distinction at Rorke's Drift and Mr Richard Heaton, grandson of Lieutenant Wilfred Heaton who served in D Company of the 1st/24th Regiment throughout the whole of the campaign and who was present at the final battle of Ulundi in July 1879.

We also appreciate the excellent turnout, not only by Regimental comrades but also by the people of Brecon, represented by the Town Mayor, Councillor Iuean Williams, which is a most fitting tribute to the memory of our distinguished predecessors, 125 years ago. Sadly our 1st Battalion is not represented today as the Battalion is deployed on operations in Iraq where I am sure our young Welsh soldiers are displaying similar fortitude in trying circumstances which brings to the fore all the advantages of our Regimental system.

In recognition of the outstanding bravery of our Regimental forebears and in respect for the Zulu warriors who also lost their lives, I would ask you to stand, please, for a moment of silence. Greater love hath no man than this, than a man lays down his life for his friends.' [1]

How proud Wilfred would have been to have known that his own grandson Richard, who had only just recovered from a hip operation, had made the long journey from Henllan to Brecon to read the Lesson during this special Service and to pay tribute to the Regiment in which his grandfather had served with such distinction. In the Havard Chapel, just off the north transept of the Cathedral, hang the Colours of the 24th Regiment which were in service during the Zulu war and which Wilfred was so proud to have carried on a number of occasions. The symbolism of these Colours, now secured in special cases to preserve them for posterity, is in many ways a fitting epitaph to all those who served with the Regiment and who gave their lives in that war of 1879. [2]

Wilfred's final epitaph is perhaps contained in a letter he received from the Commanding Officer of the 2nd Battalion South Wales Borderers (24th Regiment) in 1896, when he wrote on behalf of his officers to thank Wilfred for for his service to the Regiment and for the clock that he had presented to the Mess on his retirement:

' – you may be sure that those yet to come will know of your name independently of any inscription which may appear on your present.' [3]

Wilfred Heaton has not been forgotten and through the pages of this book it is hoped that those yet to come will continue to know of his name. May he rest in peace.

Notes

The following sources of reference are acknowledged.

Chapter 1
1. There are extensive records relating to the Heaton family, known as the Heaton Manuscripts, which are held at the County Records Office, Ruthin, Denbighshire. Extracts are quoted by kind permission of the resident Archivist, Ms Jane Brunning. Subsequent references to the Heaton manuscripts are made by their file reference and number (DD/PH). The family lineage is compiled from the Family Bible, unpublished primary source property of the Heaton family and reproduced by kind permission of Mr Richard Heaton.
2. Wilfred Heaton's school records are published by kind permission of the Honorary Archivist, Marlborough College, Mr Terry Rogers.
3. Exam results were gazetted formally by the War Office. See DD/PH 148.

Chapter 2
1. J. M. Brereton. *A History of the Royal Regiment of Wales ($24^{th}/41^{st}$ Foot) 1689–1989* (1989). Page 4.
2. Ibid. Page 42.
3. Ibid. Page 44.
4. C. T. Atkinson. *The South Wales Borderers 24th Foot. 1689–1937* (1937). Page 174.
5. Brereton. Page 120.
6. Atkinson. Page 272.
7. Jack Adams. *The South Wales Borderers* (1968). Page 82.
8. Norman Holme. *The Noble 24th. Biographical Records of the 24th Regiment 1877–1879.* Page 205
9. Philip Gon. *The Road to Isandlwana.* (1979). Page 78.
10. Ibid. Page 11.
11. See various documents on Lt William Whitelocke Lloyd held by the SWB Museum.
12. Holme. Page 208.

Chapter 3
1. The reign of King Dingane was to have a major impact upon the relationships between Boer and Zulu, which in turn had a signifi-

cant bearing on the causes of the Anglo-Zulu war. For more detail see Peter Becker. *Rule of Fear – the life and times of Dingane, King of the Zulu.* (1964).
2. Adrian Greaves. *Isandlwana* (2001). Page 60.
3. Edmund Yorke. *Rorke's Drift* (2001). Page 9.
4. Jeff Guy. *The Destruction of the Zulu Kingdom* (1982). Page 46.
5. Ian Knight. *Brave Men's Blood* (1990). Page 36.
6. Donald Morris. *The Washing of the Spears.* (1965). Page 256.
7. Knight. Page 49.
8. *Anglo Zulu War Historical Journal* Volume 1. Article on the causes of the Anglo Zulu War of 1879. Page 2.
9. Morris. Page 294.
10. John Laband. *The Rise and Fall of the Zulu Nation* (1997). Page 210.
11. Holme. Page 10.

Chapter 4
1. Holme. Page 18.
2. The criteria for the award of campaign medals is explained in more detail in the introduction to Norman Holme's book. Pages 1–5.
3. These are the views and experiences of the author, having spent a full career as an army officer. A more detailed account of life in an Officers' Mess may be found in the book *Officers Mess – life and customs in the Regiments* (1973) by Lieutenant Colonel R J Dickinson.
4. John Laffin's book *Tommy Atkins – the story of the British Soldier* (2004) makes numerous references to the Duke of Wellington's views on the standards of the British soldier.
5. Holme. Page 8.
6. Adrian Greaves. *Isandlwana* (2001). Pages 72–74.
7. For more detail on the career of General Smith-Dorrien see the book by A J Smithers. *The Man Who Disobeyed – Sir Horace Smith-Dorrien and his Enemies.* (1970).
8. Holme. Page 212.
9. *Narrative of the Field Operations connected with the Zulu Wars of 1879.* HMSO 1881.
10. For further commentary, see Michael Glover's book *Rorkes Drift – A Victorian Epic* (1998).
11. Morris. Page 385.
12. Ibid. Page 448.
13. Ron Lock and Peter Quantrell. *Zulu Victory* (2002). Page 246.
14. Morris. Page 449.
15. History of the British Courts Martial. Extract from information available on the world wide web. www.stephen-stratford.co.uk.

16. Laband & Thompson. *Field Guide to the War in Zululand and the Defence of Natal 1879.* (1983). See chapter on classification and depiction of sites, beginning at page 25.
17. Morris. Page 427.
18. This story is recounted in *The Historical Records of the 24th Regiment.* Page 226.
19. For more detail on the subject of flogging in the British Army , see chapter 9 of John Laffin's book *Tommy Atkins – The story of the British Soldier* (2004).
20. Details of the postal system were provided by Mr Simon Fenwick, historian to the Postal and Courier Service.
21. Laband & Thompson. Page 60.

Chapter 5
1. Adrian Greaves. *The Curling Letters of the Zulu War* (2001). Page 114.
2. Knight. Pages 119–121.
3. Morris. Page 477.
4. *Anglo Zulu War Historical Society Journal.* Volume 9. Article by Ian Knight on the battle of Kambula. Page 3.
5. Knight. Page 107.
6. Morris. Page 501.
7. These figures are taken from the rates of pay quoted in the Regulations for Field Forces in South Africa 1879. (DD/PH 140).
8. Extract from a letter by William Lloyd to his sister Selina. Held by SWB Museum. L1948.9.
9. See various records on soldiers letters held by SWB Museum.

Chapter 6
1. Historical Records of the 24th Regiment. SWB Museum. R46.50.
2. Morris. Page 452.
3. Extract from a letter by William Lloyd to his friend Mr Bulmer La Terriere. Held by SWB Museum. L1957.39.
4. Private Trainer made a statement after the Battle of Isandlwana. See Norman Holme. *The Noble 24th*. Page 194.
5. Ian Knight. *With his Face to the Foe.* (2001). Page 280.
6. Morris. Page 564.
7. For detail on the capture of Cetshwayo, see Ian Knight. *Brave Men's Blood.* Pages 186 – 192.
8. Holme. Page 8.

Chapter 7
1. Morris. Page 589.
2. See Jeff Guy's book *The Destruction of the Zulu Kingdom* (1979). Pages

204–209.
3. Wilfred Heaton returned to South Africa again in 1904 as Commander of the 4th Battalion Garrison Regiment.
4. See the Records of the 24th Regiment. As the commanding officer, Colonel Glyn was empowered to conduct funerals while at sea.

Chapter 8
1. J. M. Brereton. *The Brecon Beacons National Park* (1990). Page 58.
2. Guy. Page 246.

Chapter 9
1. See the Army Instruction Manual 1883. DD/PH 147.
2. This is an extract from Colonel Heaton's obituary, which was published in the *North Wales Pioneer* newspaper on 6th October 1921. DD/PH 344.
3. C. T. Atkinson. *The South Wales Borderers 24th Foot 1689–1937* (1937). Page 362.
4. Ibid. Page 368.
5. Details taken from a certified copy of Heaton's marriage certificate. SAM 004594.
6. As related by Mr Richard Heaton, grand-son of Wilfred Heaton and current owner of Plas Heaton.
7. Colonels Patton, Glennie and Pen Symons. *Historical Records of the 24th Regiment* (1892). Page 283.
8. Mr Richard Heaton recalls his grandmother as being a rather frail and poorly lady who did not seem to have enjoyed good health since her posting in India.
9. As recorded in the Heaton family bible manuscripts.
10. See Major Heaton's various letters of the period. DD/PH 148.
11. Ibid.
12. Ibid.
13. Public Records Office WO 19–7. Records of the 4th Bn Royal Garrison Regiment.
14. John Laband. *The Rise and Fall of the Zulu Nation* (1997). Page 439.
15. Correspondence between Colonel Heaton and Harriett Stokes in 1905. DD/PH 73.
16. Correspondence between Colonel Heaton and the Rev H Humphreys in 1898. DD/PH 288.
17. DD/PH 148.
18. DD/PH 344.
19. As recorded on the certified copy of Colonel Heaton's death certificate. HC904447.

Epilogue
1. A Service to commemorate the Immortal Defence of Rorke's Drift is held each year in Brecon Cathedral on the Sunday nearest to 22 January, at which such a Regimental Tribute is made on each occasion. This Service is open to the public.
2. In 2001 the Zulu War Colours, which were showing signs of considerable decay, were placed into specially designed preservation cases at considerable expense, met by the outstanding personal generosity of the late Major Basil Waters, South Wales Borderers.
3. DD/PH 148.

Select Bibliography

Unpublished Sources
The Heaton Diary of 1879. Primary source manuscript held by the Royal Welsh Museum Brecon.
The Heaton Family Bible. Primary source family tree manuscript held by the Heaton family at Plas Heaton, Henllan, Denbighshire.
The Heaton Manuscripts. Primary and secondary source documentary material held by the Denbighshire County Records Office, Ruthin, Denbighshire.
Digest of Service. 1st and 2nd Battalions 24th Regiment of Foot. Royal Welsh Museum.

Published Sources
Adams Jack. *The South Wales Borderers*. (Hamish Hamilton London 1968).
Atkinson C. T. *The South Wales Borderers 24th Foot 1689–1937*. (University Press Cambridge 1937).
Baker Peter. *Rule of Fear – The Life and Times of Dingane King of the Zulu*. (Longmans London 1964).
Brereton John M. *A History of the Royal Regiment of Wales* (24th/41st Foot) 1689 – 1989. (RHQ The Royal Regiment of Wales 1989).
Brereton J. M. *The Brecon Beacons National Park*. (David&Charles London 1990).
Edgerton Robert. *Like Lions They Fought – The Zulu War and the last Black Empire in South Africa*. (The Free Press, New York 1988).
Glover Michael. *Rorke's Drift*. (Wordsworth Editions Ltd 1998).
Gon Philip. *The Road to Isandlwana*. (Jonathan Ball Publishers, Johannesburg 1979).
Greaves Adrian. *Isandlwana*. (Cassell & Co, London 2001).
Greaves Adrian. *Rorke's Drift*. (Cassell & Co, London 2002).
Greaves Adrian & Best Brian. *The Curling Letters of the Zulu War*. (Leo Cooper, GB 2001).
Guy Jeff. *The Destruction of the Zulu Kingdom*. (Raven Press 1982)
Holme Norman. *The Noble 24th – Biographical Records of the 24th Regiment in the Zulu War and South African Campaigns 1877–1879*. (Savannah Publications 1999).
Jackson FWD. *Isandlwana 1879 – The Sources Re-Examined*. (SWB Museum, Brecon 1999).

Journal of the Anglo Zulu War Historical Society. Published by the Anglo Zulu War Historical Society . (Debinair Publishing Ltd.)

Knight Ian. *Brave Men's Blood … The Epic of the Zulu War 1879*. (Greenhill Books, London 1990).

Knight Ian. *Great Zulu Commanders*. (Arms & Armour Press, London 1999).

Knight Ian. *Great Zulu Battles 1838–1906*. (Arms & Armour Press, London 1998).

Knight Ian. *The Anatomy of the Zulu Army*. (Greenhill Books, London 1995).

Laband John. *The Rise and Fall of the Zulu Nation*. (Arms and Armour Press, London 1997).

Laband J P C & Thompson P S. *Field Guide to the War in Zululand 1879*. (University of Natal Press 1983).

Laffin John. *Tommy Atkins – The Story of the English Soldier*. (Sutton Publishing Ltd 2004)

Lock Ron & Quantrell Peter. *Zulu Victory – The Epic of Isandlwana and the Cover Up*. (Greenhill Books, London 2002).

Lock Ron. *Blood on the Painted Mountain – Zulu Victory and Defeat, Hlobane and Kambula 1879*. (Greenhill Books, London 1995).

Milton John. *The Edges of War – a History of Frontier Wars 1702–1878*. (Rustica Press, South Africa 1983).

Morris Donald. *The Washing of the Spears – The Rise and Fall of the Zulu Nation*. (Pimlico Press, London 1994).

Paton, Glennie & Penn Symons. *The Historical Records of the 24th Regiment from its formation in 1689*. (Simpkin, Marshall, Hamilton, Kent&Co, London 1892).

Smithers A. J. *The Man Who Disobeyed – Sir Horace Smith-Dorrien and his Enemies*. (Leo Cooper London. 1970).

Yorke Edmund. *Rorke's Drift 1879 – Anatomy of an Epic Zulu War Siege*. (Tempus Publishing Ltd, UK 2001).

Index

abaQulusi 68, 69
Abel, Trooper 86, 87
Abergele 122, 125, 127
Aldershot 136-138
Allahabad 135, 136
Allen, Cpl William VC 35, 109
Amathole Mountains 9
Ancram, Colonel 5
Andaman Islands 7, 134
Anglo-Zulu War 69, 96, 143
Anstey, Lt Edgar 8, 35, 54, 101
Apartheid 132
Army Hospital Corps 55, 109
Army Medical Department 55
Atkins, Tommy 21
Atkinson, Charles 8
Auctions, of personal effects 45, 53

Bambatha Rebellion 139
Bareilly 135
Base Army Post Offices 140
Battle Honours 6, 49, 50
Baxter, Lt J C 18, 35, 51
Beechwood Hotel Harrogate 140
Beesley, Mr A H 3
Bengough, Lt Col H M 41, 42, 48, 58, 75, 79, 95, 99
Bennett, Lt Levett Holt 22, 62, 86, 113, 120, 129
Beresford, Lord William VC 62, 63, 70, 95
Bettws yn Rhos 2, 120
Black, Major Wilsone 17, 47, 48, 53, 71, 74, 78, 79
Blood River, battle of 11
Boards of Inquiry etc 56-58, 65, 73, 81, 108, 111, 116
Boer War 56, 110, 132, 138
Bombay 134
Booth, Colour Sergeant VC 65

Boundary Commission 13
Bourne, Mr Douglas 144
Bradbury, Sergeant John 17
Brander, William Capt 102
Brecon 3, 7, 49, 76, 102, 118, 119, 121, 129, 130, 133, 137, 138, 142-144
Brecon and Merthyr Railway 118
Brecon Beacons 118, 131
Brecon Branch Comrades Association 142
Brecon Cathedral 49, 130, 131
Brecon County Times 76
Bromhead, Lt Gonville VC 33-37, 67, 103, 109, 136
Bromhead, Major Charles 67, 83, 135
Browne, Lt Edward VC 27, 42, 53, 58, 80, 108, 118, 119, 136
Buffalo River 26, 37-40, 63
Buller, Lt Col Redvers VC 66, 68, 91, 95, 96
Bulwer, Sir Henry 13
Burma 7, 17, 131, 134

Cape Colony 8-10, 15, 50
Cape St Vincent 113
Cape Town 8, 56, 110
Cardwell Reforms 7, 20, 133
Carey, Lt Jahleel Brenton 86 87, 91, 92
Carnarvon, Lord 12
Castle Hotel, Brecon 119, 131
Cetshwayo, King 9, 12, 13, 28, 41, 52, 64-67, 88, 89, 94, 99, 110, 143
Chard, Lt John VC 18, 33-37, 76
Chelmsford, Lord 13-15, 19, 25-35, 38, 42, 43, 51, 58, 61, 64, 68, 70, 78, 81, 86, 94, 97, 132
Chillianwalla, battle of 6, 52
Church Parade 53
Church, Florence 53, 131

Church, Major Hugh Backhouse 21, 58
Churchill, 1st Duke of Marlborough 5
Clements, Lt Arthur 27, 83, 103, 135
Clery, Lt Col C F 53, 57
Coghill, Lieutenant Nevill VC 8, 37-40, 63, 106, 116, 134, 136, 137, 142-145
Collis, Ensign 7
Colours, Queens & Regimental 21, 37-40, 63, 106, 116, 134, 136, 137, 142-145
Confederation 12, 14, 132
Connolly, James Henry 104
Courts Martial 46, 54, 86
Craney, Private 18
Cunnynghame, General Sir Arthur 9
Curling, Lieutenant Henry 63
Curragh, Northern Ireland 48

Daley, Lt James 8, 44
Dalton, James Langley VC 44
D'Arcy, Capt Cecil VC 95
Dartnell, Major 27, 28, 50, 79
Davies, The Very Reverend John 142
de Lamare Morison, Lt Col Frederick 137
de Neuville, Alphonse 38, 40
Deane, Lt Richard Grenvill 8, 50, 110
Degacher, Capt William 8, 52, 53
Degacher, Colonel Henry 52, 53, 57, 64, 71, 74, 89
Denbighshire 1-3, 127, 129, 139, 140
Dering, Daniel 4
Dering, Sir Edward 4
Dingane, King 11
Dobrie, Lieutenant Lionel 61
Drum Major 106, 107
Drumhead Service 53
Duke of Cambridge HRH 116
Dunbar, Col William 70, 78, 80, 82, 88, 108, 116, 128, 133
Dundee 67, 70, 73, 103
Dunn, Chief John 82
Durban 15-17, 27, 58, 104, 131
Durnford, Col Anthony 28-31, 41, 85
Dodds, Mr (horse) 25, 85

Elliott, Maj Gen Christopher CBE 142
Eshowe 50, 51, 68, 71
Eugenie, Princess 86, 92

Field Allowance 58, 81
Flogging 54, 55, 80-82

Flying Column 78, 88
Fortifications 44, 46, 49, 59
Franklin, Lt Reginald William 58
Frere, Sir Henry Bartle Edward 9, 12, 14
Frith, Lt F J 88, 101
Fugitives Drift & Trail 73, 85
Furlough 117-119

Gallwey, Capt 59
Gasteen, Surgeon Major 24
Gibraltar 8, 109
Gingindlhovu, battle of 71
Glyn, Colonel Richard Thomas 15, 16, 35, 38, 44, 48, 57, 58, 66, 78, 79, 83, 98, 101, 102, 106, 110, 114, 133
Great Kei River 8
Greytown 25, 56, 63, 65, 70, 105
Griqualand West 11

Hamilton-Browne, George 'Maori' 42
Hamu kaNzibe, Prince 64, 66, 69
Harness, Colonel Arthur 42, 43, 89
Harrison, Capt 107
Harrismith District 138
Hart, Lt 50
Hassard, Col Fairfax 42, 43, 51
Havard Chapel 143, 144
Heaton, Evelyn 59, 61, 62, 117, 123, 135
Heaton, Florence (wife) 135-138, 140
Heaton, Florence Catherine (daughter) 136
Heaton, Gilbert (brother) 120, 128, 141
Heaton, Hugh Edward (father) 2, 136, 140
Heaton, Hugh Edward (son) 136, 140
Heaton, John 1
Heaton, Kit 47, 48, 59, 66, 72, 79, 98, 120-123, 126
Heaton, Lt Col John Richard 137
Heaton, Richard Mr 139, 144
Heaton, Wilfred see chronology of main events
Heaton, Wilfred John (son) 135, 141
Helpmekaar 16, 19, 26, 27, 33, 35-37, 41, 42, 47, 53, 56, 59, 62, 63, 66, 68, 72, 74, 79
Henllan 1, 126, 129, 139, 141
Hicks Beach, Sir Michael 12
Higginson, Lt 37, 38, 48
Hitch, Pte Fred VC 35, 109

Hlobane Mountain 64, 68
HMS Ceylon 7
HMS Walmer Castle 19
Hodson, George 8, 54, 78
Hook, Pte Henry VC 35, 108
Horns of the buffalo formation 31, 32, 51
Howard, Colonel Thomas 5, 87

India 131, 135
Inyezane, battle of 50, 51
Isandlwana 9, 17, 26, 28, 29, 33, 36, 42, 45, 52, 53, 55, 58, 71, 75, 83, 88, 92, 100, 101, 106, 134
Isipesi Hill 27

Jones, Pte Robert VC 49, 109
Jones, Pte William VC 35, 109

Kambhula, battle of 61, 68, 69, 82
Kimberley 8, 11, 110
King Edward VII 138
King George V 140
Kopje Allein 67, 84

La Terriere, Mr Bulmer 84
Laager 30
Lloyd, George Whitelocke 9, 52
Lloyd, Selina 9, 75
Lloyd, William Whitelocke 9, 25, 48, 57, 65, 70, 74, 75, 84, 85, 96, 97, 101, 134
Logan, Lieutenant Quentin 57
Lord Battersea (Cyril Flower) 131
Lord Napier of Magdala 134
Louis Napoleon, Prince Imperial 86, 87
Lovett, Lt Harry 76, 78, 82, 86, 98, 99, 121

Magnibonium 97, 101, 102
Mail, distribution of 55, 56
Malta 138
Mangeni River 23, 27, 58
Marlborough College 2
Marter, Major Richard 99
Martini-Henry Rifle 9, 35
Mbuyazi 11
Medal - Long Service & Good Conduct 17
Melvill, Lieutenant Teignmouth VC 10, 17, 37-40, 48, 49, 54, 60, 73, 143
Middle Drift 15
Militia, Carlow Rifles 9

Militia, Royal Carnarvon Rifle Corps 3
Mooi River 25, 105
Moriaty, Captain 65
Morshead, Mrs Chiquita 113, 114
Mpande, King 11
Museum, South Wales Borderers 139

Natal, colony of 132, 143
Natal Mounted Police 27, 49
Natal Native Contingent 15, 29, 32, 41, 42
nDondakasuka, battle of 11
Newdigate, Maj Gen 78, 79
Ngwebeni Valley 31, 91
Ninth Frontier War 8, 110
Norris-Newman, Charles 63
Nqutu Plateau 28, 31
Ntombe Drift 65

Officers Mess 20, 21, 77, 80, 118, 119, 137
Oskarberg 75
O'Toole, Sgt VC 95
Outspan 23, 24, 26, 89, 90, 104, 105

Palmes, Lt George 27, 82, 106
Pearson, Lt Col 50, 51, 68
Perry, Private 7
Pietermaritzburg 16, 18, 25, 27, 42, 51, 58
Pinetown 20, 21, 101
Plas Heaton 1, 110, 126, 136, 138, 130, 000
Ponto, the dog 44
Port Natal 19
Portsmouth 116, 117, 136
Pulleine, Lt Col Henry Burmeister 16, 29, 30, 32, 45

Rainforth, Major Thomas 27, 37, 59, 64, 106
Rangoon 135
Raw, Lt Charles 31
Reed, Sara Elizabeth 10
Retief, Piet 11
Reveille 23, 89, 92, 97
Reynolds, Surgeon Major VC 58, 108, 113
Rhaniket 135
Roddy, Corporal 19
Rogers, Trooper 86, 87
Rorke's Drift 13, 18, 27, 30, 33-37, 41, 45, 47, 49, 50, 53, 57, 61-63, 66, 69, 75, 108, 134, 142

Royal Garrison Regiment 138
Royal Regiment of Wales (24th/41st Foot), The 142, 143
Royal Welsh Regiment, Band of 142
Russell, Private 19, 46

Sandhurst, Royal Military College 3, 8
Shaka, kaSenzangakhona, King 11, 31
Sihayo, Chief 13, 26, 58
Smedley, Mrs 117
Smith, The Rev George 47, 61, 101
Smith-Dorrien, Horace Lockwood 25, 26
South Africa 23, 50, 58, 72, 109, 110, 131, 132, 134, 138
South Wales Borderers, 1st&2nd Bns 5, 17, 133-137, 141, 144
Spalding, Major Henry 33, 35-37
Spring, William 8
SS Balmoral Castle 9
SS Clyde 71
SS Egypt 109, 110, 116
St Mary's Church Brecon 130
St Mary's Church Warwick 7
Stokes, Miss Harriett 138, 139
Strickland, Comm Gen Edward 19, 57

Trainer, Private J 85, 101, 107
Transvaal 11, 109
Tugela River 13, 51, 104
Tyrell, Private 54

Ultimatum 13
Ulundi 14, 29, 31, 51, 78, 90, 92, 94, 98, 101, 144
Upcher, Russell 15, 27, 26, 37, 45, 60, 61, 135
Upoko Races 100

Venables, Sara 2
Victoria Cross 44, 49, 50, 53, 65, 67, 91, 95, 108, 109, 134
Victoria, HM Queen 50, 109, 110, 143

Warnedford, Deputy Comm 25
Warwickshire 7, 133,
Welch Regiment, The 5
Wellington, Duke of 21, 22
Williams, Pte John VC 35, 109
Wolseley, General Sir Garnet 39, 94, 97, 99, 108
Wood, Col Evelyn VC 51, 64, 66, 68, 69, 88
Wynne, Mrs 55, 120, 130, 131,

Xhosa, people 8

Younghusband, Capt Reginald 52

Zulu Nation 11, 82, 132, 139, 143
Zululand 12, 14, 16, 17, 26, 44, 49, 59, 66, 75, 99, 110, 132, 139